W9-ATC-105

Gerald J. Schiffhorst
University of Central Florida

John F. Schell
University of Central Florida

THE SHORT

HANDBOOK FOR

Writers

**Instructor's
Annotated
Edition**

McGraw-Hill, Inc.

New York St. Louis San Francisco
Auckland Bogotá Caracas
Hamburg Lisbon London
Madrid Mexico Milan Montreal
New Delhi Paris San Juan
São Paulo Singapore Sydney
Tokyo Toronto

This book was developed by STEVEN PENSINGER, Inc.

This is the Instructor's Annotated Edition of *The Short Handbook for Writers*. It includes all material found in the student's edition as well as the answers on the text pages for most of the student exercises.

The Short Handbook for Writers
Instructor's Annotated Edition

1 2 3 4 5 6 7 8 9 0   FGR   FGR   9 5 4 3 2 1 0

ISBN 0-07-055345-9

This book was set in Bookman Light ITC by York Graphic Services, Inc.
The editors were Steve Pensinger and Curt Berkowitz;
the designer was Robin Hoffman;
the production supervisor was Kathryn Porzio.
Arcata Graphics/Fairfield was printer and binder.

Library of Congress Cataloging-in-Publication Data

Schiffhorst, Gerald J.
    The short handbook for writers / Gerald J. Schiffhorst, John F. Schell.—
    Instructor's annotated ed.
        p.   cm.
    Includes index.
    ISBN 0-07-055345-9
    1. English language—Rhetoric.   2. English language—Grammar—
    1950-   I. Schell, John F.   II. Title.
    PE1408.S3136   1991
    808'.042 — dc20   90-45638

logic	Check the logic of your writing. **19, 20**		
mm	Misplaced modifier: place it elsewhere so that it clearly modifies the intended word. **30**		
mo	Use the mood required by your sentence. **45**		
ms	Follow conventional manuscript form. **65**		

p   Correct the punctuation

[ ]	brackets **58**	( )	parentheses **57**
:	colon **55**	.	period **51**
,	comma **47–50**	?	question mark **52**
--	dash **56**	" "	quotation marks **58**
. . .	ellipsis **58**	;	semicolon **54**
!	exclamation point **53**		

pred	Make the subject and predicate of this sentence relate to each other logically. **31**
ps	Know the parts of speech and their uses. **34**
ref	Make this pronoun refer clearly to its antecedent. **40**
rep	Eliminate the obvious repetition. **78**
shift	Correct the shift in verb or pronoun use. **46**
sp	Proofread for proper spelling, and work on your spelling weaknesses. **66**
sub	Use subordination to relate secondary details to main ideas. **25**
t	Use the correct verb tense. **43**
trite	Replace this trite expression with fresher language. **75**
ts	Use a topic sentence to focus each paragraph on one point. **21**
u	Unify this paragraph by making all sentences relate to the topic sentence. **22**
vague	Use specific and concrete words. **70**
vb	Use the correct form of this verb. **44**
wdy	Tighten this wordy expression. **78**
ww	Wrong word: choose a more exact word. **71, 72**

About the Authors

Gerald J. Schiffhorst is Professor of English at the University of Central Florida, where he has taught writing since 1970 and has chaired the composition program. He has degrees from St. Louis and Washington Universities and is the author of two books and numerous articles on Renaissance literature.

John F. Schell chairs the English Department at the University of Central Florida, where he has been Professor of English since 1987. He has degrees from Drew and Vanderbilt Universities. Among his other publications is *Writing on the Job* (with John Stratton).

Contents

Chapter 3
Drafting the Essay 30

Chapter 4
Revising and Editing 50

Chapter 5
Writing Persuasively 68

Chapter 6
Writing Paragraphs 90

Chapter 7
Writing Sentences   121

PART II
A GUIDE TO STYLE

Chapter 8
Basic Grammar   161

Chapter 9
Punctuation and Mechanics   225

Contents

Contents

Preface

Our purpose in this book is to provide students with a handy source of reference as they write and an extensive guide to the composing process. As such, *The Short Handbook for Writers* can function both as a classroom text and as an independent tool for students responding to questions posed by their composition instructors. Readers familiar with the three successful editions of *Short English Handbook*, of which the present volume is a major revision, will see that our new title reflects not merely a new publisher but a more comprehensive view of writing. The first five chapters expand the earlier treatment of prewriting, composing, and revising to include separate discussions of the role of the reader and of persuasive writing. The three divisions of this text indicate its distinct purposes: Part I guides the student through the writing process, including rhetorical emphasis on the sentence and paragraph; Part II serves as a source of reference on matters of grammar, punctuation, and diction; and Part III presents most of the major practical writing applications that composition students encounter, from letters and literary analyses to research papers. This section includes a sample student review, literary analysis, and research paper (in MLA style).

We provide a useful source of clear, brief answers to the major questions that arise during the composing process. We present these explanations and examples in an immediately accessible form that will apply to students' needs. In the Guide to Style (Part II), we have used concise entries that state a point, explain it briefly, then present examples clearly labelled "weak/improved" or "correct/incorrect." Examples here and elsewhere in the book come from student writing. Nearly every section includes exercises for classroom or independent application. We have tried to rely as little as possible on formal terminology, but we explain essential terms both in the text and in the Glossary of Terms.

We are pleased to acknowledge the assistance of many students and colleagues at the University of Central Florida and elsewhere. Stephen H. Goldman, University of Kansas; Charles Nash, Cottey College; Mitchell E. Summerlin, John C. Calhoun State Community College; and Jane Marmaduke Woodman, University of North Carolina at Asheville, provided helpful suggestions during the revision. And we are grateful to Russell Kesler for his special assistance, as well as to Richard Adicks, Vicky Brain, Eileen Oswald, Sharon Johnston, Gail Pentz, and Susan Strasshofer. Lynn Butler Schiffhorst made an invaluable contribution, along with our editors, Steve Pensinger and Curt Berkowitz, whose support and guidance made the book possible.

Gerald J. Schiffhorst

John F. Schell

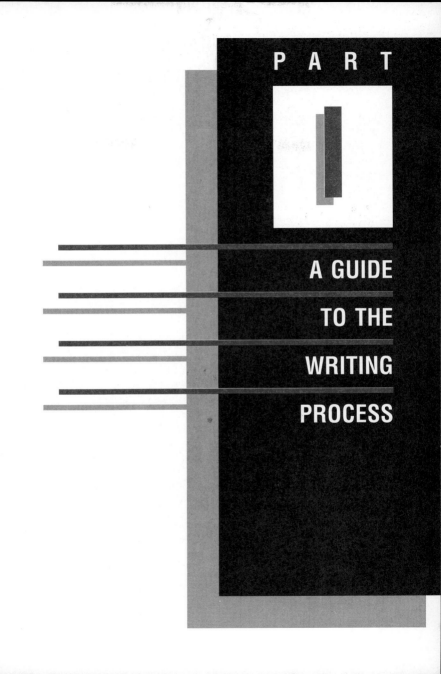

PART

1

A GUIDE
TO THE
WRITING
PROCESS

CHAPTER

1

Discovering and

Exploring Ideas

Overview

Instead of reading this book straight through, you will probably refer to various chapters and entries as you need them. Even so, to put the individual entries in perspective and to help you get the most from the time you spend writing, we will begin with an overview of the whole subject of writing.

We are not going to present a simple, foolproof formula guaranteed to make you a competent writer. Unfortunately, there is no such formula. Writing is like playing tennis: you learn and improve by doing—by practicing, by listening to criticism, and by practicing some more. Good writing does more than just avoid blunders. It holds the reader's interest. When you write well, you begin by thinking out what you want to say. Then you say it, in clear, logical sentences and carefully chosen words, expressing your thoughts and feelings so that your audience will understand them just as you want them to be understood.

Most writing—certainly all the writing we will be concerned with here—has a purpose and a method suited to it. Writers tell stories: they say what happens (narration). Or they argue: they speak for or against something (argument). Or they describe: they tell how something looks or sounds or moves (description). Or they explain: they tell how something works (exposition) or why something happens (analysis). As you plan what you want to say in a paper, you will also be deciding which of these five approaches you will use. This does not mean that you will choose one approach and leave the rest in storage. You may be called on to explain, argue, describe, analyze, or narrate, or explain and argue, or describe and narrate, or do all of these in one paper. Nevertheless, the assignment or your own purpose or a combination of your purpose and your material will usually make one approach predominant. For example, you may start out by describing ways in which consumers are deceived by television commercials and then end up arguing that there should be stricter regulation of such advertising. Since the emphasis in this case should fall on the argument, your purpose in describing commercials is to prepare your reader to believe as you do about regulation.

In an essay on Al-A-Teen, for example, your main purpose might be to explain what this support group does and how it functions. In so doing, you might compare it with Alcoholics Anonymous, or you might classify various programs for substance abusers and their families in relation to in-patient or out-patient treatment centers. You might also analyze different theories of teenage alcoholism and drug abuse, using quotations from magazine and newspaper articles dealing with the causes of these problems. Perhaps you could attend an Al-A-Teen meeting and then describe the range of people you met or write a narrative account of your visit. Finally, you might conclude an essay with your opinion of the issues involved: Is Al-A-Teen helping to solve the problems faced by adolescents who live with substance abusers? Still, your essay would remain mostly exploratory: to explain the role of Al-A-Teen, based on your experience and reading.

To a certain degree, all such writing must be persuasive. It must persuade readers that it is worth their time and attention. What you have to say will get a fair hearing only if you make sure it deserves one. Writing that deserves to be read is the kind we will be concerned with throughout this book.

Writing is a process of generating ideas; and the first four chapters divide this ongoing process, for convenience, into prewriting, drafting, and revising. At each stage, focus on a few things at a time. Allow time to plan and develop ideas by learning to think on paper, and do not worry about editing or correcting what you write until the composing process has run its course. Since writing is a complex activity, the stages often overlap or double back: you will simultaneously generate and react to your work while considering your purpose and reader. But you must first find something to say.

1   Explore what you want to say.

Most writers have experienced the frustration of being unable to think of a fresh idea—or of discovering one too late. Thinking through some of the many possible subjects for writing and exploring what we already know about those subjects can keep us from becoming "stuck" with nothing to say. Anything can be turned into material for writing; how to do so through invention, the first stage in the writing process, where you explore your subject, is the topic of this chapter.

If you are new to college or university life, for instance, you might jot down whatever comes to mind as you think about your experiences as a freshman. Here are one student's notes:

big campus	a lot of reading
dorm living	major—in what?
freedom—on my own	pledge a fraternity?
working—how many hours?	crew team
large lectures	parties

You could then underline some of the more promising points on such a list, ones that could easily be developed with examples. If living away from home appeals to you as a topic, you could write about the need to budget your time so that daily chores do not consume too much of it. Or you could compare high school with college, perhaps with a younger sister or brother in mind. Or you could consider the pros and cons of Greek life or the problems of working while pursuing a degree. Listing ideas in the order they occur to you is an easy way to get started. Such invention strategies are helpful both in locating subjects and in exploring them before you write your essay.

Sometimes, however, a subject is readily available or assigned. For example, you are upset by an editorial about the state legislature and write a letter to the editor. Or your employer asks for a report on computer safety devices. Or your instructor suggests five topics for an essay. Yet even when the subject is provided or limited for you, you will have to determine your own approach and decide what to say about it. In any case, careful planning is essential; successful writers seldom produce effective work without some form of invention.

In exploring what to say about a subject, try out some of the following invention strategies to determine which works best for you.

Discovering and Exploring Ideas

1. *Brainstorming* is one of the simplest ways to begin the writing process. You can generate ideas by talking about possible topics with a friend or group of friends. The result will be uneven, but ideas will emerge. If you don't have a friend willing to brainstorm with you, try taking notes or using a tape recorder, talking freely about your subject for fifteen minutes. Then play the tape back, noting any important ideas. To explore a point you have discovered, try another fifteen minutes of tape recording on that point.

2. *Freewriting* is like tape recording with a pencil and paper. Jot down your thoughts about your topic, writing continuously for fifteen minutes without stopping. Try to record your thoughts as fast as they occur. Ignore correctness or neatness. If you get stuck, write "I'm stuck" and keep going. After fifteen minutes, select anything from your notes that looks worthwhile. When you discover something promising, you can use the freewriting exercise again on this new selection. Here is an example of a student's freewriting exercise:

> My mind is a blank—I can say something about AIDS, Kenny's cousin has AIDS, he said he thinks AZT is working—but it costs a lot and the government no longer pays for it, he doesn't know if his cousin will continue to take it or go broke, what if he dies simply because he can't afford it? I read that the drug company that makes AZT is getting rich, but the drug was first discovered in a

government project with taxpayers money—it doesn't seem right that the drug company is now making money off of it. What else? What else? I seem to be stuck. What else about AIDS? How bad will it get before they find a cure? I'm scared when I think of the future. I wonder if other people in my class are scared. We never talk about it.

Even in this two-minute excerpt, several possible points emerge for further exploration: the federal government's role in health crises, drug companies' profits, and reactions to AIDS among the writer's classmates.

Freewriting is most successful if you try to capture your mind in action without planning, structuring, or editing.

3. *Clustering* can also help you to generate ideas and to see the relations between them. Instead of sentences, clustering uses single terms, which are easier to jot down quickly. And instead of moving down the page, you begin clustering by writing down a possible subject in the middle of the page inside a circle (or balloon). From there you can take off in any direction with another term. Each new balloon may give rise to additional ideas, which get attached to the balloon that sparks them.

Again, work freely and quickly for fifteen minutes; then look at the clusters to see which look most promising. From this exercise, you could explore the causes and effects of population growth in Florida.

Clustering

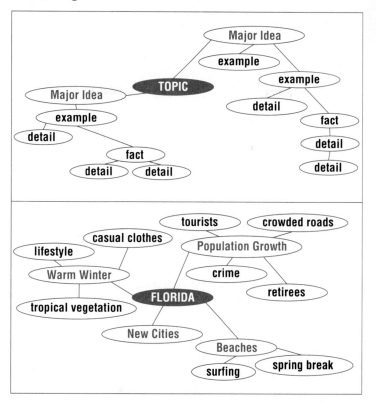

4. *Asking questions* can help you recall specific experiences or attitudes. If, for example, the subject of beards arises, you can ask yourself:

Do I like beards on most men? Why?
Do I like only certain types of beards? Which ones?
What types of men look good in beards, and what types do not?

Such exploratory questions involve classifying, analyzing, and persuading as you determine your own feelings about the subject. Various possible ideas can emerge:

A beard, as long as it is neatly trimmed, can enhance any man's appearance.

Beards suggest maturity and masculinity.

Beards not only look messy and uncomfortable but also make men look old before their time.

Asking questions about the meaning of a word, the design of an object, or your reactions to a work of art can produce numerous topics for writing.

5. *The pentad* is an especially valuable form of asking questions. According to this technique, developed by Kenneth Burke, every human action is influenced by five elements: act (what), scene (where, when), agent (who), agency (how), and purpose (why). Act refers to anything that happens (or could happen)—whether physical, intellectual, or emotional—or anything that is the result of an activity (an award, a completed paper). Scene is the setting or background of the action. The agent is the person (or force) responsible for (or influenced by) the action. Agency is the method that makes a thing happen, and purpose is the reason or motive for an action. These five elements parallel the journalist's familiar questions *who, what, where, when, how,* and *why;* but they also extend the possibilities for invention since the terms of the pentad can be compared and related: the agent's purpose and the effect of the scene on the agent, for example.

You can use these five terms to analyze current, historical, or fictional events; to explore characters in novels or films; to learn more about the people involved in a narrative; or to analyze your audience in an argument. The pentad, however, is not applicable to things (computers, for example).

Imagine, for a moment, that your college or university has announced a new policy to test incoming students for drugs. Those who test positive must undergo counseling while their admission is delayed. As a student senator, you are asked to write a column in the campus newspaper opposing this ruling. You think through the topic in terms of the pentad:

What was done? (act)	new ruling? unconstitutional act? bold initiative?
When/where was it done? (scene)	after long consultation? in private? on campus?
Who did it? (agent)	governor? legislature? president of college? outsiders?
How was it done? (agency)	by open vote? secret agreement? outside pressure?
Why was it done? (purpose)	to protect young people? to keep out undesirables? to earn votes? to appear strong? innovative? innocent of drug dealing?

When we compare and relate the five terms, here is what happens when we think about the act (mandatory testing) in terms of the scene (university):

How does the campus setting influence this act?
Is the university being "used"?
Are students being singled out because they are unsympathetic victims?
Do officials hope the students will protest, to turn public opinion against the students?

When we consider the agent (who does the testing) in terms of agency (how the testing will be carried out), we develop these ideas:

How will the university implement this rule?
Who will do the testing?
What will the university test for?
What will be done about faulty tests and positive results caused by legal medication?
Where will the money come from for such an expensive program?
Will faculty and staff also be tested? If not, why are students singled out?
What about everyone's constitutional right of privacy?

This example shows some of the many questions that can be generated when each of the five terms is considered in relation to the other four.

6. *Cubing* means examining a subject from six perspectives (a cube has six sides):

   1. Describe the subject. (What is its content?)

   2. Compare it. (What is it similar to, different from?)

   3. Associate it. (What does it remind you of?)

   4. Analyze it. (Explain how it was made)

   5. Apply it. (Explain how it can be used)

   6. Argue for or against it. (Take a stand)

   Write briefly (for three to five minutes) about the subject from *each* of the six points of view, beginning with what you know. Unlike the pentad, this exercise can be used for objects (a car, building, sculpture) as well as for persons, events, and ideas.

7. Writing informally in a *journal* can provide valuable ideas for assigned essays. Unlike a diary or class notebook, a journal is a record of interesting impressions and experiences that you could share with others. It provides an opportunity for private writing and thinking. Some suggestions for writing in a journal:

a. Find a quiet spot where you can write for about fifteen minutes a day, freely recalling what you have observed and read. Do not worry about correct form. You can mention the people you met, the ideas you discussed, the movies or lectures you attended, the food you ate—but noting your reactions, explaining why you liked or disliked what you experienced.

b. Write about your progress in your writing and in other classes: what are you learning? what are your feelings about your work?

c. Write personal reactions to any independent or assigned reading: why did you like or dislike a work? Paraphrase or quote memorable passages.

d. Write descriptions of people or scenes you have observed.

e. Keep a record of a major local or national event (such as a political scandal) as it unfolds over several weeks.

Since writing is a way of learning, journal entries will help you observe and reflect on your experience. And they will often be of use in other more formal writing; ideas derived from books and other media can become subjects for essays.

EXERCISE

1. Using freewriting or clustering, generate ten to twelve possible ideas about one of the following subjects:

year-round school	childbirth at home
colorizing black-and-white movies	computers in the classroom
	walking for exercise
latchkey children	reducing caffeine intake
living with an alcoholic parent	acid rain
	divorce

2. What types of questions could you ask about each of the following subjects to generate possible writing topics?

the greenhouse effect

using drug testing to screen job applicants

increasing fees to provide more campus parking

toughening laws for drivers who drink

raising taxes to reduce the federal deficit

animal rights

low-income housing for the homeless

sex education in schools

portrayal of minorities on TV

the rights of smokers

rising medical costs

3. Consider the following brainstorming list a student made for the topic Living in Florida. Underline points that she could develop into writing topics:

warm year-round, no winter
beaches, surfing
tourists, crowded roads
retirees
casual clothes, lifestyle
palm trees, tropical vegetation
newer, cleaner cities

4. Try talking for fifteen minutes into a tape recorder on one of the following subjects to generate topic ideas:

rock music and hearing damage
using animals in laboratories
the increasing use of midwives
bodybuilding for women
violence in music videos
buying on credit
vacationing with the family

5. Explain which prewriting strategy—listing, clustering, or cubing—would be the most effective for you in exploring these subjects:

horror movies, New Age music, teenage suicide, planning a wedding, jogging

6. To use the pentad, imagine a person (yourself, a friend, or a fictional character) acting to resolve a crisis. With this image in mind, try to answer as many of the following questions as apply:

What is the person doing?
How did he or she get involved?
What is the person trying to accomplish?
How will the person accomplish these goals?
What obstacles does the person face?
What action is the person trying to take?
What other actions are possible?
How do the setting, time of the event, and others involved in it affect the person's actions?

Develop other questions relevant to your imagined scene.

7. Write in your journal one of the following:

a. Recall the best piece of writing you have ever done—a letter, speech, college essay—and reconstruct the method you used to plan and develop it. Talk about the problems you faced and the ways you solved them.

b. Write a dialogue in which you imagine two people talking about a current social issue. Label the speakers A and B (or give them names). To keep the conversation moving fast, use questions and brief responses. Aim for spontaneity; write quickly without extensive planning.

c. Write about the ideas you have learned from your favorite class, and comment on their importance.

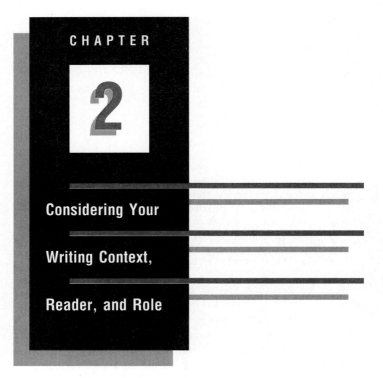

Considering Your

Writing Context,

Reader, and Role

In collecting information for an essay, you initially focus on your own observations, memories, and thought processes. But your aim as a writer is not just to get facts and ideas on paper but to communicate them to a reader for a purpose. This chapter discusses the ways in which your intentions are shaped by communicating to others. People are involved in all aspects of the writing act: the human occasion for the writing, the real or imagined audience, and the human agent, the writer. Each of these—the occasion of the writing, the audience, and the writer—influences both the content and the form of the writing.

2 Consider the writing context.

Every writing act responds to a specific occasion or context and, in so doing, determines its purpose. A technician takes notes while reading an article to understand and retain important information. A police detective writes up the facts of an unsolved case to find a key to the solution. Writing is not spontaneous, like breathing; it is a willed act in response to a given situation.

What You Write

Your reason for writing greatly influences what you write, too. For instance, guilty after a fight with your date, you sit down and write an apology. This situation calls for a personal expression of your feelings. But if a shirt you bought from a mail-order house has a flaw, the letter you write in response is factual, providing the information necessary to correct the error. And if you decide to write a letter in your newspaper's "Personals" section soliciting a date, your writing will be persuasive, making yourself appealing to another person.

Why You Write

We often begin to write without first identifying what it is we wish to accomplish. For example, a simple letter home may seem to be purely informational. But on further reflection, we may discover that the letter is really an attempt to explain a failing grade. Or the sarcastic letter to the college paper, after more careful thought, may prove to be defeating our own intention of getting the editor to change her point of view.

As a writer, always be sure of your purpose. Is your aim to persuade? to inform? to scold? to disclose your feelings? to investigate? Different purposes call for different strategies, so know your aim before you begin.

How You Write

The context also helps to determine *how* you write; many situations have conventions that are often taken for granted. You would not, for instance, type an apology to your date on business stationery, using formal style; whereas a letter to your insurance company might well be formal.

College Writing

College writing is also determined by the context. Writing up a biology experiment must conform to the conventions of lab reports, and a review of a book for a history course must meet the expectations of book reviews. Before beginning any kind of writing assignment in any of your classes, be sure you know the context and follow the conventions of the assignment.

3 Consider your readers.

The greatest influence on the content and form of a piece of writing may well be the audience. Children's fiction, for instance, tells stories that are appropriate for young minds in a simple, direct style. Novels written for an adult audience, on the other hand, often treat mature subjects, using irony, ambiguity, and symbolism. The sophistication of the audience determines the difference.

Because we usually write to communicate some feeling or idea to another person, that person becomes central to the writing act. Nearly every piece of writing is aimed at a specific audience. Whenever we write, we should be actively imagining our readers, not writing *at* them but creating a dialogue with them that meets their expectations and needs.

You should think of these readers as intelligent people who want to be informed and pleased. You are addressing people who want to solve a problem, make a decision, or learn something new. They do not want you to repeat what they already know. They expect original approaches to ideas, clearly organized essays that are easy to follow, and writing that is free of errors in grammar and mechanics. They are sure to think less of you if they find any lack of care in the form and content of your writing.

Non-Academic Writing

When writing outside the classroom, the issue of audience is important but relatively easy to address because you have a clear idea of your readers. If you are writing a memo to the person across the hall at work, you can be friendly; you can assume that the two of you share interests and information. If the same information is included in a report for a customer outside your office, your tone becomes less relaxed and you assume less knowledge and interest on the reader's part. If exactly the same information is written for a professional journal, there is again a change. Now you use a more formal style and include more background information, references to other articles, as well as significant attempts at keeping your audience's interest.

Academic Writing

When you respond to an assignment from your instructor, your audience may be imaginary. In such cases you create a fictional and sympathetic audience and write to him or her. Your instructor, of course, will have a significant interest in the information you provide.

Having a sense that your work is directed to specific

readers—your instructor, your classmates, your fellow employees, citizens, club members, and other possible readers—will help you establish your purpose in writing.

Identify Your Audience

The one constant audience for academic writing is the person who assigns it. This is an easy audience to identify. Whether you are writing a physics exam, a marketing report, or even teacher evaluations, the product of your efforts will be directed to your instructor.

When you are assigned writing aimed at readers in addition to your instructor, take time to identify the audiences involved. To do this, think of yourself as the center of the activity and follow your writing as it leaves you and passes through other hands.

For instance, your instructor assigns you the task of writing an editorial for your school newspaper. Before you begin to write, imaginatively trace the journey of your writing after it leaves your hand. First, your boyfriend or girlfriend may volunteer to type the essay for you: Audience Number One. Then, of course, your essay will find its way into the hands of the editorial board, which will consider it for publication: Audience Number Two. If it is published, the obvious audience comes into play, your fellow students: Audience Number Three. However, faculty, staff, alumni, and parents also have access to the school newspaper: Audience Numbers Four, Five, Six, and Seven. And should you be unlucky enough to libel someone, your writing may go to court: Audience Number Eight.

Identify as many of the types of readers as you can who may read the following pieces of writing:

- a letter to the regional McDonald's office complaining about a local manager

- a complaint to the college president about your math teacher

- a short autobiography to accompany your application to medical school

- a letter to the local newspaper complaining about rising property taxes

Define Your Audience

Have you ever written a nasty letter to a company that cheated you or to a public personality who angered you? That sort of writing is intended to make you feel good and your reader feel bad. But most writing tries to create a common ground between the reader and writer. Writers—in order to persuade, entertain, or teach readers—try to convince the audience that they have mutual backgrounds, interests, beliefs, aspirations, and needs. Successful writing reflects a feeling of concern for the reader and elicits the reader's trust; it wants to generate a dialogue. To do this, writers must not just identify their readers; they must learn what their readers are like. In short, a good writer defines the personalities of his or her readers. For example, are your readers:

young or old?
male or female?
Southern, Eastern, or Western?
of average intelligence or above average?

In addition to these traits over which your readers have no control, consider those characteristics which they have chosen. Are they:

single or married?
urban or rural?
liberal or conservative?
people who prefer to work with their hands or their minds?
religious or non-religious?

Most important, think about how your readers relate to the subject matter about which you plan to write. What is their level of knowledge about your subject? Must you provide extensive background information? Must you define terms, identify aspects, explain concepts; or will you insult your readers by explaining things they know?

Consider the level of knowledge each of these audiences has about the following subjects, discussing what would and would not be appropriate in an essay:

Audience	Subject
college students	MTV
senior citizens	skateboards
miners	United Mine Workers of America
college students	United Mine Workers of America
senior citizens	MTV

In addition to your readers' knowledge, their interest in your subject is also important. For example, if your subject is important to them, you will immediately have their attention. If not, then you will have to work harder to get that interest.

Finally, is your subject one toward which your audience is favorably inclined, or is there a likelihood they will disagree with you? If they favor what you say, you will approach your topic more aggressively than you would if you knew you had a hostile audience.

Asking yourself these questions can help you create a vivid picture of your audience in your mind and can aid you in writing to "real" people in convincing prose. Try to think of readers as partners in the writing process, people who ask questions, require information, and need to be satisfied.

If you imagine your readers as people seriously interested in what you have to say, and if you imagine that they see you as a competent, self-assured friend, your tone will be friendly, relaxed, and conversational, as it will be in most informal essays. If you see yourself as the expert and your readers as learners, as in a research report, your tone will be more formal (see **67**).

Your Instructor

Although you may be writing for a variety of audiences, your composition instructor will still evaluate that writing. Because your instructor *must* read what you write (you have a captive audience), you might unconsciously assume that you need not excite, interest, or persuade your instructor. But every reader wants to be delighted with fresh insights and with original or amusing approaches to familiar subjects. This is especially true of busy, critical readers—and of teachers who have evaluated thousands of student essays.

To avoid putting both you and your instructor to sleep, try to see your instructor simply as another human being. As you get to know this person, what idea of his or hers would you like to change? What important issue would you like to disclose to this person? What fascinating point would you like to explain to this human being? What would you like to think through, consider, or test with this person? Analyze your audience—your instructor—to discover those subjects that you might argue or investigate with him or her.

At the same time, this human being is still your instructor, an audience to whom you must demonstrate your competence in the handling of your material, the structuring of your thought, and the honing of your style.

EXERCISE

1. Read the introduction to your college catalog. From that introduction, deduce what kinds of students your college hopes to attract.

2. Write the introductions to three other college catalogs, each with a different audience in mind. When you are finished, analyze the effect of the audience upon your writing.

3. Although you are doing poorly in school and are in bad financial shape, you wish to join Pi Pi Pi sorority

or fraternity. Write a letter to the following people in which you persuade them (or discuss with them) your joining Pi Pi Pi: your father; your instructor in statistics, which you are failing; your best friend.

4. Write a realistic character description of your instructor, using the techniques of audience definition we have discussed above.

5. Imagine writing about year-round schools to an indifferent or hostile audience. What approach to the topic would you take? What would be your purpose?

6. As a member of a health club or gym, you notice various types of bodybuilding and exercise activities. You wonder what the benefits of working out on bodybuilding equipment are for a person your age as opposed to engaging in aerobics, running, jogging, or walking. You interview dedicated bodybuilders, weekend joggers, and aerobics instructors; and you read several fitness magazines to determine the reasons people choose a particular form of exercise and the effect of this exercise on the body. What type of readers would benefit from the results of your investigation?

7. While working part-time for a bank, you notice that many customers have problems with their monthly statements. As a business and computer science major, you decide to investigate a new computer program for your employer. You compare the features of several systems and then propose to write a report to your boss recommending that a new software package to streamline customer accounts be adopted. What assumptions about your reader's needs should you make?

8. Choose a problem on your campus—class size, inadequate housing, a parking policy, for example—and write a letter to the college president recommending a solution.

9. Describe possible readers for each of the following topics. Explain what they would know and what they would need to know about each topic.

Why People Develop Phobias
How Movies Are Rated
How Colleges Recruit Athletes
Why the Sky Looks Blue
Causes of the Wall Street Crash of 1987
Reasons for Building a Wellness Center in Your Community
Reasons for Changing the Zoning in Your Neighborhood

10. Choose a topic from column 1 and an audience from column 2. Decide how you would approach each audience in writing on each topic.

1	*2*
The Need for Public Housing	senior citizens
The Great Depression	college students
Japanese Industrial Cooperation	hairdressers
Lowering Tuition Costs	first graders
The Popularity of *Star Trek*	business leaders

4   Consider your role as writer.

Each of us assumes various roles in life—as someone's child, grandchild, or parent; as a member of some civic, social, or religious group. Similarly, as a writer you may assume one of many different roles. You may be an adult writing to children or a child (no matter how old) writing to your parents. Or you may be an expert writing to amateurs or an angry person trying to communicate that anger. The role you assume in a piece of writing has a major influence upon what you write.

Be Aware of Your Role

Are you addressing your readers as a college student, part-time waiter, rock musician, tennis player, or family member? Selecting one of the roles you play in everyday life means drawing on specific experiences and interests, and these roles affect the way you "talk" to your readers. Here, for example, is one student's list of roles:

college freshman	guitar player
consumer	amateur auto mechanic
taxpayer	fraternity member
U.S. citizen	Big Brother
Catholic	computer programmer
son	swimmer
brother	soccer player

Each of these roles could suggest possible topics and readers:

Topic: Safety Tips for Beginning Divers
Readers: People interested in learning to dive

Topic: Majoring in Computer Science
Readers: Most college students

Topic: The Problem of Date Rape
Readers: Parents, all college students, general readers

If this same student were to write in favor of a gasoline tax increase to fund highway repair, he could call upon his roles as citizen, consumer, and taxpayer to address any one of the following groups of general readers, each of which would require different approaches and information:

truckers	other college students
legislators	other interested citizens
motorists	those with an opposing view

Be consistent throughout a composition in the role you choose to assume. If you write as a trombone player, stick with that role rather than—in the same essay—also trying to be a streetwise kid. If you write as a student researcher on cognitive psychology, keep in mind that you are not an expert on your topic and that you are reporting the results of your reading. When writing an exam, remember that you are a student trying to reveal your mastery of the subject matter. Be consistent in displaying your knowledge and understanding.

Whether you write as a creditor seeking a loan extension, an outraged citizen, or a well-prepared student, be aware of the identity you take on. If you are an authority, act like one. If you are committed to your subject, don't be afraid to show it. If you lack information, locate the facts or data you need before you proceed. If you are not enthusiastic about your subject, don't pretend you are; you will probably sound insincere. If you are not an expert, don't pose as one because the chances of being found out are almost certain.

Know How Your Audience Perceives You

It is important that you anticipate how your audience will respond to you and your subject. The way an audience perceives you as a writer influences how you approach your topic, what level of detail you need, and what tone you should use.

If your readers respect you as an authority, you will not have to establish your expertise as fully as you would if they thought of you as a beginner. Of the following student topics, determine which ones reflect a student's experience. Ask yourself, how does the reader's perception of your expertise affect what you will write about each topic?

The Benefits of Joining the Glee Club

The Personal Gains of Ethical Conduct

Motivating Sales Using the "Fear" Appeal

Lafayette, Paris, and the French Revolution

Also work toward creating a sense of trust between you and your readers. Is your writing objective and disinterested? Do you have some personal bias toward your subject? Is your tone reasonable and mature?

Finally, does your audience like you? If your readers don't like you, they won't feel any commitment to what you write, no matter how expert or how credible an author you may be. Since readers are usually busy people, they respond favorably to a writer who can:

- present information clearly

- structure ideas so readers can easily follow them

- avoid obnoxious or insulting language

- provide all the details an audience needs

- be generous, understanding, and modest

- hold the reader's interest by freshness of thought

Being aware of who you are in each writing act and anticipating how your audience sees and reacts to you is an important initial step in the writing process.

EXERCISE

1. Choose any piece of advertising and discuss the ways in which the writers have tried to make you react favorably to the product or the corporation.

2. Using the same piece of advertising, look at ways in which the writers have tried to create an impression of expertise and an impression of trustworthiness.

3. Letters to the editor are often a good place to find examples of writers who fail to analyze their purpose. Look at some of these letters: first determine the purpose of each writer and then determine if the letter fulfills that purpose.

List at least one type of reader to whom an essay on each of the following topics might be directed. Consider also what role the writer might assume.

1. Freezing Nuclear Weapons Production
2. Legalizing Gambling as a Source of State Revenue
3. Joint Custody in Divorce Cases
4. Reasons for the Nursing Shortage
5. Student Evaluations of Faculty

CHAPTER

3

Drafting

the Essay

This chapter will help you compose the first draft of an essay. Having collected information and considered your purpose and reader, you now come to the point when you must focus and arrange this information. Begin by reading over your prewriting material to see what interesting insights or connections you can explore. Look for points to be developed, subdivided, and deleted. Next, make the subject your own by turning it into a manageable topic, one you know and feel something about. Before you write, you will probably ask yourself these basic questions, which are covered in the following pages:

How can I limit my subject?

What is my main idea?

How will I plan the essay?

How will I begin?

5 | Limit your topic.

Before you write the first draft, examine your subject for a topic that will interest your reader and that will be possible for you to handle. Consider whether you have enough information about your topic to develop it effectively. Do you have sources available? Do you have enough time to investigate it? Return to your prewriting strategy to narrow your subject. If, for example, you had begun with a broad subject such as physical fitness, your prewriting might have helped you limit your focus to aerobics. Now, with further thought, you find that this is also too broad. Continue to narrow your topics:

Aerobics
↓
Benefits of Aerobics
↓
Benefits of Aerobics for Weight Reduction

Many beginning writers choose the broadest possible topic because they fear that they have too little to say. In fact, a more limited topic will be easier to develop and will provide more opportunities for specific details. For instance, if you were to write about the meaning of love or the value of education, the result would likely be a series of general statements that would be both boring and unconvincing. Choose instead your experience in caring for a terminally ill relative or the benefits of your summer study in Europe. For an essay on the latter subject, you realize that you cannot include everything that occurred during your summer abroad; so you select one revealing or unusual episode:

Not: My Summer in Europe *or*
The Advantages of Studying Abroad

But: Why I Will Always Remember Getting Lost in Venice *or*
My Problems in Communicating with the French

There are several ways to narrow a subject. You might ask yourself: What aspect of the subject do I know the most about? What aspect most interests me? What aspect would most interest a reader? Your prewriting might also have helped you narrow the subject. For instance, in listing features of "football safety," you might have subdivided this subject into specific areas, such as head injuries, improved helmets, artificial turf, and the role of coaches. Any one of these points can become a limited topic for a short essay:

Broad subject: Football Safety
Still too broad: Reasons for Football Injuries
Limited topic: The Role of Artificial Turf in Football Injuries

Broad subject: Public Television
Still too broad: How Public Television Differs from the Commercial Networks
Limited topic: Superior Coverage of Public Events on Public Television

Broad subject: Modern Technology Harms the Environment
Still too broad: Industrial Chemicals Produce Water Pollution
Limited topic: Acid Rain, Caused Mostly by Coal-Burning Factories, Kills Lakes

To convince others that what you write is worth reading, you must first be interested in the topic yourself. Picking a topic you know and feel something about will make planning and developing the paper easier and more pleasant. It will also give the finished paper an authenticity, authority, and enthusiasm that will capture and hold your reader's interest. (If a topic is assigned, make sure you are comfortable with it before you start to write.) You must understand just what is being asked of you, and you must know—or find out— enough about the subject so that you can handle it with some confidence.

If you are given a general topic, begin by studying the broad assignment ("For your classmates, write an explanation of a process or a technique that you have found useful") and the specific suggestions ("Possibilities range from planting tomatoes to adjusting a carburetor to housebreaking a puppy").

Here are examples of topics that students chose for papers addressed to an audience of classmates:

Inappropriate:	A Simple Method of Determining Chi-Square with a Pocket Calculator
Appropriate:	A Foolproof Method of Balancing a Checkbook with a Pocket Calculator
Inappropriate:	Recent U.S. Policy in Central America
Appropriate:	Reasons for U.S. Involvement in El Salvador

The first inappropriate example assumes a stronger background in statistics than most students have. It would be appropriate for a group of students who use chi-square in interpreting research data, but not for students in the average writing class. The second inappropriate topic deals with a broad subject that most students could treat successfully only through extensive research. A thorough paper on that topic would require more time and space than the typical college essay permits.

The first appropriate topic has a broad appeal. Many of us know nothing about chi-square, but almost all of us know about unbalanced checkbooks. The second appropriate topic is more sensible in scope than the overly ambitious topic on Central America as a whole, and it gives the writer more opportunity to present personal judgments.

A. *Which of the essay topics below would be appropriate for an audience of college students? Mark those that would be appropriate with* A, *those inappropriate with* X.

A 1. The Differences between Health Clubs and Gyms

A 2. The Need for Low-Income Housing

X 3. The Divisive Effect of the Russian Revolution

X 4. The Importance of Molecular Psychology

A 5. Why Religious Cults Are Attractive to Young People

B. *Examine the following essay topics. Mark those that are well limited for an essay with* L, *those too broad with* X.

X   1. Racism in America

X   2. The Greenhouse Effect

L   3. Reasons for the Nursing Shortage

L   4. The Need for Motorcycle-Helmet Laws

L   5. Why Many Young People Distrust the Police

X   6. Solar Energy

X   7. Recent Changes in the Family Structure

L   8. How to Play Soccer

L   9. The Right of Teachers to Strike

L 10. Violence in Music Videos

6   Clarify your purpose with a thesis statement.

Stating your main idea—your thesis—will help you define your purpose in writing: to inform, analyze, describe, or argue, among others. What, you can ask yourself, will I say about my topic? What main point do I hope to make in my essay? Although your prewriting exercises will probably have focused on such questions, it is important to solidify your central idea as you begin to write.

Sometimes it is helpful to write out for yourself: "In this paper I hope to _____." Such a statement, which is *not* included in the paper, expresses your goal as well as some plan for achieving this goal. Rather than stating, "My purpose is to write an essay on animal research," define more explicitly your goal, plan, and audience: "My purpose is to persuade my classmates of the need for stronger government regulations on the use of animals in scientific research." This more clearly focused statement includes a basic writing strategy: to persuade.

In organizing your material, ask yourself what your basic aim in presenting the topic is: to explain how a thing works, to analyze its parts, to define what it means, to describe what it looks like, to tell what happened to it, or to argue for or against it. Often in an essay you will use several of these rhetorical strategies. When you decide on your principal rhetorical aim, you can often discern a method of organization, such as listing events in chronological order or citing the causes of a problem in the order of their importance. Often the topic itself will suggest a method of organization: an essay on how to prepare for a job interview would follow a step-by-step order; an essay analyzing the differences between a novel and a film would employ comparison and contrast.

Having decided what you want to do, construct a sentence that expresses the main idea you intend to present to the reader. This thesis statement should reflect a clear, definite commitment that expresses your stand on the topic. Your statement of purpose will help you formulate a tentative thesis statement: "Better government regulations are needed to reduce the suffering of animals used in laboratory research." Such a statement, subject to change, will guide you as you compose, helping you to make sure that the essay will make one main point. Including the thesis in the introduction of the paper will help the reader see at once your most important point.

A thesis statement does not announce what you are going to write about ("This paper will discuss teacher strikes"). It specifies the point you will make about the topic. For example, you may want to say:

> Teachers' strikes are justifiable because of inadequate compensation.

Or: Although teachers have a right to strike, the students should not be punished in the process.

Or: Teachers should exercise their right to strike only when all other alternatives fail.

Each of these thesis statements serves three functions:

1. It identifies the limited subject and thus provides a test for what material should go into your essay.
2. It makes clear your attitude toward the subject.
3. It focuses the reader's attention on the specific features of the subject that you will discuss.

The inadequate thesis statements that follow perform only one or two of those three functions:

Inadequate: The health fields are very promising today.
Improved: Many new, well-paying, challenging positions are opening up in medical technology.

Inadequate: Police officers today are different from the way they used to be.
Improved: As increasing numbers of college-educated men and women join police forces, the old stereotype of the big dumb cop is rarely used.

The inadequate thesis statements do not provide a limited focus or indicate the writer's feelings or stance: Why are health fields promising? How are police officers different—

and what does the writer think of this change? The revised statements answer such questions by revealing a more specific approach to the topics. The improved thesis statements point to the kind of material that should be presented in the paper and indicate the writer's attitude toward the topic and the reader. Such thesis statements make it much easier to locate information. For instance, if you were developing the essay on jobs in medical technology, you would know that you need data on recent developments in the field, on salaries, and on jobs that call for more than routine performance; and you would know that you should ignore information with no bearing on these matters.

Despite the importance of a thesis statement, you need not feel bound to the first one you write. If you come upon contradictory information or if your attitude changes as you think about the topic, you can always revise your thesis. You might, for example, decide to change your thesis statement on the new breed of police officers to something like this:

> The change in big-city police forces today results not so much from college graduates entering police work as from policemen and policewomen taking advantage of opportunities for advanced education and specialized training.

A good thesis statement, one that is complete and specific, will guide you in developing and supporting it. It will help you know what to emphasize and what to exclude. An effective thesis clarifies your aim: you know why you are writing on the topic and what it means to you. Since nearly all our writing tries to persuade the reader to accept our views, try to think of your topic in arguable terms, as one side in a debate. Sharpening your topic with an argumentative edge will help you clarify your stance and purpose.

EXERCISE

A. Study the thesis statements below. Mark with W *those that would work well for an essay of 300 to 500 words.*

Mark with X those that need to be more specific. Then revise those you have marked X so that they are suitable for a short essay.

w 1. A Southerner who moves to a big city in the North must adjust to a different, faster-paced style of life.

x 2. Dolphins have their own complex language.

w 3. Despite their obvious difference, snow skiing and waterskiing require the same basic skills and provide the same kind of thrills.

x 4. Racism on American campuses has not diminished.

w 5. Network television's exit polls seriously affect voters' attitudes.

x 6. Computer crime is a growing problem.

x 7. Abortion should be a woman's prerogative because she alone should have control over her own body.

x 8. Ultralight aircraft can be dangerous.

x 9. Madonna's songs use religious imagery.

x 10. A home can be altered to accommodate the physically handicapped.

B. For each of the following broad subjects, suggest a more limited, clearly focused topic that would be appropriate for a short essay. Then construct a thesis statement that includes your attitude toward the topic (that is, what you think about it). For example:

Focused topic: Negative Attitudes toward the Elderly in Television Situation Comedies

Thesis: Television situation comedies create as well as mirror negative attitudes toward the elderly.

1. Drinking and Peer Pressure

2. Nonsmokers' Rights

3. Talk Radio

4. Space Shuttles
5. The Problem of Homelessness
6. Relief for High Tuition Costs
7. Men versus Women Shoppers
8. Living in a Small Town
9. College Students and Soap Operas
10. Studying Foreign Languages

7 Plan your draft with a rough outline.

As you begin to write, you need to consider a plan to help you group the various points you have developed. Your first (rough) draft allows you to think through the topic fully, concentrating on the larger issues of content and organization, not style. Sometimes you may begin writing at once, referring to your prewriting notes, and sketch out the body of the essay before returning to the introduction. More often you will first need a rough outline to give you a clear sense of direction, to make sure that your essay has a logical sequence the reader can follow.

Most writers make rough outlines before they compose, and they continue to organize as they write. They use outlines to guide the development of their ideas and do not feel restricted by them. Outlines are meant to be changed, not followed slavishly. Rough outlines, consisting of phrases arranged to show some relationship, can emerge from your prewriting material, as in this example:

Thesis: Most New Age beliefs are not new.
        1. Predicting the future with tarot cards and astrology

2. Searching for peace and world harmony
3. Examining the self

Conclusion: People often forget the ancient forerunners of New Age thinking.

Such an outline suggests the overall plan of the typical essay with its beginning, middle, and end.

Introductory paragraph

Body paragraphs

1. First point
2. Second point
3. Third point, etc.

Concluding paragraph

With your thesis in mind, write out three or four major points in the order that seems most logical. As you write, you can sort the supporting information (facts, examples, details) under the headings in your list. Again, these headings are flexible: if you discover considerable new material, you may find yourself adjusting your outline—or simply composing freely, with the rough outline as your initial guide.

Here is a sample thesis statement with two rough outlines—one unsuccessful, one more effective.

Thesis: The hearing loss caused by rock music is a problem with few solutions.

Ineffective outline:
1. High-decibel noise is part of rock music
2. Parents' warnings about hearing loss
3. Stereo earphones worse than concerts
4. Turning down the volume not likely
5. Regular hearing checkups

Effective outline:
1. Deafness from high-decibel noise
2. Many rock musicians' hearing damaged

3. Stereo earphones endanger hearing
4. Fewer loudspeakers at concerts needed
5. Ear protectors for performers and fans needed

The second rough outline is superior because each point develops from, and clearly relates to, the thesis statement, whereas the first outline contains less relevant points (2, 4, 5).

EXERCISE

7

Study the thesis statements and rough outlines below. Mark each outline that would be helpful with H, unhelpful with X.

x 1. *Thesis:* Alcoholism has become a major health problem.

    Rough outline: 1. Nearly 40 million Americans cannot control their drinking
          2. Teenage drinking rises
          3. Cost of alcohol-related crimes increase
          4. Alcohol-related crimes increase
          5. Brain cells and liver damaged

H 2. *Thesis:* There are many types of prejudice other than religious and racial.

    Rough outline: 1. Small-town roots vs. urban sophistication
          2. Big-name schools vs. lesser-known ones
          3. Physically handicapped people vs. non-handicapped
          4. Southern accents vs. Northern accents
          5. Wealthy families vs. middle-class families

x 3. *Thesis:* Most students find that living on campus is preferable to living at home.

Rough outline: 1. Cafeteria food is one drawback
2. Opportunities to make more friends
3. Developing independence
4. Proximity to classes and libraries
5. Learning to live on a budget

H 4. *Thesis:* The hidden dangers of jogging can make it a harmful means of exercise.

Rough outline: 1. "Runners' knee" results from excessive pressure on the knees
2. Pounding hard surfaces hurts the feet
3. Shinsplints are a common muscle injury
4. Lower back pain results from an imbalance of back and abdominal muscles
5. Dehydration of the body can lead to heatstroke

X 5. *Thesis:* A student's academic responsibilities should take precedence over job commitments.

Rough outline: 1. Large numbers of college students have part-time jobs
2. Tuition costs make jobs essential for many students
3. Scheduling classes to suit employers' demands can cause problems
4. Finding adequate study time is a major challenge
5. Off-campus jobs often prevent involvement in college activities

A thorough topic outline can provide a complete point-by-point layout of your entire essay. A sentence outline can do even more. It can give topic sentences to organize your explanations for all of your points. Detailed topic or sentence outlines are excellent guides to organization and can be especially helpful in preparing a long paper.

To develop a good topic outline, start by using the points on your rough outline as the major divisions (labeling them with Roman numerals I, II, III, etc.). Then develop subdivisions (labeling them A, B, C, etc.) for each. Although two levels may be enough for a short paper, a third level (labeled 1, 2, 3, etc.) will help you organize details in longer projects. Sometimes even a fourth level is useful (labeled a, b, c, etc.).

Topic outline

Thesis: Businesses should not use polygraph tests to screen job applicants.

I. Why businesses use polygraph tests
   A. To keep employees from stealing
   B. To determine the honesty of job applicants

II. What kind of businesses use polygraph tests

III. How the polygraph test works
   A. Records one's physical response to questions
   B. The response pattern interpreted by an examiner
   C. Is not a "lie detector"

IV. Why businesses should not use polygraph tests
   A. Potentially good employees frightened away
   B. Lack of scientific evidence that tests are accurate
   C. Unreliability of examiners
   D. Unethical uses of confidential information
   E. Illegal invasion of privacy

A sentence outline is included with the sample research paper (pages 374–375).

8 Your introductory paragraph should focus the reader's interest on your thesis.

A good introduction serves two important functions: it attracts the reader's interest and focuses that interest on the thesis. Therefore, to write a good introduction, you need to know what your thesis is and why your reader might care about what you have to say. If you can be sure that your reader is already interested in your topic, and if your essay is short, then you hardly need an introduction. Start with the thesis statement and move to the first point:

> Anyone who earns over $10,000 a year should be aware of
> three simple techniques for saving money on income taxes.
> The first and most obvious of these . . .

To treat the same subject in a longer paper, in more than a few paragraphs, you might need to mention all three techniques in the introduction so that the reader would know what to expect. Then the next paragraph could begin discussing the first technique.

If your reader needs background information to understand why your topic is significant, provide that information in your introductory paragraph. If, for example, you were going to report on new techniques for catching shoplifters at the store where you work, you could first discuss what shoplifting costs the average consumer and then lead your reader to the specific case of your store and finally to your thesis statement.

The pattern just discussed for the introductory paragraph on shoplifting is the most reliable way of introducing college papers:

General statements related to topic and to reader's interests
↓
Any necessary background material
↓
Thesis statement

Sometimes you will start with your thesis and include an outline of your main points in the introductory paragraph:

> *Citizen Kane* is my candidate for the greatest movie ever made. Orson Welles' 1941 classic remains unsurpassed for several reasons. One is the appeal of the theme, with its examination of power and of idealism corrupted by wealth. This political fable of an American magnate is told in an imaginative series of flashbacks and flash forwards that suggests the mystery of the character's failure. The innovative use of light and sound also contributes to the film's technical brilliance.

8

The body paragraphs would analyze the theme and techniques in detail.

A more effective way to capture the reader's interest is to open with an interesting example, experience, or anecdote. Sometimes a quotation or proverb is effective:

> "It is better to be silent and thought a fool than to open your mouth and remove all doubt." I remember this old saying whenever I prefer to listen rather than speak in class. . . .

Instead of stating his thesis—that football is unnecessarily brutal—this student begins with his own experience:

> I spent the Christmas of my senior year in the hospital with my neck in a brace, wondering if the cut nerves in my right arm would leave me permanently crippled. In the next room, a classmate was recovering from spinal surgery to correct a massive herniation that made him, a strong young man of 21, immobile. He took a year to recover; I spent three months in traction. We still undergo therapy and face further hospitalization. Although we both survived, we paid a terrible price for playing football.

The revision stage of the writing process provides the best opportunity to produce a good introduction. After you have completed a first draft and have clarified your ideas, you can return to the opening and rework it. Consider these introductory paragraphs:

First draft: Elvis Presley, who died in 1977, lives in the minds of many of his fans and in the pages of tabloids, which proclaim his reincarnation. Books, too, recount psychic experiences involving the dead singer and stories of his reincarnation. Visitors pour into his home and buy memorabilia, making his estate much more valuable than it was when he was alive. To thousands of loyal worshippers, the King is not dead. He and the Elvis phenomenon have become larger than life.

Revised: Each year on August 16, the anniversary of his death, the faithful converge on Memphis to hold a candlelight vigil at the shrine of Elvis Presley. Many of them look forward to his return or recount psychic experiences in which Elvis appears to them. Books and tabloids proclaim, "The King lives!" adding fuel to the reports of his reincarnation. Millions of dollars are spent on statues, records, pictures, and other memorabilia because of a belief that if Elvis is not alive, he is a saint. Elvis worshippers have formed a religious cult unlike anything associated with other dead celebrities.

In revising, the writer has developed an introduction with specific examples that clarify the idea of a religious cult.

EXERCISE

1. A student's essay on open adoption begins with the following paragraph. What could you do to rearrange some of the sentences and add material to provide a more colorful introduction?

Whereas most people take their heritage for granted, adopted people often experience a sense of dislocation or anxiety about their identity. Open adoption allows children to fill in these blanks, giving their lives continuity. Most adopted children live with the question: "Who am I?" They wonder if they were wanted or whether there was a good reason for their natural parents to give them up.

2. Here are a thesis statement and topic sentences for the three main paragraphs of a short essay. Write an introduction.

Thesis:	Today's popular music is so varied that no one type is dominant.
First topic sentence:	The distinctions among rock, soul, salsa, and Country-Western are often blurred.
Second topic sentence:	Popular composers often borrow from other stylists.
Third topic sentence:	Many performers are hard to categorize.

9 Your concluding paragraph should reemphasize your main points.

The conclusion should state your thesis in different words and reemphasize its importance. Merely repeating your ideas is unnecessary and tedious, but a concluding paragraph can summarize the main points of a long essay. Here is the conclusion of an essay on the importance of fairy tales:

Because parents are often uncomfortable dealing with evil and fear, fairy tales are indispensable for young children. In a society where the family structure has changed, children need the reassurance provided by stories in which love overcomes the fear of death. They need to hear stories that confront the anxieties of the real world through characters who overcome obstacles and live "happily ever after."

—Marian Engels (student)

Sometimes you can recommend a course of action or solution to problems presented in the paper, as in this ending of an essay on hiring the disabled:

> Businesses have made many improvements to enable disabled people to work comfortably, and new laws and programs have helped them secure jobs. Architectural barriers have been eliminated to help the disabled. As a result, businesses should be willing to hire more disabled people and provide proper facilities for them. Since disabled people have shown that they can function in the business world, shouldn't they be given every chance to contribute to society?
>
> —Mary Herder (student)

Whether you cover all of your main points or just your thesis, follow these guidelines in writing concluding paragraphs:

1. Do not introduce new topics; everything you present should emphasize points you have already made.
2. Do not repeat the same words and examples you have used earlier.
3. Make your writing forceful; do not overestimate the importance of what you have said, but do not hesitate or apologize, either.

Though it should be concise, a conclusion cannot be so vague and general that the reader feels let down, as in this ending of a literary analysis that compares two short stories:

First draft: These two stories, despite their many differences, have much in common. They show how two writers, using different subjects and styles, can say similar things.

To satisfy the reader with an appropriate conclusion, the writer should present the reason for the comparison of the stories and sum up what the analysis has revealed:

Revised draft: These two stories, though different in subject and tone, force us to think about what a successful life is. By presenting their readers with failures, both authors imply that success does not consist in possessing material goods but in living according to the enduring values of love, selflessness, and honesty.

9

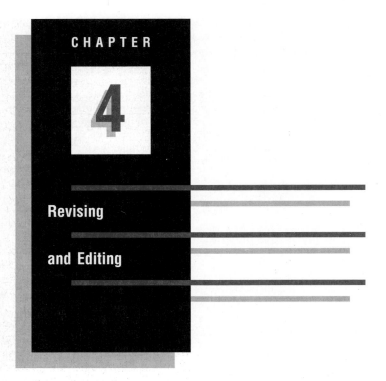

Revision means to "look again," to rethink and clarify what you have written. You "step back" from your work to examine it afresh. Revision does not mean recopying or correcting errors but recognizing that your draft is unfinished, that words and ideas can be added, deleted, or rearranged. A good writer is never satisfied with a first draft and never forgets that writing entails rewriting. Rarely will you submit an essay without making changes in its content as well as in its structure and style. If you assume that nearly every piece of writing can be improved, you will not hesitate to drop entire paragraphs, to condense, shift, and rearrange. As you revise, you are examining your initial ideas, purpose, and audience to get a more objective perspective on your work; after you revise, you will edit, making changes and corrections on the final copy.

Revision occurs throughout the writing process. After you complete a sentence, for example, you read and react to it, considering whether to expand on it or delete from it. But most rewriting occurs after you have written a first draft. You read that draft with your own intentions in mind, and you also read with your reader in mind. You consider what you have produced and what might be missing to satisfy the reader's needs. Reading your own work objectively and considering the comments of other readers will help you discover if your meaning is clear and if your structure and style express your meaning effectively.

As you read your first draft, you may need to change your thesis, purpose, and writing strategy as you compare what you have written with your original intention. As you proceed from large overall concerns to specific sentence and word changes, your focus will shift from yourself as writer to the reader. First, read what the draft says, then read from the reader's viewpoint, and finally read with an eye for problems to be solved.

Here are some basic tips for revising:

1. As you write, leave plenty of space for changes.
2. When you revise, try to work from a typed or printed, not handwritten, draft so that you can approach your work more objectively.
3. Revise in stages, setting the draft aside for a "cooling off" period; when you return to it, you can then view it critically.
4. Read each draft aloud; if a sentence sounds awkward, rework it until it sounds right. Listen also for omissions and repetitions.
5. Let someone else read your drafts and react honestly to your ideas and style. Collaborative work is espe-

cially helpful as you revise. The comments of your fellow students and instructor can help you develop a more objective view of your work.

6. You should be willing to discard anything that does not relate to your purpose and thesis. But revising does not entail changing *everything;* your prewriting will have produced some useful material.

7. Save all of your drafts, but do not waste time by re-copying the whole paper after each stage of the revision process.

In making your work clearer for your reader, you make it clearer for yourself. This point has been made by Donald M. Murray, who suggests a three-stage "clarification" process. With each reading, he says, the writer should focus on a different aspect of the writing:

1. meaning
2. structure
3. style

10   Revise for overall meaning.

Consider the major areas of your essay before being concerned with the minor ones. First, read your draft quickly for content and ideas. Try to be objective about it, ignoring word choice and other details as you ask yourself these questions about the content:

1. What is my main point?
2. Does everything in the draft relate to this point?
3. Do I have enough solid evidence to develop this point?

4. What else does the reader need to know?

5. Is the draft too short? too long?

6. Are there parts I could cut?

7. Does the draft follow through on what the title and introduction promise?

To make sure that your essay has unity, compare your thesis and introduction with the body of the paper. If they do not match, rewrite the introduction or delete paragraphs that stray from the main point. Use arrows to indicate any paragraphs that need to be switched.

11 Revise for structure.

Read the draft quickly again, this time with your method of organization in mind. Again, avoid questions of style and try to be as objective as you can. Focus on whether each part of the essay is developed well and is in the right order as you ask yourself these questions:

1. Is my title effective?

2. Will my introduction capture the reader's interest? (see **8**)

3. Do I have a clear statement of purpose and a thesis? (see **6**)

4. Is every paragraph related to my thesis?

5. Does each paragraph make one point? Is each paragraph fully developed? (see **21, 24**)

6. Am I using facts and examples, not merely general statements, to support my thesis? (see **17**)

7. Have I defined my major terms? (see **16**)

8. Am I bringing myself into the paper too much, distracting the reader from the subject?

9. Does the conclusion sum up the main points and return to the thesis? (see **9**)

At this stage in the revision, look for any irrelevant information that can be cut. Then examine your paragraphs; if they are skimpy, consider what examples or facts you can add from your prewriting. Remember that making changes is easier than starting from scratch.

To make sure that your essay is effectively organized, make a rough outline or, if you prefer, briefly summarize each paragraph. This will allow you to stand back from your work and see if your points flow naturally and proceed logically and if each point is properly developed.

12 Revise for style.

Then, after a short break, read the draft a third time for style. Now that the content is well established and the structure is firm, read the essay slowly out loud, line by line. Examine your sentence patterns and word choice. Ask yourself these questions:

1. Are my sentences all starting the same way? If so, could I use subordination and variety (combining)? (see **25**)

2. If any of my sentences contain series or lists, are the items grammatically parallel? (see **33a**)

3. Are there any unnecessary repetitions, wordy phrases, clichés, or jargon? (see **29, 75, 77**)

4. Are there any words whose meanings I am unsure of? Is my diction appropriate to my audience and purpose? (see **67, 71**)

5. Have I avoided unnecessary passive verbs? (see **28e**)

6. Are my tenses consistent? (see **46a**)

7. Have I deleted all unnecessary words and phrases? (see **78**)

8. Do I lead the reader smoothly from one point to another and from start to finish?

9. Does the paper sound like me speaking to the reader?

12a   Check the point of view.

As you polish your essay, make sure that you have selected the proper person and that you have not shifted person: first person *(I, we)*, second person *(you)*, third person *(he, she, it, one,* or *they)*. Most academic and professional writing uses third person because it emphasizes the subject, not the writer.

Weak: I found as I watched the movie that the plot was implausible.

Revised: The plot of the movie was implausible.

In this example, the use of *I* distracts the reader from the subject. Some beginning writers mistakenly think that *I* is never suitable in college writing and go out of their way to avoid it:

Weak: It is this writer's contention that the compact disc has not entirely replaced the record album.

Improved: The compact disc has not entirely replaced the record album.

Or, if your audience lends itself to a more informal tone:

For me, the compact disc has not entirely replaced the old, familiar vinyl record.

12

The *I* point of view is appropriate if you are writing from your own experience. In this example from a personal narrative, the writer is the subject:

> I went to the woods because I wished to live deliberately, to front only the essential facts of life, and see if I could not learn what it had to teach, and not, when I came to die, discover that I had not lived.
>
> —Henry David Thoreau

The *you* point of view, which emphasizes the reader, is used in instructional materials, such as this book, which talks directly to the student. The indefinite *you* (referring to anyone in general) is inappropriate:

> College helps you become a well-rounded person. (see **40b**)

12b Rely on topic sentences.

In revising for style, examine the topic sentence of each paragraph in your draft to see if the sentence clearly defines the doer (subject) and the action (verb). By asking *who, what, where, when, how,* and *why,* you can give each paragraph a more specific focus and place the emphasis where it is needed.

Weak: There were numerous differences between the presidencies of Carter and Reagan.

Revised: The presidencies of Carter and Reagan differed most in their views of federal power.

The first topic sentence above is weak because it fails to address *how* the presidencies of Carter and Reagan differed. The following paragraph is poorly developed because the writer did not ask any of the basic questions about the doer, the action, and the purpose:

Beginning life on a college campus is exciting yet difficult and frustrating in many ways. For the first time there are new ideas, responsibilities, and attitudes that are challenged. Yet with these challenges come many problems for the new freshman.

The first sentence has no doer: who is beginning life? The writer uses *there are* (in the second sentence) rather than a human subject, such as "the freshman for the first time encounters new . . ." The use of *many ways* and *many problems* gives the reader no mental picture. To revise this vague paragraph, the writer examines each sentence to see how it can become more specific and draws on her experience to generate examples. Here is a later version of that paragraph with final revisions included:

A freshman's ~~One's~~ introduction to college life is often *less*

exciting ~~as well as~~ *than* difficult and ~~very~~

frustrating. I spent most of my first day at the

University standing in lines, ~~I waited~~ first at

registration, ~~and~~ then at the bookstore. *When* I

returned exhausted to the dorm after getting none

of the classes I *had* wanted, ~~and~~ *I* went to the

cafeteria, hoping to *find* ~~see~~ my roommate, but ended up

eating alone. That night I was ~~really~~ ready to

~~call it quits and~~ go home. But now, after two

weeks here, I have learned to cope with dorm

                                      _to_
problems and͜enjoy the independence. Having made

new friends͜~~in my classes and at several parties~~

I/find college challenging and fun. My experience
                    freshmen the hassles of
shows that, if ~~one~~͜can handle͜the first week,

they can manage to enjoy⌐life i/n college⌐
                               ⊙

Revising should also help you develop your own style. Your
aim is to express your convictions clearly and honestly, not to
try to impress readers with a formal, stilted style of borrowed
phrases and unfamiliar words. Pay close attention to sentence structure (chapter 7) and word choice (see **71**), simplify
wordy phrases (see **78**), reduce the passive voice (see **28e**),
and reword for emphasis (see **28**).

Not: There is no reason TV cameras should not have a place
        in our courts. *(confusing double negative)*

But: TV cameras should have a place in our courts.

Not: The house was purchased for $52,500, but Carlos sold it
        for $89,900. *(shift from passive to active)*

But: Carlos purchased the house for $52,500 but sold it for
        $89,900.

Rather than worry about an inadequate word length, imagine
that you will be rewarded for the words you can delete. Consider the advice of Strunk and White in *The Elements of Style:*
"A sentence should contain no unnecessary words, a paragraph no unnecessary sentences, for the same reason that a
drawing should have no unnecessary lines and a machine no
unnecessary parts."

13 Use collaboration in revising.

Writing need not be an entirely solitary activity. By having others respond to your work, you can receive valuable help, and you can see that your instructor is not your only reader. By reading another's paper, you can also become a better reader of your own work.

Friends and family members can react to your work as outsiders; fellow students, who know the assignment and the standards for evaluating it, can approach it more objectively as insiders who know the problems involved with incomplete drafts. As partners, they can help you reexamine your ideas.

Here are some suggestions for collaborative revising:

1. Make helpful, positive suggestions and comments. Your aim is not to "play teacher." Recognize, too, that the criticism you receive is directed at your work, not at you. Respect others' responses, but know that you must decide what to accept and what to reject.

2. Be prepared with a legible draft and with specific questions about your own work.

3. Do not focus on errors, style, or word changes.

4. If your instructor divides the class into groups, you can focus on three or four specific aspects of your partners' work. For example, you can determine if there is a clear purpose and thesis, adequate development, and an introduction that captures your attention and indicates how the paper will be structured.

5. Independently of the class, you can exchange a draft with another student and agree to examine each other's work before it is due. Rather than trying to focus on everything, examine the introductory paragraph, the first sentence of each subsequent paragraph, and

the conclusion to determine if the structure is clear and logical. Or you can work with your partner to develop some of your own criteria for evaluating each other's writing. Try writing a short summary of the student's thesis and purpose; then write a short comment, indicating your assessment of the paper's strengths and weaknesses.

14 Revising with a word processor.

Most writers are more objective and critical when reacting to typed or computer-printed drafts than to handwritten ones. Writing undergoes an important transformation when you move from reading your own scrawl to seeing your words in type, and you become aware of problems not apparent before. Revising from a typed or printed copy can help you spot smaller stylistic problems as well as larger problems of organization and development.

If you compose your initial drafts with a word processor, you are ahead of the game. You know that modern technology has greatly simplified the time-consuming retyping once required for revision. Microcomputers can make it easier for you to make multiple changes in your drafts. With the text on the computer screen, it is easy to add, delete, or rearrange elements. Word processing packages generally allow you to add merely by typing in new material and to delete by using a "delete" key. Most writers, however, think it best to edit on hard copy (paper), which they mark up before entering the changes into the computer. Proofreading, too, is best done from the hard copy before you print the final text. Remember, you should not rely exclusively on your spelling check, which cannot help you distinguish between easily confused words (*their* and *there,* for example). Writers must be responsible for editing their own errors and correcting their own spelling.

Whether you revise by working on-screen or by marking the printout, be sure to save and print copies of each stage of your essay. You may wish to return to earlier drafts as you rethink the assignment.

15 Edit for errors.

The final stage in revising is editing the final draft for correctness. If your work is to make a good impression, a thorough word-by-word examination of your completed essay for errors and omissions is essential. No matter how interesting the topic, no matter how imaginative its development, if the essay contains errors, the reader is sure to think less of your work and to be distracted from what you say.

The proofreading stage is the time not for major changes but for checking typing errors or slips of the pen. Put the draft aside for a while; then read it carefully, looking at individual words, not at whole statements. To locate misspellings and omissions, read backwards, starting with the last word. Check for repeated words as well as for spelling, punctuation, and grammatical errors. Check the dictionary for the meanings of any words you are unsure of. To change a wrong or misspelled word, draw a line through it and write the correction directly above. If you have omitted a word, place a caret (∧) below the line at the place where the omission occurs and then write the word directly above the caret. If you have a number of such corrections, you should retype or recopy the page. The following passage includes most of the frequently used proofreading marks:

    Most of us have difficulty

proof reading our own work properly   **close up**

because of the way we read it: for

content. Our eyes no**rm**ally move **reverse**

across a line of pr**in**t in a series

of "jumps" that Allow us to focus*on* **lowercase/insert**

one point of information, then

another. <u>in</u> proofreading, we must **caps**

interrupt|this normal reading-for- **separate**

information method and read *the* words as **insert**

words, concentrating on form

(spelling, grammar, etc.), on not **transpose**

meaning.

EXERCISE

A. Revise this paragraph by clarifying the subjects and verbs in any sentences that are vague or impersonal and by reducing wordiness.

~~Explaining~~ the many differences between rugby and

involve
football ~~comes down to a question of~~ professionalism.

~~Though there are many differences between the two~~

~~sports, the outstanding difference is that~~ rugby~~,~~ is unlike

professional football~~,since it~~ is engaged in merely for the love of the game. Participating in the sport means that

rugby players need ... *themselves*

outside jobs ~~are necessary~~ to support ~~the players and their~~

pay their . *Because it is an*

~~hobby.~~ And expenses on the road ~~must be paid by the~~

amateur sport, rugby has trouble

~~players. The difficulty in attracting large crowds to support~~

attracting large crowds in America

~~rugby in this country is no doubt due to the fact that it is~~

and is therefore less popular.

~~an amateur sport that is less well promoted and therefore~~

~~less popular than football.~~

B. Revise the following sentences by simplifying them.

1. ~~What~~ the machine ~~does is to~~ enable*s* the blind to

   read without Braille.

2. Sam ~~possessed the knowledge~~ *knew* that he was in

   trouble.

3. ~~It is~~ the characters who distort moral standards.

   ~~that~~ the author condemns

4. ~~What~~ Shakespeare is suggesting ~~and conveying to~~

   ~~us, his audience, in this particular play, is~~ the

   power of sexual jealousy *in this play.*

   because

5. ~~The reason why~~ I was late ~~was due to the fact that~~ I

   overslept.

6. ~~In the case of~~ <u>engineering</u>/ ~~it can be assumed that~~

   students will have to work ~~very~~ hard ~~indeed.~~
   The idea

7. ~~It has been suggested~~ that lasers can be used to

   destroy enemy missiles/ ~~and this idea~~ caused much

   concern in the 1960s.

                                          creates   mood.
8. ~~The mood created by~~ the album ~~is~~ a mellow ~~one.~~
      preferred

9. She ~~indicated her preference for~~ the white wine.
   We can better comprehend

10. ~~A basic part of our comprehension of~~ the character
                                      if we inquire
    of Shylock in *The Merchant of Venice* ~~is dependent~~
                                   of
    ~~upon our inquiring~~ into the role ~~played by~~ Jews in

    the society of Shakespeare's ~~time.~~

*C. If you write with a word processor, explain the
advantages that your word processing package offers for
revising. Write a paragraph to a student unfamiliar with
your software package. Or write a paragraph for your
instructor explaining how you revise using your word
processor.*

*D. Examine these drafts of a student paragraph, noting
where and why changes were made.*

First draft with major revisions:

~~IN PRAISE OF HALLOWEEN~~ HASSLE-FREE HOLIDAY By Lynn Adams

There are no "shoulds" at Halloween time and
It has a lighthearted quality that other holidays lack.
no expenses to speak of. A costume can be as

plain as a paper bag with eyeholes, and a party

can be as simple as candy and games. Halloween

doesn't demand days of cooking or weeks of

shopping, and it isn't associated with heavy

drinking. ~~It is a day to pop corn and dangle~~

~~spiders.~~ It doesn't force families to travel or

, thus preventing tension and hurt feelings.
plan elaborate get-togethers. ~~The best thing is,~~
Fortunately,
it leaves many people indifferent to it, and they

play an important role in keeping this holiday

hassle free. If you don't like going to work as

~~a witch, clown,~~ Frankenstein, or Cinderella, you

can be yourself without being called "Scrooge" or

having "Bah! Humbug" hissed at you behind your

back. ~~Don't we need a day when people just come~~

~~together to relax?~~ ~~Isn't it surprising,~~ *It is appropriate* that this

hassle-free day that celebrates dark, frightening

things is free of fear and darkness.

*On Halloween, people who like one another get together to
have fun and be silly or grotesque, qualities we need in
our ~~busy,~~ overworked, ~~serious,~~ practical ~~daily~~ lives.*

15

Second draft with style revisions:

HASSLE-FREE HOLIDAY   By Lynn Adams

~~B~~*Because* ^There are no "shoulds" ~~at~~ *around* Halloween ~~time~~ and

few major
~~no~~ ^expenses, ~~to speak of.~~ ^*I*t has a lighthearted

quality that other holidays lack. A costume can

be as plain as a paper bag *pierced* ^with eyeholes~~; and~~ a

party can be as simple as~~candy and games.~~ ^*ducking for apples.*

Halloween doesn't demand days of cooking or weeks

nor is it
of shopping, ~~and it isn't~~ associated with heavy

to
drinking. It doesn't force families to travel or ^

plan elaborate get-togethers, thus preventing

also
tension and hurt feelings. Fortunately, it ^leaves

these people
many people indifferent, ~~to it,~~ and ~~they~~ ^play an

important role in keeping this holiday hassle

people
free.   If ~~you~~ ^don't like going to work as

they   *themselves*
Frankenstein or Cinderella, ~~you~~ can be ~~yourself~~

hearing
without being called "Scrooge" or ~~having,~~ ^"Bah!

their   *s.*
Humbug" ~~hissed at you~~ behind ~~your~~ back ^ On

friends
Halloween, ~~people who like one another~~ get

--
together to have fun and be silly or grotesque~~/~~ ^

that get too little attention
qualities ~~we need,~~ ^in our overworked, practical

ironic   *holiday*
lives. It is ~~appropriate~~ that this ~~hassle-free~~

the shadowland of ghosts, skeletons,
~~day~~ that celebrates ~~dark, frightening things is~~

and monsters is so unshadowed by distress
~~free of fear~~ ^and darkness.

Final draft:

HASSLE-FREE HOLIDAY   By Lynn Adams

Because there are no "shoulds" around Halloween and few major expenses, it has a lighthearted quality that other holidays lack. A costume can be as plain as a paper bag pierced with eyeholes; a party can be as simple as ducking for apples. Halloween doesn't demand days of cooking or weeks of shopping, nor is it associated with heavy drinking. It doesn't force families to travel or to plan elaborate get-togethers, thus preventing tension and hurt feelings. Fortunately, it also leaves many people indifferent, and these people play an important role in keeping this holiday hassle free. If people don't like going to work as Frankenstein or Cinderella, they can be themselves without being called "Scrooge" or hearing "Bah! Humbug" behind their backs. On Halloween, friends get together to have fun and be silly or grotesque-- qualities that get too little attention in our overworked, practical lives. It is ironic that this holiday that celebrates the shadowland of ghosts, skeletons, and monsters is so unshadowed by distress and darkness.

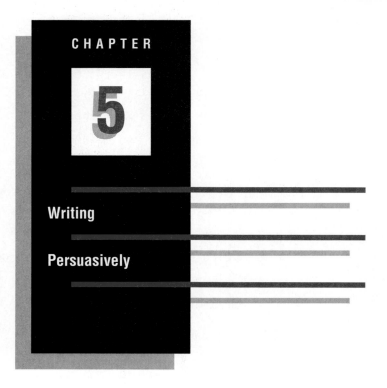

CHAPTER

5

Writing

Persuasively

Successful writing is convincing as well as interesting. To be convincing, you must provide evidence to support your thesis and make sure that your reasoning is logical.

Most of the essays you write will be argumentative since the thesis statement you choose reflects your stance on an issue or topic, and it is a stance that must be proved. Such writing assumes that your reader will not automatically agree with your views. So your aim is to win over the audience. You can do so by establishing your own authority and credibility, that is, by being reasonable: using logical arguments that are clearly and forcefully stated, exploring issues fully, and presenting facts and examples to support your position. Often you must anticipate your reader's objections to your arguments and refute them objectively.

Convincing writing not only relies on the full exploration of your subject but also demands that you create a reasonable and credible voice. Present your views in a fair, balanced, honest manner. Convince your readers that you are well informed about your subject, that you are sincere in what you write, and that you are being candid with them.

Persuasive writing, essentially, is the art of appearing logical and objective. This chapter will help you achieve this end.

16 Define your terms.

Having a clear understanding of the important words and concepts in your thesis and sharing this information with the reader are essential to logical writing. As Cicero wrote 2,000 years ago, "Every rational discussion of anything whatsoever should begin with a definition to make clear what is the subject of the dispute."

Many issues you will deal with as a writer involve the precise definition of key words. For instance, our courts have tried to grapple with the definition of *pornography* as well as *religious freedom* and *affirmative action;* the controversy over abortion depends on a definition of *human life* and when it begins. Political discussions of democratic governments in the Third World require a definition of *democracy.* In much controversial writing, the definition is the most important element.

Writers must anticipate the readers' need to understand any new or technical term, any vague or ambiguous word, or any legal term they may not know. If you introduce a term of your own or use an old term in a new way, you must define it. Equivocal words, having several possible meanings, can cause problems; a word such as *intelligence* will require extensive definition. Make sure that your definitions are not so broad or so narrow that they result in vagueness. Also avoid circular definitions in which a key term is repeated: "A hacksaw is a saw used to hack wood."

Definitions must be logical. One way to create a logical definition is to place the thing being defined in its general class or genus, then to explain its difference from other things in that class. "A telephone is an instrument for communication" is not a satisfactory definition since it is not limited solely to the thing being defined: there are many instruments for communication. The definition must be expanded to limit the class of the object ("instrument") so that it includes the telephone and nothing else. You can define words in many ways, for example, by using synonyms, antonyms, analogies, past usage, and examples.

17 Use solid evidence.

To be convincing, an essay must include adequate evidence. Evidence consists of acts, examples, personal testimony, and other information relevant to your topic that supports your thesis. In selecting evidence, first be sure to distinguish carefully between facts and opinions. Be suspicious of unprovable, uninformed opinions that have no factual basis:

Americans are more materialistic than Europeans.

College students are more politically liberal than their parents.

Whereas facts can be verified, opinions are personal judgments that may or may not be verifiable, depending on the supporting facts. That the U.S. Civil War occurred between 1861 and 1865 is a fact documented in reliable sources. That the causes of the Civil War were economic rather than political is an opinion that would require evidence before readers would accept it. Make sure that your opinions are informed, that is, based on good sense or facts which can be verified by research, observation, or experience. Uninformed opinions, on the other hand, reflect popular beliefs and cannot be verified.

Uninformed opinion: Crazy ideas get their start in California.

Informed opinion: Florida is a dangerous state for lightning strikes.

Conclusions based on mere opinion (unless the opinion is that of an unbiased expert) are usually unreliable, whereas conclusions based on facts (hard evidence) can stand up under scrutiny.

17

You can generate evidence by brainstorming and by using other prewriting strategies (see **1**), and you can locate evidence by examining library and other sources that agree, as well as disagree, with your view. Do not ignore evidence that seems to conflict with your views. Present it honestly, and strengthen your position by showing that there is opposing evidence, which need not weaken your argument. Refute other views by showing that your position is more reasonable. Include your own experience, but realize that many of your readers may have had different experiences. So you will have to put yourself in their place and anticipate objections. In assembling evidence, then, consider your audience. If your thesis is that elderly drivers should face tougher standards than younger drivers, do not write merely for those who would likely agree with you (such as college students); remember those readers (such as senior citizens) who would be likely to challenge your views. In collecting and presenting evidence, be as skeptical as your readers are likely to be.

Consider the reader's response to this statement: "Eighteen is a reasonable drinking age, and our legislators should lower the legal drinking age in our state." Remember that assertions alone are not convincing. Without seeing some evidence, the reader is likely to say, "Eighteen is not a reasonable age," and so reject the conclusion. But evidence—such as facts, examples, personal testimony, and other relevant information—can transform this opinion into an arguable thesis.

To be persuasive, evidence must be up to date, sufficient, unbiased, and representative. For instance, a single example will not be convincing, nor would most evidence derived from only one group of people. Experts are an important source of evidence, but since they are likely to disagree with one another, it is important to consult more than one.

Statistical evidence is probably the most effective logical tool. Advertisers rely heavily on statistics ("four out of five doctors"), and legislators use them to defend their positions ("violent crime has increased 14 percent"). Statistics, however, must be examined critically. Some statistics are manipulated or misleading. It is often impossible, for example, to prove or disprove certain "facts," such as that an alcoholic drink kills 5,000 brain cells. And when you read about "average income," ask yourself whether it is a mean or median average. Moreover, a pollster can control statistics by controlling the information from which they are drawn. And the fact that a majority of citizens polled on an issue favors that issue does not mean that your reader will also favor it.

Like statistics, facts are an important source of evidence but must be checked for accuracy. To determine within reasonable limits what is factually reliable, consult encyclopedias, dictionaries, almanacs, and other standard reference sources.

Examine carefully the published sources you consult, remembering that not everything in print is authoritative (see **81**). Some publications—such as those sponsored by or advocating particular political, religious, or business interests—are likely to be biased. Often writers with little background in a subject publish books, as some health and diet books attest. Articles in popular magazines are often written by non-experts; even noted authorities writing outside their fields lack authority. Be suspicious if the published authority:

- is not objective, fails to acknowledge opposing views

- does not distinguish fact from opinion

- is not published by a reputable publisher or is out of date

- is not recognized as a reliable source by other authorities (in book reviews, etc.)

EXERCISE

Decide if each of the following sentences states a fact (F) or opinion (O). Rewrite statements of opinion as fact.

Example

Opinion: Joan is a bright student.

Fact: Joan is a scholarship student who makes excellent grades in difficult subjects.

o 1. Chan is a stylish dresser.

o 2. Woody Allen's early movies are wonderfully funny.

F 3. Canada has fewer drug problems than the United States.

o 4. This course is too difficult.

o 5. This camera is expensive.

o 6. Bran cereal is the best source of fiber.

F 7. Fifty million Americans walk every day for exercise.

o 8. Wealthy people pay fewer taxes than middle-class people.

18 Be reasonable.

Being reasonable means listening to all sides of an issue, researching it thoroughly, and thinking it through before drawing conclusions. Reasonable writing also requires moderation. Since readers will be turned off by extreme positions ("children should not be allowed to play contact sports"), try to find a middle ground between the extremes in any controversial topic. Recognize facts and examples that seem to contradict your views and mention them in your argument. Refute opposing views by showing why your position is stronger. In refuting opinions you disagree with, do not attack those who hold the opposing views; instead, give your reader good reasons to reject those views as weak or unsound. If you cannot show logically why your opinions are preferable to others, you need to do more thinking and reading, or consider changing your thesis. Conceding that the opposition has some valid points comes from recognizing that arguable issues are not black or white, all right or all wrong. By avoiding a one-sided presentation, you can win your readers over by presenting yourself as a well-informed writer who has prepared a case as fairly and completely as possible.

EXERCISE

A. *Examine the following statements. Mark with* R *those that appear reasonable; restate those that appear unreasonable.*

1. Exposure to television violence contributes directly to criminal behavior.

2. The fall of the Roman Empire was due to a decline in moral standards.

3. Safety belts reduce injuries in auto accidents.

4. TV commercials for beer lead to adolescent alcoholism.

5. The United States has lost its role as preeminent leader of the industrial world.

B. *Definitions*

1. Use your dictionary and your own experience to define one of the following words: *propaganda, happiness, love, education, philosophy.*

2. Examine the following definitions, and reword those that are illogical:

   a. Shakespeare's works are *classics* because they are the standard against which drama is judged.

   b. An *election* is when people vote.

   c. A *leftist* is a person whose political position is radical or liberal.

C. *Reword the following statements so that they become moderate:*

1. Women have no place in the armed services.

2. Today's young people lack the sound moral values of their elders.

3. Television viewing is addictive.

4. Parents with young children should not own guns.

5. Wealthy people have a better chance of getting elected to Congress than other people.

18

Effective writing requires logical reasoning. Reasoning is a way of thinking in which one statement leads a writer to reach a conclusion. For instance: "The rate of inflation has come down; therefore, the cost of new housing will come down, too." The first statement establishes a fact that allows for the conclusion. It isn't sufficient to present an opinion ("I think housing costs will soon be lower"); you must present a reason that allows you logically to reach your conclusion.

Logic is concerned with the way we move from assumptions to conclusions. It does so in two ways: by induction and by deduction. Inductive reasoning moves from the particular to the general, drawing a conclusion about an entire class of things by examining specific examples. If, for example, while driving down the highway you see ten stalled Hondas, you might conclude that Hondas aren't reliable. You are applying inductive reasoning to your observations, proceeding from specific examples to a more general conclusion. In such instances, we rely on the inductive leap, a conclusion based on probability. Since you have seen only a fraction of the existing Hondas in the world, it would be safer to conclude that *some* Hondas are unreliable since you are only aware of the ten you observed, not the others that are probably reliable. To be absolutely certain of your conclusion, you would have to examine *every* Honda.

Facts, statistics, and informed opinions lead inductively to generalizations. A generalization is a logical "leap" you make from the particular evidence to the larger conclusion. When using inductive logic such as this, be sure your generalizations are based on adequate evidence; a single example or observation will not be convincing.

Inductive reasoning often begins with a question or hypothesis that you try to answer or prove by gathering evidence before you draw an inference or conclusion. For example:

Question:	How did I get a dent in the rear of my car?
Hypothesis:	The car was hit while I was shopping.
Evidence:	There was no dent when I parked the car an hour ago in front of the store.
	I parked on the side of the street away from oncoming cars.
	There is no room for a car behind mine.
	But there is a driveway behind my parking place.
Inference:	Someone backed out of the driveway and hit my car while I was shopping.

I will never be absolutely certain of what happened, but my inference is reasonable. As this example shows, induction allows you to make conclusions with incomplete information; its drawback is that you will never be completely certain of your conclusion. Here is another example. Educators would agree that there is a correlation between poor study habits and poor grades. Many case studies would support this conclusion. But do poor grades result *only* from poor study habits? Are there not some exceptions that would make the generalization "bad grades are caused by bad study habits" false?

Careful writers try to secure as much information as possible and as many examples as possible to make the inductive leap as narrow as they can. And they qualify their conclusions with terms such as *probably, most, it seems, experiments suggest,* etc. For example: "Bad grades are most often caused by bad study habits."

Another method of reasoning, *deduction,* works in a way that is the opposite of induction. It begins with a general premise or assumption and moves to a specific conclusion. The conclusion *must* be true if all the statements in the arguments are true: "If all trees have roots, then this tree has roots." Unlike induction, deduction can be irrefutable in an argument and so is more persuasive. But deductive logic requires the argument to be structured according to long-established forms. The principal form is the *syllogism*, consisting of a general statement or major premise (which is part of our general knowledge of the world), a related but more specific statement called a minor premise, and a conclusion derived from these premises:

All dogs are animals. *(major premise)*
Barney is a dog. *(minor premise)*
Therefore Barney is an animal. *(conclusion)*

Such a conclusion is valid and true; no other conclusion would logically follow from the two premises. If they are true, the conclusion must be true. But if the form of the syllogism is wrong, the argument is not valid and the conclusion not sound:

All dogs are animals. *(major premise)*
All horses are animals. *(minor premise)*
Therefore all dogs are horses. *(conclusion)*

The two premises are true, yet the conclusion is absurd. The syllogism does not work because horses are not included in the major premise, and therefore there is no relation between major and minor premises.

If the major premise is false, the conclusion will be false:

All dogs are black. *(major premise)*
Barney is a dog. *(minor premise)*
Therefore Barney is black. *(conclusion)*

Your arguments, of course, will be more complex, but the principles are the same. If your readers accept your major and minor premises, they should accept your conclusions. So it is important to make sure that your generalizations are sound before drawing conclusions. If you were to state that "liberal arts graduates are successful people" as the basis of

Writing Persuasively

an essay favoring liberal education, you would need to ask yourself these questions:

Is this generalization certain or only probable?
Have any studies been conducted to prove it?
What exceptions can I think of?
What do I mean by "successful"?
Would my readers immediately accept my premise?

A single case study or example will not be a strong enough basis for making a generalization convincing unless you can show that your example is truly representative.

Most argumentative writing uses a combination of induction and deduction. Deductive premises are arrived at by induction. This logical process can be found in many conversations. For example, a friend tells you, "All the students who have worked at Ernie's restaurant have had to drop out of school, so I've decided that Ernie's is not a good place for students to work. And I won't take a job there because I intend to graduate."

Your first step is to examine the logic behind this conclusion. You will want to know whether it is a *coincidence* that students who work at Ernie's drop out of school or whether working there is the major *cause* of their poor academic performance. To make this distinction, you ask your friend if he knows of students who worked at Ernie's and how many he knows; if he says that he has only heard about them or knows only a few of the dozens of student employees, you conclude that his reasoning is based on coincidence. If he should know all the students who have worked at Ernie's in the past two years, each of whom complained of the owner's unreasonable demands on his employees, then it is logical to conclude that working there would be unwise for a student. But this is unlikely. Deduction requires that you start with knowledge that has been tested over the years. Ernie's employee practices have not been scientifically studied; thus the premise that "all students who have worked at Ernie's . . ." is unprovable, and so his conclusion is not logical.

An alternative, practical approach to logic is a method devised by Stephen Toulmin. Toulmin logic is concerned with persuading or arguing for some conclusion, some claim you wish to make. Toulmin says that every argument has three parts: claim, evidence, and warrant.

First, you must clearly present the conclusion, or *claim,* that you want the reader to accept. Although the conclusion usually comes at the close of a written passage, you must begin there, stating precisely what you are arguing for, stating your claim fully and correctly. Here are several sample claims:

1. I think that Penn State will beat USC in the Sugar Bowl.
2. The United States defense budget plays an important role in the American economy.
3. Sororities are of more benefit to a college campus than fraternities.
4. Our university should build three more parking lots.

These claims or conclusions require some *evidence.* To persuade readers to agree with your claims, you must offer substantial reasons, data, and facts in support of those claims. For example:

1. The Penn State offense and defense have a superior record compared with that of the USC Trojans.
2. The defense industry, the largest employer in the United States, contributes billions of dollars to the economy.
3. Sororities are more than twice as likely as fraternities to be involved in community service.
4. The university has sold 2,000 more parking permits than there are parking spaces on campus.

Much more evidence for each of these four claims could be found. In the football claim, for instance, you might also compare the offensive and defensive yardage of each team, the number of points scored as well as given up, the length of time each had possession of the ball, and statistics from games in which the two teams played the same opponent. In most cases, the more evidence you provide, the more likely the reader will agree with the claim.

In addition to the claim and the evidence, a third step exists in Toulmin logic: the *warrant,* an unstated assumption, which is the most likely to be overlooked. It is a logical bridge connecting the evidence to the claim. This third element allows the evidence to be used for the claim the writer makes; it "warrants" the conclusion from the evidence given. In the football example, the unstated assumption of the argument—the warrant—is that previous performance will determine future performance. That assumption warrants the conclusion that Penn State will win; it is the bridge between the evidence and the conclusion.

Here is a diagram of the Toulmin method:

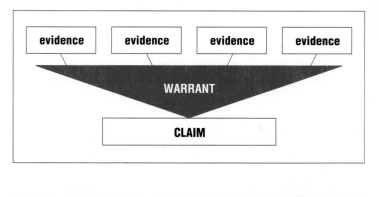

19

A. Examine the four examples of student claims above, and discuss the warrant for each. In each case, how might you oppose the claim by attacking the warrant? In the football example, if Penn State had played only weak teams and USC only strong ones, their prior records could be inconsequential in predicting the outcome of their meeting. The warrant that prior records will determine future success is therefore not valid. What are the warrants for the other three arguments, and how can you contradict them?

B. Examine the following statements. Mark D for those that were arrived at deductively and I for those arrived at inductively.

D 1. Warren G. Harding was one of our least effective presidents.

D 2. The 1920s were marked by a rebellious reaction against the horrors of the First World War.

I 3. The media are a threat to democracy because of their power.

I 4. Big cities can be dangerous.

D 5. Executions should be televised to make crime less glamorous.

C. Examine the following statements. Write a paragraph on each, explaining whether the reasoning is sound or unsound.

1. Voting is a waste of time because there is no way to know for sure if any of the candidates will do a good job.

2. The biblical story of creation and the theory of scientific evolution cannot both be right.

3. "Winning isn't everything. It's the *only* thing." (Vince Lombardi)

4. Power corrupts people and so power is evil.

5. Handguns don't kill people; *people* kill people.

D. Examine the following student editorials. Write a response indicating why you do or do not find each logical.

1.   One of our varsity athletes recently applied for employee compensation, demanding benefits for a knee injury he suffered while practicing basketball. Since the university awarded him a basketball scholarship, he claims that the school should pay him for an operation he needs to repair the knee he injured "on the job." However the case is decided, it again raises questions about the amateur status of college athletics.

College athletes often have their priorities mixed up. If they think that an education is one of the rewards they should receive for being a good athlete, they forget that scholarship aid should assist them in the only real "job" they have: to be students, to learn to think, to sharpen and develop their knowledge in many areas, and to receive the education that a university is supposed to offer. Just as a scholarship student majoring in history is not being paid to major in history, a college athlete is not being paid to play a game. While we all should support our varsity teams and other sports, we should remind ourselves that in the term *intercollegiate athletics*, we should emphasize *collegiate*, not *athletics*.

2.   Are students consumers? Are their rights threatened when they cannot withdraw from classes whenever they choose? Such questions deserve a logical response.

College students deserve to expect competence from their professors, but just because they pay to attend college, students are not thereby consumers since education is not a commercial service. Students pay tuition to place themselves in a situation of possible learning, which is a self-activity on their part, not a guaranteed product. Whether students learn or not is ultimately their responsibility. Professors direct the learning process but do not sell or produce academic services. Moreover, schools exist for students,

19

not for *a* student or just a few students. Since in any society certain relative individual goods must sometimes be sacrificed for the good of the whole, students do not have the right to withdraw from courses at any time without academic penalty. Since education is not a business, students' rights are not those of consumers.

20 logic   Avoid logical fallacies.

Fallacies are errors in reasoning that often look defensible but are deceptive; they weaken any argument. Examine carefully your own work as well as what you read for logical fallacies, some of which are listed here.

Faulty (or hasty) generalization. Overgeneralization, the chief fallacy in inductive reasoning, results from drawing a conclusion based on inadequate evidence. To say that "physicians are wealthy" or that "students are apathetic" is to assume that there are no exceptions; absolute terms—such as *all, every,* etc.—are implied. When you hear such generalizations as "older people are poor drivers," you must ask yourself: Is there sufficient evidence to justify the statement? Are no older drivers competent? Avoid sweeping statements: "Legalized gambling opens the door to organized crime." Such statements become more defensible if they are qualified and made specific: "According to current FBI reports, several states that legalized gambling have had an increase in organized crime." Note the use of *several* (or *some, few, many*) rather than *all, none, every.*

A common type of overgeneralizing is *stereotyping,* applying labels to persons or groups, irrespective of individual differences. When you hear ethnic or racial minorities, teenagers, or Southerners referred to without exceptions and with no contradictory evidence cited, you know that prejudicial stereotypes are at work.

Non sequitur. This term means "it does not follow." This chief fallacy in deductive reasoning involves a conclusion that does not follow from the premise(s). Consider the following advertisement: A Hollywood celebrity uses brand X toothpaste; therefore, using brand X will make you more attractive. The advertiser could just as logically claim that using it would make you famous, too. The crucial word in this fallacy is *therefore* (or *thus, so,* and related words). It should indicate that you are making a logical deduction.

To avoid *non sequiturs,* test the logic of your statements. The toothpaste advertisement actually says that (1) the celebrity uses the toothpaste, (2) the celebrity is attractive, (3) therefore, by using the toothpaste, you will be more attractive. For this chain of reasoning to make sense, it would have to be established that the attractiveness depended entirely on the whiteness of the celebrity's teeth and nothing else.

20

Post hoc. *Post hoc, ergo propter hoc* means "after this, therefore because of this." This fallacy assumes that because one event comes before another in time, the first event causes the other. It is not logical to conclude that because one event (an election) occurs before another (an increase in crime), there is a causal link between them (the election did not cause crime to increase). If your grades improved after you began dating someone new, you could not claim that this change in your social life caused the grades to improve. You would need more direct evidence: did your date tutor you or insist that you study? Many superstitions are based on the *post hoc* fallacy: "Since I wore a blue suit the day I was hired, I will always wear blue when I want a job."

Begging the question. This fallacy assumes as true something that needs to be proved. It begs the question to say that "democracy is the best form of government because the majority is always right in a democracy." How do we know that the majority is always right? One form of question begging is the circular argument: "The university must raise its admission requirements because it is important for the university to have proper academic standards."

Avoiding the question. Emotional appeals can be persuasive, but good writers do not distract readers from the issue at hand by making irrational emotional appeals, including flattery, patriotism, pity, or fear: "If guns are outlawed, only outlaws will have guns." Rationalization is a way of denying the real reason for a failure: "I flunked out of college because the courses were boring." Another aspect of this fallacy is the snob appeal found in much advertising: "Sophisticated drivers demand the best: Mercedes SL."

Faulty dilemma. This either-or fallacy oversimplifies issues by assuming that there are only two possible alternatives: "If the city does not raise taxes, it will be bankrupt." Current expenditures, for example, could be reduced to avoid bankruptcy.

False analogy. Analogies (comparing items that are similar in one or more respects but dissimilar in others) can provide an effective way to clarify a point and can even be persuasive. But analogies are not acceptable as logical proofs: "Reelect Governor Smith. Why change horses in midstream?" Such folk sayings cannot logically be applied to real-life situations nor can historical parallels. For example, any parallels that may exist between ancient Rome and contemporary America cannot be used to prove that our country is doomed to undergo a similar decline.

Ad hominem. This term means "to the man." Trying to discredit an argument by attacking someone who upholds it or trying to win an argument by praising someone who shares your view is illogical. For example: "I cannot support the new tax proposal; it has been endorsed by a man who ignores his wife and children." Ideas should be judged on their own merits, not on the merits of those who support them. *Ad hominem* arguments are based on emotion rather than reason. The same is true of arguments suggesting that new or expensive products are necessarily better than others and arguments that appeal to age: "I had to walk five miles a day to school. There is no reason you need a car." What was right in the past may not be right now.

Argument to ignorance. The most common form of this fallacy is to assume that something is true because it has not been proved wrong. No one has proved that UFOs do not come from other planets, but that does not prove that they do. The burden of proof is always on the writer to support an assertion, not on others to disprove it. Another form of this fallacy is to overwhelm one's readers with statistics or scientific jargon they cannot understand or unnamed authorities ("reliable sources") with which they are unfamiliar.

20

EXERCISE

A. Identify and explain the error in reasoning in each of the following statements:

1. The state has recently abolished capital punishment, and the results are disastrous. Serious crimes have risen by 30 percent in the six months since the law was passed. **post hoc**

2. John certainly did not steal the jewelry because he is an honest man. **begging the question**

3. This is the most expensive candy available anywhere; obviously, it is the best. **non sequitur**

4. The Senator's views are worthless; he was charged with perjury ten years ago. **ad hominem**

5. Eastern-bloc athletes are the best athletes in the entire world. **hasty generalization**

6. Contemporary readers with intelligence or discriminating taste, like you, are certain to subscribe to *Elegance* magazine. **avoiding the question**

7. Studies show that college students from coastal areas tend to be liberal, whereas those from the Midwest tend to be more conservative in their values. Church attendance must be higher in the Midwest. **non sequitur**

8. Crime has increased in New York City 300 percent since the United Nations moved there. This proves that the U.N. is a bad influence. **post hoc**

9. The political direction of this country will never get off dead center until more members of our party are elected. **begging the question**

10. Since hunters oppose legislation for gun control, Mr. Brown, who voted for gun control, cannot be a hunter. **non sequitur**

11. The President is the captain of our ship of state, steering our country toward peace. To vote him out of office would be a mutiny. **false analogy**

12. Mr. Sanchez, a corporate attorney, must be affluent; income in his profession averages over $80,000 a year. **hasty generalization**

13. The fact that the Bermuda Triangle mysteries were never solved shows that they have a supernatural origin. **argument to ignorance**

14. Should the local police department stop the investigation and just wait for the next murder to be committed? **begging the question**

15. The traffic is moving so slowly that there must be an accident up ahead. **non sequitur**

16. Since young men can be drafted at eighteen, they should be allowed to drink at that age. **non sequitur**

17. Five state legislators were arrested for crimes last year; you can't trust politicians. **hasty generalization**

18. Our college must either attract more students or fire some faculty members. **faulty dilemma**

19. If I graduate from college with honors, I'll get a high-paying job. **non sequitur**

20. If I don't graduate with honors, I won't get a high-paying job. **non sequitur**

B. Locate five advertisements that are based on logical fallacies. Write a short paragraph on each, explaining how it is illogical.

Writing

Paragraphs

Writers use paragraphs to build sentences into blocks of thought that can then join other paragraphs to develop the main idea of an essay or other piece of writing. A paragraph can introduce a thesis (the main idea of a paper), develop one of the points supporting the thesis, conclude the discussion, or supply a transition between parts of a fairly long paper. The paragraphs that support the thesis often correspond to the points in a rough outline; for example, you might begin an essay on ways of controlling inflation with a paragraph outlining three main solutions to the problem. Then, in three longer paragraphs, you would discuss each of these solutions in turn.

Paragraphs come in various sizes. The length of a paragraph depends on the difficulty of the subject, the size of related paragraphs, and the background of the intended audience. An essay consisting of very brief paragraphs (of fewer than three sentences each) will suggest inadequate thought. If your paragraphs are frequently fewer than one hundred words long, you are probably not giving them the development they deserve. More important than paragraph length, however, is making sure that each paragraph develops essentially one point.

A good paragraph presents enough facts and examples to satisfy the reader that its topic has been properly developed; and it does so in sentences that fit together, or cohere, to form a single unit. The following sections examine the main qualities of effective paragraphs.

21 ts Use a topic sentence to focus each paragraph on one point.

21

The topic sentence of a paragraph states the central idea that the rest of the paragraph clarifies, exemplifies, or otherwise supports. It promises what is to come. A good topic sentence is therefore useful to both writer and reader. The writer can use it to guide the development of the rest of the paragraph; the reader uses it as a clue to what lies ahead. Though a topic sentence is often the first sentence in a paragraph, it sometimes follows a transitional opening sentence. It may even appear at the end of a paragraph that leads the reader to a climactic conclusion. Experienced writers often do not give every paragraph a topic sentence, but beginning writers are usually well advised to use topic sentences consistently and to make them easily recognizable.

A good topic sentence identifies the subject of the paragraph and the specific issue to be developed. When the focus is blurred, the topic sentence offers no sense of direction to the reader, who may suspect that the writer himself was not sure where the paragraph was heading. In the following examples, note how the sharpened topic sentences point to the supporting sentences:

Not Focused: Television does more than present entertainment and advertising.

Sharpened: *Television not only distributes programs and sells products but also preaches a general philosophy of life.*

A more specific topic sentence will help you find examples and details to develop the paragraph.

Not focused: The Thunderbird is a classic automobile.

Sharpened: *The appearance of the 1957 Thunderbird is both striking and simple.* The body is devoid of heavy amounts of chrome that tend to be ostentatious. The style, with its low-slung design and smooth curves, is very sleek and aerodynamic. The tail fins, which begin at the door handle and continue straight back to just over the taillights, are tasteful and not as outlandish as the fins of the 1960 Cadillac, for example. Even though many people refer to the Thunderbird as a sports car, its rear wheel skirts still retain the aura of a luxury automobile. The side porthole hardtop as well as the low-profile hood scoop are stylish additions to a classic car.

—Scott Wilson (student)

Not focused: Video games are useful for young people.

Sharpened: *Video games give many young people their first experience with computer technology.* In fact,

21

despite many parents' objections, these games play a large part in educating youth for our Information Society. Students lacking formal instruction in computers usually find that a video game is the first computer they learn to control. And the skills involved in playing the game can help prepare them for more complex computer systems. Whereas many upper-middle-class children have computers at home, less fortunate youngsters must learn about this technology in video game arcades, which have been criticized by parents as a waste of time and money. Adults who see contamination in these games should realize the educational value they can provide.

In a first draft, begin every paragraph with a topic sentence. A topic sentence will help you make sure that the paragraph accomplishes its purpose. When you revise your early draft, you may want to move the topic sentence to another position or get rid of it entirely. Occasionally you may wish to place the topic sentence at the end of the paragraph to give it special emphasis.

21

EXERCISE

A. Examine the following topic sentences, marking with E those that would effectively develop the following central idea (thesis statement) of a whole essay: "Adolescent suicide is an alarming problem that cries out for solutions." Mark with X those that would NOT be effective.

x 1. There are thousands of attempted suicides each year among teenagers.

E 2. Understanding what causes teenagers to consider suicide may help prevent it.

E 3. The quest for escape from pressures and fears is a common cause of adolescent suicide.

x 4. Suicidal personalities develop as the result of several factors.

E 5. Though many young people use suicide as a threat, it should be seen as a call for help.

B. Rewrite the following topic sentences to give each a sharper focus. Then use one as the topic sentence for a paragraph you write.

1. White-collar crime is more harmful than most people realize.

2. Traffic lights in low traffic areas are more than a nuisance.

3. Immigration to the United States presents many problems.

4. Commercials in movie theaters are not popular.

5. Many citizens oppose the production and sale of cheap handguns.

C. Construct a topic sentence for the following paragraph, and decide where it should be placed. Explain your reasoning.

21

Where the American West actually began often depended on when one asked the question. In the seventeenth century, the West began practically at the Atlantic seashore. Later, in the time of Jefferson and Hamilton, the West was anywhere beyond the Appalachian Mountains. In the nineteenth century, Charles Dickens got no farther than St. Louis, nine hundred miles short of the Rockies; he went home convinced that he had seen the West and declared it to be a fraud. And in modern times, we think of the West as a stretch of landscape beginning with the Rockies and stretching to the Pacific. Or we think of what the movies have made into a stereotype: the one-street town which suddenly appears on the horizon. Such towns, which could still be found in Arizona and Nevada as late as the 1940s, are now gone or have become tourist traps. But all is not lost, for the West also remains a state of mind: the idea of El Dorado, of getting away from it all, of leading a new and luckier life under the big sky.

---

22 u Make all other sentences relate to the topic sentence.

If a paragraph is to perform its function, it must meet two principal criteria: unity and coherence (see also **23**). In a unified paragraph, every sentence contributes to the central idea. Every detail supports the topic sentence to produce a single, unfolding idea.

Examine each sentence in your paragraphs to make certain that it follows from and develops the topic sentence. Details not directly relevant to the central point do not belong in the paragraph. For instance, if your topic sentence were, "I support our university's policy of recruiting student athletes because it benefits the students academically and the school economically," your supporting sentences would deal with the advantages to student athletes and to the university recruitment budget. Sentences about the problems raised by the policy of building winning teams would violate the unity of the paragraph. To write about these problems, you would need a new paragraph.

The first step in achieving paragraph unity is to construct a clear, specific topic sentence. The next step is to develop, throughout the rest of the paragraph, the idea that the topic sentence expresses. When you revise your rough draft, eliminate all irrelevant points, no matter how interesting or well stated they are. The two underlined sentences in the following paragraph violate unity:

Psychoanalysis, as developed by Sigmund Freud at the end of the last century, was originally a therapy, but it eventually evolved into a theoretical system. As a therapy, psycho-analysis experienced its greatest popularity in this country during the 1950s and 1960s. According to Freudian theo-rists, along with or underneath the conscious mind, we have an unconscious mind, a type of mental energy we are unaware of. Therefore, nothing that happens, consciously or unconsciously, is without some cause. Another basic part of psychoanalytic theory is that, in everyday life, we often use defense mechanisms to hide from unpleasant truths about ourselves. In his celebrated break with Freud, C. G. Jung rejected the idea that major problems can be traced to sex-ual disturbances.

EXERCISE

A. Underline any sentences in these paragraphs that violate unity.

1. Despite criticism, producers of beer and wine spend many millions of dollars each year to advertise their wares on television. This results in great profits for major ad agencies and TV networks. It is hard to imagine sports programs without beer commercials. Still, many consumer groups have tried to curb such commercials because they see a link between the advertising of alcohol and excessive drinking. They are concerned about the increase in highway acci-dents caused by the drunk driving of teenagers and young adults. They contend that beer and wine ad-vertisements encourage alcohol consumption and abuse. Others argue that advertising largely promotes brand loyalty and that peers' attitudes and behavior have more influence on teenage drinking than TV advertising. Thus the controversy over banning alco-hol commercials goes on. But alcohol itself is not likely to be banned.

2. The ancient Greeks took sports seriously. All men took daily exercise, and their gymnasium was the social center of their lives. The competitive nature of

22

Greek society, seen in contests for the best tragedies, influenced sports, where the aim was to win. To finish second was considered a disgrace since the ancients thought that the glory of winning elevated the victor to a godlike status. The successful athlete was a privileged figure, achieving fame as well as fortune. Despite popular myths to the contrary, the Olympic victor was not an amateur, content to receive only a crown of olive leaves. Nor were wars halted every four years for the Olympics. Women were excluded from men's games, which were closely tied to religion and art and were performed by nude contestants. National prestige was reflected in the Panhellenic competitions, although team sports, involving the sharing of glory, were absent.

3. Gorée, the island on the West African coast closest to North America and the Caribbean, has a special place in black history. It was the last piece of Africa seen by millions of people before they were transported from liberty to slavery. Gorée is located near Dakar, the capital of Senegal. For more than three hundred years, slaves embarked from this island to the sugar and cotton plantations in America and the West Indies. Before being sold, captives were held in a windowless, airless concrete building that testifies to the subhuman conditions of slavery; if they were not marketable, captives were cast into the nearby Atlantic Ocean. From this building, a tunnel led directly into the holds of ships that carried more than twenty million people into slavery. In recent years, many descendants of slaves have made a pilgrimage to Gorée to see grim reminders of past inhumanity.

22

B. *Decide which of the following sentences belong in a unified paragraph that begins with this topic sentence: "A computer can play chess because of the nature of the game itself." Mark those sentences that belong with* B, *and mark those that do not with* X.

B   1. Chess is a game involving millions of possible positions.

B   2. Each piece moves in an orderly fashion according to fixed rules.

X   3. This game has been popular since the thirteenth century, though its origins are even older.

B   4. Chess also has a fixed objective: to trap or checkmate the opponent's king.

B   5. Moreover, chess has been so refined by human trial and error that it has been widely written about.

X   6. In fact, hundreds of books on this game of skill are available.

B   7. Since master games have been recorded and analyzed, the strategies are well known.

B   8. For example, the expert player knows which pawn formations are likely to be strongest, the advantages of various openings, and so on.

B   9. It is a game with assigned numerical values, a rook being worth five points, for example.

B 10. All of this highly quantified information can be entered into a computer.

23

23 coh   Provide coherence within and between paragraphs.

For an essay to be effective, it must be coherent: its parts must be linked and must fit together. The content of your paragraphs should lead the reader from the beginning of your essay to the end in some logical order. When you move from one paragraph to a different paragraph, include signals that show the relationship between the two. These signals are transitional devices to indicate, for example, that you are moving from an introductory paragraph that states a problem to supporting paragraphs that cite causes and effects, offer solutions, or provide examples.

In a paragraph, coherence is the natural flow from one sentence to the next. The sentences interlock so that the first idea leads to the second, the second to the third, and so on. You cannot write a succession of isolated sentences and expect your reader to supply the words and phrases that tie them together. You must make the reader feel that by the end of the paragraph you have made your point clearly and smoothly.

23a Achieve coherence by following a clear order.

The first step in achieving coherence is to follow a clear, logical order. That is, point *A* might precede point *B* because *A* happened before *B,* because *A* led to *B* or caused *B,* or because *B* illustrates *A.* Or your purpose might determine the order: you might put *A* first to give it special prominence; you might lead up to point *G,* leaving it until last for emphasis. Always try to find a pattern that will seem sensible both to you and to your reader.

The main patterns involve the order of time, space, and climax as well as the general-to-specific and specific-to-general order. In all cases, the structure determines the coherence.

Time order. Paragraphs that relate a series of incidents or steps in a process often follow a naturally chronological order. The first example is a narrative; the second, a factual explanation of a process.

First: The most terrifying day in my life ended with what seemed to be a miracle. It began with an incoherent yell, a panicky scream that pierced the quiet summer afternoon. It was the sound of my six-year-old son

	outside the kitchen window. As soon as I reached the
Second:	place in the yard where he stood, I realized that he was
	yelling, "Dad fell! Dad fell!" Mark's face was white, and
	while I knew what he was saying, it took a few minutes
	for the meaning of the words to sink in. He stood
Third:	sobbing and pointing toward the tree. Then I saw my
	husband lying motionless next to the ladder beneath
	the giant oak, his ax on the ground. Almost without
Fourth:	thinking, I ran to the telephone and then began the
	long agonized wait for the ambulance, a wait that
	fortunately turned out to be much worse than what the
	paramedic told me: my husband was going to make it.

The principle of sonar depends upon the propagation of sound waves through water. Everyone is familiar with the rings produced when a pebble is tossed into a lake. So, too, vibration from a sound sets into motion a series of encircling waves. This vibrating source *first* pushes or compresses the molecules adjacent to it, causing a high-pressure area. On the backward motion, the water is decompressed, and the molecules move apart to produce a low-pressure area. This motion *then* causes more distant molecules in the high pressure region to move apart, pushing more distant molecules into a compressed state. This process continues in an expanding, circular motion as do the ripples caused by the pebble.

Spatial order. An arrangement in space (from top to bottom, left to right, and so on) is often possible in descriptive paragraphs, such as the following excerpt from *The Elephant Man and Other Reminiscences:*

From the intensified painting in the street, I had imagined the Elephant Man to be of gigantic size. This, however, was a little man below the average height and made to look shorter by the bowing of his back. The most striking feature about him was the enormous and misshapened head. From the brow there projected a huge bony mass like a loaf, while from the back of the head hung a bag of spongy, fungous-looking skin, the surface of which was comparable to brown cauliflower. On the top of the skull were a few long lank hairs. The osseous growth on the forehead almost occluded

23

one eye. The circumference of the head was no less than that of the man's waist. From the upper jaw there projected another mass of bone. It protruded from the mouth like a pink stump, turning the upper lip inside out and making the mouth a mere slobbering aperture. This growth from the jaw had been so exaggerated in the painting as to appear to be a rudimentary trunk or tusk. The nose was merely a lump of flesh, only recognizable as a nose from its position. The face was no more capable of expression than a block of gnarled wood. The back was horrible, because from it hung, as far down as the middle of the thigh, huge, sack-like masses of flesh covered by the same loathsome cauliflower skin.

—Sir Frederick Treves

Climactic order. Some material will suggest an order of increasing importance. In this example, the sentences lead up to the highest point of interest.

In the center of the grove an oak stood, tall and stately but bulging in the middle. On this venerable bulge a pair of ravens had taken up residence for so many years that the tree was known as the "raven tree." Children often tried without success to get at the nest, the difficulty of the task whetting their appetites. But when they climbed up to the swelling, it jutted out so far beyond their grasp that they found the undertaking too hazardous. And so the birds lived on, building nest after nest in perfect security until a February day when the grove was to be cleared. Men came with their saws, the woods echoed the clamor, but the mother raven remained on her nest, even when the tree began to tilt. At last, when it gave way, the bird was flung from her nest, whipped to the ground by twigs. She deserved a better fate.

—adapted from Gilbert White

General-specific. Paragraphs often begin with a general statement or topic sentence (see **21**), followed by supporting details and examples. But many writers start with the specific and end with a general comment that summarizes the point of the paragraph, as in this example:

Christopher Nolan is spastic, mute, and bound to a wheelchair. Brain-damaged at birth, he cannot operate his limbs. Until the age of ten, blinking was his sole means of communication. Then, sensing their son's luminous mind and desire to communicate, his parents secured a muscle-relaxing drug that freed him to use a special typing stick affixed to his forehead. With such an unlikely device, Nolan has become one of the most acclaimed contemporary Irish writers. His books have been praised as the work of an original word-smith who explores human consciousness with imaginative insight.

By contrast, this paragraph offers a good example of the general-to-specific pattern:

Among the vices of age are avarice, untidiness, and vanity, which last takes the form of a craving to be loved or simply admired. Avarice is the worst of those three. Why do so many old persons, men and women alike, insist on hoarding money when they have no prospect of using it and even when they have no heirs? They eat the cheapest food, buy no clothes, and live in a single room when they could afford better lodging. It may be that they regard money as a form of power; there is a comfort in watching it accumulate while other powers are dwindling away. How often we read of an old person found dead in a hovel, on a mattress partly stuffed with bankbooks and stock certificates!

—Malcolm Cowley

EXERCISE

A. *Rearrange the sentences in the following paragraph. Provide coherence by choosing and following a specific order (time, space, climax, or generalization).*

(1) When air particles are made white-hot by lightning, they reach temperatures as high as 30,000 degrees Centigrade. *(2)* Under such intense heat, the nitrogen combines with the oxygen in the air to form soluble nitrogen oxides. *(3)* Rain dissolves these oxides and carries them to the earth as di-

luted nitric acid. *(4)* This is the pungent odor we smell in the air of a thunderstorm. *(5)* Lightning touches off a series of chemical reactions in the nitrogen needed to sustain plants. *(6)* About twenty-two million tons of this essential nutriment float over every square mile of the earth, but it is unusable, insoluble, in its aerial form. *(7)* When it reaches the earth, the nitric acid reacts with minerals there to form nitrates on which plants can feed. *(8)* Although lightning kills more people in the United States than any other natural disaster, it is also essential for plant life. *(9)* Lightning, then, may frighten people, but it transforms the upper air into "fertilizer" for plants.   **8, 5, 6, 1, 2, 3, 4, 7, 9**

B. Rearrange the sentences in this paragraph so that you provide coherence by following a specific-to-general order:

(1) Schools and textbooks should recognize the role played by religion in our country. *(2)* Religious liberty was a major goal of America's founders. *(3)* It is easy to forget that the Plymouth Colony was settled by Puritans, Rhode Island by Baptists, Maryland by Catholics, Virginia by Episcopalians, Pennsylvania by Quakers—all for religious reasons. *(4)* Yet many students believe that religion has had little to do with the development of the nation. *(5)* A recent study found that textbooks devoted more space to cowboys and cattle drives than to religion. *(6)* Some educators are concerned about religious indoctrination in public schools. *(7)* But effective teachers can talk about religion without promoting a specific belief. *(8)* A knowledge of religion is essential to understanding art, music, literature, and politics and to understanding recent events in the Middle East and Asia.   **5, 3, 2, 4, 6, 7, 8, 1**

C. Rewrite the following paragraph so that it follows a climactic order:

The war that began in 1914 changed the shape of Europe and marked the beginning of the modern world. World War I, called the "war to end wars," began the bloodiest century in history. Britain alone lost 765,000 men, more than twice the number killed in World War II. Ten million people were killed in battles or in the cross fire, and sixty-five million men participated in the fighting. The Great War led to the Russian Revolution, the rise of Nazism in Germany, and another world war. It was a war that wiped out the flower of Europe's young manhood. The consequences were as devastating as the carnage.

D. Arrange these sentences into a coherent paragraph.
Begin by numbering them in a logical order.

(1) To give a computer an interpretation of its symbols would only result in more uninterpreted symbols. *(2)* Many intelligent people apparently believe that computers can think or will soon be able to do so. *(3)* Simulation is not duplication; a computer that prints "I am depressed" is obviously incapable of this or any other human feeling. *(4)* The same is true of other mental states because a computer cannot interpret or attach meaning to the symbols it uses. *(5)* They assume that computer simulations of mental processes actually produce these processes. *(6)* Only the human users of the computer can interpret symbols. *(7)* The simple fact that a computer attaches no meaning to the symbols it manipulates shows that the computer is simply a useful machine, incapable of rivaling human intelligence. *(8)* Of course, a computer can simulate hurricanes, five-alarm fires, or the flow of currency in a depressed economy. *(9)* But no sensible person thinks that a computer simulation of a fire will burn down the neighborhood.   **2, 5, 8, 9, 3, 4, 1, 6, 7**

23b   *Use transitional devices to improve coherence.*

On reading over your rough draft, you may find that, logical as your pattern is, the sentences do not flow from one to the next. Sentence A ends with a thump. Then sentence B starts up. And so on. You may need transitional devices to bridge the gaps. These devices connect the sentences and bind the paragraph into a single, coherent unit. The most common transitional devices are presented here.

Pronouns. Since each pronoun refers to an antecedent, a pronoun and its antecedent form a link. You can often make a paragraph cohere merely by using pronouns properly. On the other hand, incorrectly used pronouns can weaken coherence (see **39–41**). In the following examples, notice how pronouns in the second sentence of each pair provide coherence by referring to the important subjects in the first:

> *Diet books* continue to proliferate. *They* appeal to the anxieties of our weight-conscious society.

> *Patients* must fast for twelve hours before the test. *They* should also avoid red meats for seventy-two hours before coming in.

Repetition. Substituting a pronoun for a noun is actually a kind of repetition. Direct repetition of a word or expression will give a similar effect:

> *Exposure to too much sun* can damage the skin. This *damage* is irreversible and can result in skin cancer.

Use direct repetition with care. Overdoing it will give an awkward, immature ring to your writing ("*Daily receipts* are taken to the central office. *Daily receipts* are then tallied . . ."). You can get much the same transitional effect by using synonyms or slightly altered forms of the repeated expressions:

> *Jimmy Carter* has been busy since leaving the White House. *The former President* has traveled widely to help the needy and homeless.

Transitional terms. Transitional terms make a paragraph coherent by relating ideas. Like pronouns, many of these terms come to mind automatically, but the thoughtful writer carefully chooses among them. Here is a partial list of common transitional terms:

1. *Time words:* next, then, after, before, during, while, following, shortly, thereafter, later on, the next day, secondly, finally
2. *Place words:* over, above, inside, to the left, just behind, beyond
3. *Contrast words:* however, but, nevertheless, on the other hand, nonetheless, notwithstanding, on the contrary, conversely, yet
4. *Cause-effect words:* so, therefore, thus, accordingly, consequently, as a result, hence, because of this
5. *Addition words:* and, furthermore, moreover, likewise, similarly, in a like manner, too, also
6. *Emphasis words:* indeed, in fact, especially, most important
7. *Summary words:* in other words, in short, to sum up, in conclusion
8. *Example words:* for instance, for example, that is, in particular

The following examples illustrate the use of transitional terms:

Indulgences developed from the medieval

church's concept of penance as a substitute for

Time   punishment due to sin. *At first,* the penitent was

required to make a pilgrimage or perform an act of

Contrast   charity. *But* such activities were only substitutes for

the real punishment, and it was a simple step to

Example	make further substitutes for the original ones. *For*
	example, the sinner could make his penance by
	paying the cost of going on a pilgrimage rather than
	actually making a trip. In an age when travel was
Repetition	both expensive and dangerous, *such* a monetary
Effect	substitution was sensible. *As a result,* the sinner
	suffered financially, and the church could use his
Effect	money for acts of charity. *Thus* indulgences were
Repetition	born. The opportunities for abusing *this* practice of
Contrast	giving money in place of penance, *however,* were
Repetition	numerous. *Indulgences* were frequently criticized,
Pronoun	and Luther's famous attack on *them* was one
Contrast	among many. *Yet* the principle is sound and
	difficult to attack without undermining the entire
	theology of penance.

—adapted from Donald J. Wilcox

	Sometimes it seems that Thomas Jefferson the
Pronoun/ **Example**	man hardly exists for us. *He* seems, *that is,* to be
	mainly a symbol of what we as Americans are or

23

Pronoun	think we are. *He* appears almost to have been
	invented so as to reveal something about ourselves.
Emphasis	No one else in our history, *in fact,* embodies so
	much of our democratic heritage and so many of
Contrast	our democratic hopes. *Yet* the man himself has
	proved to be a fascinating, complex character, the
	worthy subject of several recent biographies.

Transitional sentences and paragraphs. Pronouns, repetition, and transitional terms can provide coherence within paragraphs and can even link two consecutive paragraphs; but to link two paragraphs that differ significantly in content, you occasionally will need a transitional sentence or even a short paragraph. If, for instance, you have devoted three or four paragraphs to the theories of one authority and are ready to shift to those of another, you will probably need a sentence to help the reader make the transition. For example: "A critic who approaches Shakespeare's plays differently, however, is Maynard Mack, who. . . ."

If you have written three paragraphs on the ways in which your municipality can provide safer drinking water and are now ready to shift to differing views on the subject, you might use a short transitional paragraph:

> Several experts, however, disagree with these solutions and believe that the problem has been exaggerated. As we will see, their views have one thing in common: cost.

Here are two versions of a student's paragraph. In the first, transitional devices are omitted. In the second, they have been inserted and italicized.

Less effective: There is no Nobel Prize for mathematics, and mathematicians rarely make the headlines. It is not a glamorous profession. There are no exotic, expensive pieces of equipment—no cyclotrons, body scanners, or electron microscopes—for the public to identify with. Research tools are plain. Pencil, paper, chalk, and a calculator are about all one needs. In a time when some scientists' names—Einstein, Jung, Freud, and others—have become household words, few people could name even one great modern mathematician. Mathematics is so basic to most scientific subjects that it has been called the language of all experimental dialogue.

More effective: There is no Nobel Prize for mathematics, and mathematicians rarely make the headlines. It is not a glamorous profession. There are, *for example,* no exotic, expensive pieces of equipment—no cyclotrons, body scanners, or electron microscopes—for the public to identify with. *In fact,* research tools are plain. Pencil, paper, chalk, and a calculator are about all one needs. *And* in a time when some scientists' names—Einstein, Jung, Freud, and others—have become household words, few people could name even one great modern mathematician. *Yet* mathematics is so basic to most scientific subjects that it has been called the language of all experimental dialogue.

Note how the four transitional devices make explicit the connections between the ideas. The final transition—*yet*—clarifies the contrast between the final, climactic sentence and the preceding points.

EXERCISE

Add appropriate transitions to make these paragraphs more explicitly coherent.

1. The benefits of shale oil production are more numerous than the drawbacks. **First of all,** Oil shale has been found to

   produce an effective fuel, in both liquid and gaseous

   forms. Shale oil represents **, in fact,** a potential, long-range

   source of fairly secure oil and gas. **Furthermore,** Numerous

   by-products can be derived from oil shale processing.
   But There are some disadvantages, particularly for the

   environment. These negative features concern socio-

   economic impact, surface disturbance, pollution, and

   water supply. **Moreover,** There are some legal questions con-

   cerning government control of shale oil processing.

   Experts believe **, however,** that the future is bright for the shale

   oil industry.

2. Whales are special both because of their size and

   because of their innocence. **For example,** The blue whale is the

   largest creature to have lived on our planet. It easily

   outclasses the dinosaur, which was so small by com-

   parison that it could have easily passed through a

   whale's jawbone. The tongue of a blue whale weighs

more than an elephant. It emits whistles louder than
the noise of a jet engine and thumps comparable to
earthquakes. _{Yet} The whale is completely non-aggressive
toward people and, like the dolphin, is known for
acts of mercy. **In fact,** Whales have been known to lift ship-
wrecked sailors to safety on their backs. Since the
whale's instinct is to bring help, the term *killer whale*
is **thus** a misnomer.

---

24 dev Develop paragraphs fully.

The main point of a paragraph must be clarified or supported
if that paragraph is to be interesting and convincing. Effective
development is quite different from "padding": think of development as growth and increasing depth, not as mere expan-
sion. This section shows some of the various ways that writers, depending on their subject and purpose, develop effective
paragraphs.

24a   Examples

Including examples and details is the most frequent way to
achieve good paragraph development. They provide readers
with the specific information they need to understand the

controlling idea. Merely asserting a point is never sufficient; each idea must be developed with facts and examples. Although too much detail is sometimes a problem, bad writing usually suffers from too little detail rather than too much. Short paragraphs often indicate lack of effort or thought.

In the following passage, notice how the example of elephants helps to make the author's initial point concrete and convincing:

> Animals seem to have an instinct for performing death alone, hidden. Even the largest, most conspicuous ones find ways to conceal themselves in time. If an elephant missteps and dies in an open place, the herd will not leave him there; the others will pick him up and carry the body from place to place, finally putting it down in some inexplicably suitable location. When elephants encounter the skeleton of an elephant out in the open, they methodically take up each of the bones and distribute them, in a ponderous ceremony, over neighboring acres.
>
> —Lewis Thomas

In the following example, the weak paragraph is general, whereas the improved version is developed with specific illustrations:

Weak development: In most earlier cultures, salt was viewed not only as a preservative but also as a powerful religious and symbolic substance. Valued because it was essential to life, salt had such a symbolic significance that it came to represent health, virtue, and friendship. From biblical to medieval times, there are references to salt in many cultures. At the same time, this valuable substance contributed to a number of fascinating legends and superstitions.

Improved development: In most earlier cultures, salt was viewed not only as a preservative but also as a powerful religious and symbolic substance. Valued because it was essential to life, salt had such a symbolic significance that it came to represent health, virtue, and friendship. Moses, for example, commanded the Israelites to sprinkle offerings of wheat with salt. And since covenants were usually made over a sacrificial meal, the expression "covenant of salt" was established. Arabs who shared bread and salt with a guest were committed to protecting him, and the Persian expression "untrue to salt" means disloyal and ungrateful. This valuable substance also contributed to a number of superstitions. Some medieval Frenchmen said that the devil was often seen without a tail because courageous folk had once sprinkled it with salt. The devil was so agonized by the virtuous substance that he chewed his tail off.

24

EXERCISE

Study the two pairs of short paragraphs below. Mark the paragraphs that are well developed with W and those that are poorly developed with X.

x 1A. Picture, if you can, a dark blue fjord in Alaska. The snow-capped mountains rise high into the sky around the water, and their reflection is clear on the still surface. A lone whale suddenly interrupts the tranquil scene. Just the tip of its head shows, and soon the air is alive with spray. Soon you think the whale is gone, but it comes up again. Its large brown eyes remind you of a lonely hound dog's, and its mouth is curved into what looks like an eternal smile. Then it slides gracefully back into the water the same way it came, leaving barely a ripple on the surface.

—Greg Weekes
student

w 1B. Picture, if you can, a dark blue fjord in Alaska. The snow-capped mountains rise high into the sky around the water, and their reflection is clear on the still surface. Patches of evergreens dot the shoreline, and all you can sense is the cold silence of a still spring day. A lone whale coming up for air suddenly interrupts the tranquil scene. Just the tip of its head shows, and soon the air is alive with spray. As it dives again, you catch a glimpse of its tail, strong and powerful, speckled with barnacles. The huge fin slips silently beneath the water, and you think the whale is gone. But it soon comes up again, this time in a position almost perpendicular to the surface. Its large brown eyes remind you of a lonely hound dog's, and its mouth is curved into what looks like an eternal smile. Then it slides gracefully back into the water the same way it came, leaving barely a ripple on the surface.

—Greg Weekes
student

x 2A. A New York City taxi seems designed to test the endurance of the most patient rider. The experience of traveling in one of these legendary conveyances is often irritating to the passengers, whether they be Manhattan natives or tourists. The drivers are often insulting, ill-informed, and unhelpful. What is worse, they drive too fast in heavy traffic and jolt the hapless rider along countless potholes in cabs which almost always seem to lack shock absorbers. The result is discomforting and nerve-racking. Similar conditions exist in other major cities; but for sheer violence, no taxi ride can compare with one in New York.

w 2B. A New York City taxi seems designed to test the endurance of the most patient rider. The drivers are known for their ability to insult the passenger in colorful language, to refuse to open doors or help with luggage, and to know little about landmarks or shortcuts. More distressing to the hapless victim is their tendency to speed into the most heavily-trafficked streets while either bearing down on the accelerator or snapping on the brakes as they thump over roads so full of potholes that they resemble moonscapes. While the passenger reaches for a tranquilizer, wondering what happened to the shock absorbers, he is forced to sit like a nervous yogi—eyes shut, fists and teeth clenched, knees taut. Though similar conditions exist in other major cities, for sheer violence no taxi ride can compare with one in New York.

24b   Comparison and Contrast

Comparison notes the similarities of two subjects; contrast, the differences. Writers most often discuss both similarities and differences, following one of these two methods:

1. *Subject by subject* presents all the details of one side of the comparison or contrast first and then the details of the other side.

Thomas Jefferson had an insatiable curiosity that made him a sort of Renaissance man. The third American president, author of the Declaration of Independence, and founder of the University of Virginia was also an architect, inventor, musician, and scholar of philology, meteorology, archeology, astronomy, chemistry, and anatomy, among other fields. The idea that such a man could master all knowledge and put it into practice was an invention of the Italian Renaissance, as seen in the career of Leon Battista Alberti, whose interests parallel Jefferson's. Alberti, also a self-confident innovator, studied languages, law, and mathematics and wrote treatises on painting, sculpture, and moving weights. In 1444, he wrote the first book on architecture since antiquity; a classical scholar, he was concerned with the practical application of his studies. His relaxations were the same as Jefferson's: music and horsemanship. Although Jefferson, unlike Alberti, was a politician and statesman, the similarities between the two men show that Jefferson's achievement owes much to the Italian Renaissance and its dream of the universal man.

—adapted from Kenneth Clark

2. *Point by point* moves back and forth between the subjects, item by item:

The proliferation of lawsuits in the United States in the last decade is in marked contrast to the practice in Britain, where people are generally more reluctant to sue. In America, the prevailing view is that problems can be solved and that the system can be made to work for the individual. The British, on the other hand, tend to be not only less aggressive but also more pessimistic about human nature. Unlike Americans, they do not believe that the world can be radically improved. Because, in this older view, people are seen as flawed, their society is seen as always imperfect. Americans, by contrast, retain much of their traditionally idealistic anything-is-possible optimism. Perhaps for this reason, there are more legal efforts to alter the course of events through the courts in the United States than in the United Kingdom.

24c Definition

A definition explains the meaning of a word or concept by placing it into a general class and then supplying details that distinguish it from other things of the same class. Writers often expand upon dictionary definitions, using examples or comparison and contrast to distinguish one thing from another and thus provide a thorough explanation of an idea or term, as in this paragraph:

> The word *gentleman* originally meant something recognizable: one who had a coat of arms and some landed property. When you called someone "a gentleman" you were not paying him a compliment, but merely stating a fact. If you said he was not "a gentleman" you were not insulting him, but giving information. There was no contradiction in saying that John was a liar and a gentleman; any more than there now is in saying that James is a fool and an M.A. But then there came people who said—so rigidly, charitably, spiritually, sensitively, so anything but usefully—"Ah, but surely the important thing about a gentleman is not the coat of arms and the land, but the behaviour? Surely he is the true gentleman who behaves as a gentleman should? Surely in that sense Edward is far more truly a gentleman than John?" They meant well. To be honourable and courteous and brave is of course a far better thing than to have a coat of arms. But it is not the same thing. Worse still, it is not a thing everyone will agree about. To call a man "a gentleman" in this new, refined sense, becomes, in fact, not a way of giving information about him, but a way of praising him: to deny that he is "a gentleman" becomes a way of insulting him. When a word ceases to be a term of description and becomes merely a term of praise, it no longer tells you facts about the object. (A "nice" meal only means a meal the speaker likes.) A *gentleman,* once it has been spiritualised and refined out of its old coarse, objective sense, means hardly more than a man whom the speaker likes. As a result, *gentleman* is now a useless word. We had lots of terms of approval already, so it was not needed for that use; on the other hand if anyone (say, in a historical work) wants to

use it in its old sense, he cannot do so without explanations. It has been spoiled for that purpose.

—C. S. Lewis

24d Analogy

A writer uses analogies to make comparisons of items that seem to have little in common. Analogies help make something that is unfamiliar or complex easier to understand, as in this example:

> The South today might be compared to a man who has had a bad toothache for as long as he can remember. In fact, it has never occurred to him to imagine life without this constant pain. Then, suddenly, the pain disappears. At first, he doesn't know what has happened; then, realizing his good fortune, he enjoys his new, painless existence. But he soon discovers that he faces a new problem: what to do now that he no longer has the pain to worry about. In a similar way, Southerners have recently discovered that they are no longer obsessed with the problem of race that for so long was part of the very connotation of the word *South*.
>
> —adapted from Walker Percy

24e Classification

Classification organizes material into categories to reveal the nature of each category. A writer might wish to show the differences and relationships among the categories, as in explaining three types of instrumental music; or an author might outline several psychological theories before indicating which one she will discuss. In the following example, a student lists three reasons why student evaluations of faculty are biased:

> Student evaluations of faculty are biased for several reasons. First, students' grade expectations influence their rating of an instructor. Those who are likely to receive a high grade will be more favorably disposed toward the instructor

24

than those expecting low grades. A second area of bias is more subtle. It involves age, sex, and appearance. A study in the *Journal of Educational Psychology* found that unattractive, middle-aged female instructors and unattractive, elderly male instructors frequently received lower ratings than their younger, more attractive counterparts. Related to this is a third factor: that men generally are rated higher than women because of gender stereotyping that associates masculinity with success and authority. For these reasons alone, it is apparent that any effort to conduct student evaluations of faculty will be far from objective.

—Cynthia Wilson (student)

24f Cause and Effect

Cause-and-effect paragraphs explain why something happened. They may proceed from cause to effects or may simply list the causes of an obvious effect. For example, a writer might explore the reasons for the Wall Street Crash of 1929 without showing that the crash was disastrous. The following paragraph deals with some effects of the 1983 breakup of the Bell System.

Many telephone customers continue to view the court-ordered breakup of the giant Bell System as a costly mistake. They complain about complicated bills that reflect additional charges built into telephone service. They are frustrated by the need to buy and repair their own equipment. Although the increased competition that followed the breakup has resulted in some benefits, such as clearer connections and new services, local telephone rates have risen substantially. These higher rates offset any advantages typical residential customers see in a service they once could take for granted.

EXERCISE

Write a paragraph using each of the following methods of development. Use your own topics or those suggested.

1. *Examples:* political cartoons, peer pressure and drugs, life in the Peace Corps, TV addiction, solar energy

2. *Comparison and contrast:* AM and FM radio stations, American and Chinese food, waterskiing and snow skiing, small-town colleges and urban universities, two jobs (cars, restaurants, professors, fraternities)

3. *Definition:* natural foods, New Age, intelligence, a soap-opera addict, an ideal teacher

4. *Analogy:* animal rights, campus racism, voice messaging, cults

5. *Classification:* recreational vehicles, concerts, health clubs, diets, music videos

6. *Cause and effect:* recycling trash, declining math and science scores among U.S. students, need for more low-cost public housing, public opinion polls, year-round school

24

Writing

Sentences

Since the sentence is the primary means of expressing ideas, look carefully at each sentence you write to make sure it is clear, emphatic, and mature. Chapter 8 focuses on correct grammatical patterns; this chapter focuses on effectiveness, describing ways to express your thoughts with skill and style.

The principal types of sentences (see also **35**) are as follows:

1. Simple sentence (one subject and one predicate)

   I have never visited Asia.

2. Compound sentences (two or more independent, or main, clauses)

   I have never visited Asia, but I hope to do so next year. (coordinate)

3. Complex sentence (one independent clause and at least one dependent, or subordinate, clause)

   Although I have never visited Asia, I hope to do so next year. (subordinate clause + main clause)

4. Compound-complex sentence (at least two independent clauses and one dependent clause)

   Although I have never visited Asia, I hope to do so next year; I already have a vivid sense of what it is like. (subordinate clause + two main clauses)

   Although I have never visited Asia, I have often imagined it, and I hope to see the real thing next year. (subordinate clause + two main clauses)

25

25 sub | Use subordination to relate secondary details to main ideas and to improve stringy or choppy sentences.

Two or more ideas can be connected in a sentence by two means: *coordination* or *subordination*. Coordination gives the ideas equal grammatical emphasis; subordination presents one as the main idea and puts the other(s) in a dependent or de-emphasized relationship to the main idea. Therefore, your sentence structure should depend upon the relationship you want to show between your ideas. Notice how the meaning subtly changes in the following sentences:

Two sentences: Politicians can say extreme things. They must say them so that no one pays close attention.

Coordination: Politicians can say extreme things, but they must say them so that no one pays close attention.

Subordination: Although politicians can say extreme things, they must say them so that no one pays close attention.

Subordination: Politicians can say extreme things if they say them so that no one pays close attention.

Subordination can allow you to include a number of details in one sentence, some of which you need but do not wish to emphasize. In this sentence, the emphasis is in the main clause, the subordinate *(italicized)* elements adding additional information:

> I noticed the visitor, *a tall, gray-haired man in a three-piece suit,* then continued to instruct the children, *who did not appear to enjoy the lesson.*

25a Use subordinate clauses to relate secondary details to the main idea.

Relative pronouns *(who, whom, which, that)* and subordinating conjunctions (such as *because, since, although,* and others in the list below) introduce subordinate clauses and signal specific relationships between them and the main clause. Notice how each subordinate clause below has a different relationship to its main clause:

Effective: *Although* Jessica had spent six hours cramming for a philosophy test, she felt unprepared.

Effective: Jessica, *who* had spent six hours cramming for a philosophy test, felt unprepared.

Effective: *After* she had spent six hours cramming for a philosophy test, Jessica still felt unprepared.

Effective: *Because* Jessica spent only six hours cramming for a philosophy test, she felt unprepared.

The following list of common subordinating conjunctions shows the variety of relationships that subordination can indicate:

Cause: since, because, if, so that, in order that

Contrast or concession: although, though, whereas, while

Time: when, whenever, as, before, since, after, as long as, once, until, while

Place: where, wherever

Condition: if, unless, whether, provided that, as long as

Manner: as, as though, as if, how

Similarity: as . . . as

Some subordinate clauses can be used in the same way as nouns (as subjects or objects):

Churchill said *that Dulles was like a bull with his own China shop.* (clause as direct object)

Some subordinate clauses can also function as modifiers—as adjectives or adverbs. An adjective clause modifies (or qualifies) a noun or pronoun and most often begins with a relative pronoun:

Churchill said that Dulles was like a bull *who always carried his own China shop.* (clause modifies *bull* and thus functions as an adjective)

An adverb clause modifies a verb, adjective, adverb, verbal (such as a gerund or participle), or the rest of the sentence:

25

When Churchill spoke, people listened. (clause modifies the verb *listened*)

Be sure to place your main idea, the one you want to stress, in the independent clause, and, when possible, put the main clause last.

Although I read much more quickly now, I remember less.

Do not destroy the emphasis in a sentence by putting the main idea in a subordinate clause:

The American Medical Association issued a report *which warned that many doctors have ignored nutrition.*

Improved: According to an American Medical Association report, many doctors have ignored nutrition.

25b *Use subordination to improve long, stringy sentences.*

One mark of an inexperienced writer is frequent use of rambling, stringy sentences composed of a series of main clauses strung together with *and* or other coordinating conjunctions. If you subordinate one or more clauses, you will usually make your meaning clearer and the sentence more readable:

Ineffective: Some women are happy just being at home, *and* they argue that a woman's place is largely in the home *and* that mothers who work should feel guilty.

Effective: Women who are happy just being at home argue that a woman's place is largely in the home and that mothers who work should feel guilty.

Ineffective: Mr. Jackson built the company's reputation, *and* he believed in hard work, *and* he was committed to high quality.

Effective: Mr. Jackson, who believed in hard work and high quality, built the company's reputation.

Effective: Mr. Jackson, who built the company's reputation, believed in hard work and high quality.

Ineffective: He began the descent to the ocean floor *and* felt as though he were in a dream, *and* he sensed that, like someone jumping from a skyscraper, he was floating rather than crashing.

Effective: As he began the descent to the ocean floor, he felt as though he were in a dream in which he sensed that, like someone jumping from a skyscraper, he was floating rather than crashing.

25c Use subordination to improve a series of short, choppy sentences.

Numerous short, choppy sentences are another common sign of an inexperienced writer. Such sentences are awkward to read and fail to show relationships among their ideas. Notice in these examples how subordination improves upon the short, choppy sentences:

Ineffective: Roger wanted very much to play the bass. He taught himself twenty-two songs. Then he took lessons.

Effective: Roger wanted so much to play the bass that he taught himself twenty-two songs before he took lessons.

Ineffective: Alice expected to enjoy *The Color Purple.* She failed to understand it at first. Then she saw the movie.

Effective: Although she expected to enjoy *The Color Purple,* Alice failed to understand it until she saw the movie.

25

25d Avoid excessive subordination.

Too many subordinate structures in a sentence can make it awkward, monotonous, or even confusing:

Ineffective: Their apartment is in unit seventy-nine, which is the second unit on the right overlooking the garden that is behind the parking lot.

Improved: Their apartment is in unit seventy-nine, the second unit on the right; it overlooks the garden behind the parking lot.

Ineffective: She bought a cattleya, which is a type of orchid, which is used in many corsages.

Improved: She bought a cattleya, the orchid used in many corsages.

In these examples, notice how you can eliminate non-essential information (and wordiness) by deleting *which is, which are,* and so on at the beginning of a clause.

EXERCISE

A. Read the following sentences. Mark E for those that are effective and X for those needing less or more subordination.

25

x 1. Lightning kills about one hundred people a year in the United States, and it is the leading killer among natural disasters and is more deadly than floods and hurricanes combined.

x 2. The Prohibition movement was largely the product of religious reform. It attacked alcohol as a moral evil. It resulted in the Eighteenth Amendment.

x 3. America's moon landing occurred in 1969, and it

revitalized U.S. science and technology and brought many industrial and military benefits.

x 4. About twenty-five million Americans have dyslexia, which is not a disease but a learning problem, which requires classes to help dyslexic students.

x 5. Two men stand on the side of the road. They are shirtless. One of them is pointing at the sky.

x 6. The boy got delayed, so by the time he arrived at the fair, it was closing, so he was unable to buy anything.

x 7. Politicians use fancy words that they think will impress voters, who are generally sharper than the politicians think.

x 8. The soldiers did not continue. This was not because they were tired. They were without command. It was not because they had no place to go. They had no one to lead them.

x 9. Thieves stole two dozen cases of Scotch. They stole it from a liquor store in Cleveland. The theft took place yesterday. They left less-expensive whiskey behind.

e 10. Our regular dentist, Dr. Cox, is on vacation; we called Dr. Parnell, who shares an office with Dr. Cox.

25

B. *Rewrite the sentences above marked* X.

C. *In the following selection, a paragraph by a noted writer has been reduced to a series of short sentences. Combine as many of these as you think appropriate, using subordination whenever possible.*

I was growing up in Newark in the forties. At that time we assumed that the books in the public library belonged to the public. My family did not own many books. Nor did they have much money for a child to buy them. So it was good to know that I had access to any book I wanted. The only reason for this privilege was my municipal citizenship. I could get books from that grandly austere building downtown on Washington Street. Or I could secure them from the branch library. I could walk to it in my own neighborhood. No less satisfying was the idea of communal ownership. I mean property held in common for the common good. I had to care for the books I borrowed. I had to return them unscarred. And I had to return them on time. The reason was that they were not mine. They were everybody's. That idea had as much to do with civilizing me as any I was ever to come upon in the books themselves.

Compare your version with the original paragraph:

When I was growing up in Newark in the forties, we were taught, or perhaps just assumed, that the books in the public library belonged to the public. Since my family did not own many books, or have very much money for a child to buy them, it was good to know that solely by virtue of my citizenship, I had the use of any of the books I wanted from that grandly austere building downtown on Washington Street, or the branch library I could walk to in my neighborhood. But even more compelling was this idea of communal ownership, property held in common for the common good. Why I had to care for the books I borrowed, return them unscarred and on time, was because they weren't my property alone, *they were everybody's.* That idea had as much to do with civilizing me as any idea I was ever to come upon in the books themselves.

—Philip Roth

25

Use coordination to give equal emphasis to two or more points.

Two or more independent clauses may be joined by coordination to create one compound sentence that gives equal grammatical emphasis to each clause (see **34h** and **36**). A compound sentence is less choppy than two separate simple sentences that contain the same information. And compound sentences signal to the reader the similarity or equivalence of the material in the independent clauses.

Effective: Those who write clearly have readers, but those who write obscurely have critics.

Effective: The team ran onto the field, and the crowd cheered for two minutes.

Coordination implies an equal relationship between the clauses. If the content of one clause is more important than that of the other, subordinate the less important clause.

Ineffective: It was raining, so we had to leave extra early for the airport.

Effective: Since it was raining, we had to leave extra early for the airport.

26

Use coordination to combine sentences.

Parallel coordinate phrases can help you develop mature, expressive sentences. Instead of constructing separate sentences, skillful writers often combine and relate sentence elements so that a single sentence carries more weight.

You can add colorful or clarifying details to a sentence by adding modifiers to the subject or to the predicate or to the sentence as a whole. You can do this by adding modifiers in front of the main clause to form a periodic sentence (see **28c**), or you can pile up modifiers after the main clause rather than use a string of short or choppy sentences.

Ineffective: Space satellite images have many uses. They alert California growers about the cotton bollworm. They inform farmers about screwworms that destroy cattle and poultry in Mexico. And they help chart the destruction of the Mediterranean fruit fly.

Effective: Space satellite images have many uses, alerting California growers about the cotton bollworm, informing farmers about screwworms that destroy cattle and poultry in Mexico, and helping chart the destruction of the Mediterranean fruit fly.

Effective: By alerting California growers about the cotton bollworm, informing farmers about screwworms that destroy cattle and poultry in Mexico, and helping chart the destruction of the Mediterranean fruit fly, space satellite images have many uses.

The repetition in sentences that all begin alike can be eliminated by creatively combining them into one richer, more complex sentence. Too many modifiers, however, can overload a sentence and make it hard to read; also, not every sentence need be developed in this way. But combining can be especially valuable in generating effective descriptive and narrative sentences.

Ineffective: Steven stands on the bridge. He drops pieces of wood upstream. He times how long it takes them to come out the other side and calculates the rate of flow.

Effective: Steven stands on the bridge, dropping pieces of
                   wood upstream, timing how long it takes them to
                   come out the other side, calculating the rate of
                   flow.

                                                    —Margaret Atwood

1. *Noun phrases* can develop a sentence by vividly restating a noun in the main clause:

   Sandra refinished the old *cabinet,* a tall Victorian piece of
   carved walnut marked by years of use.

2. *Verbal phrases* can provide details of the action, object, or scene mentioned in the main clause. In a
   narrative sentence, verbal phrases enable a writer to
   picture simultaneously all the separate actions that
   make up the action named in the main clause. The
   following sentence is broken to distinguish the verbal
   phrases from the main clause that follows them:

   Holding his breath until he was about to burst,
   gulping down a quick glass of water,
       Jeff frantically tried to kill his hiccups before another
       spasm occurred.

3. *Absolute phrases,* like the indented phrases in the
   sentence below, can also add details to a single sentence, often by developing one aspect of the subject:

   The German Shepherd growled menacingly,
       his huge white teeth bared,
       his eyes alert for the slightest false move, and
       the hair on his neck raised as a warning.

   Note that the use of coordinate modifiers involves
   parallelism (see **33**).

27

A. Develop each of the following into one sentence, using coordinate noun, verb, or absolute phrases.

1. The band marched onto the field, Its red uniforms
   ing
   glisten~~ed~~ in the afternoon sun, Its spirited music cre-
   ing
   at~~ed~~ excitement in the packed stands.

2. The dog's dish is unguarded, Its owner is sound
   asleep, Its contents ~~are~~ scattered on the ground.

3. I pictured myself sending a 350-yard drive screaming
   down the fairway, ~~I then imagined myself~~ chipping
   the ball effortlessly onto the green, And ~~I dreamed of~~
   nonchalantly depositing it right into the middle of the
   cup before tipping my hat to a cheering gallery of
   onlookers.

4. It was nearly dark when we arrived at the motel, It
   ~~was~~ a faded cream-colored Holiday Inn/ ~~It was~~
   perched on the edge of the busy interstate, Its gaudy
   lighting
   flashing sign ~~lit~~ up the evening.

5. The campus traffic cop stood in front of my car, ~~He~~

27

looming up before me, His eyes ~~were~~ hidden under his
hat, His silent stance suggesting that I was a criminal.

*B. Combine the following groups of sentences, using
whatever method works best, to form an effective sentence.*

Ineffective: Jerry's room was a mess. The floor was littered
with empty beer cans. The bed was piled high
with dirty clothes. The desk was stacked with
books.

Effective: Jerry's room was a mess, its floor littered with
empty beer cans, its bed piled high with dirty
clothes, its desk stacked with books.

1. The freshmen wrote silently, Some paging nervously
through pocket dictionaries, Some glancing anxiously
at their watches, Others filling page after page with
words.

2. When The Christmas piñata opened, It showering the children with toys and candies, They scrambled and
squealed, ~~They~~ nearly knocking one another over.

3. The tempting aroma of coffee drifted up the stairs, It
~~was~~ a welcome reminder of home to the sleepy students, ~~It was~~ a suggestion of warmth on a cold morning.

4. The gull flew above our heads, ; Its white wings ~~were~~
   gently spread apart, ; Its feet disappear**ing** beneath the
   body of white feathers.
5. The storm was violent, ; Its thunder roar**ing** over the
   roof, ; Its rain lash**ing** at the windows over my bed.

---

28 emp | # Use word order and sentence length for emphasis and variety.

Effective writing not only expresses ideas clearly and relates them to one another appropriately but also emphasizes the most important ideas. Skillful writers also vary the structure of their sentences.

28

28a Emphasize an important word by placing it at the beginning or end of the sentence.

The most emphatic position in most essays, paragraphs, or sentences is at the end. The next most emphatic position is the beginning, so you can emphasize key words by starting and ending sentences with them. Since semicolons are much like periods, words immediately before and after semicolons also receive emphasis. Notice how altering the key words in the following examples improves the emphasis.

Ineffective:	The only real evil is ignorance, as Diogenes said. (leaves the reader thinking about Diogenes, not about what Diogenes said)
Ineffective:	It was Diogenes who said that the only real evil is ignorance. (empty words at the beginning of sentence)
Effective:	Diogenes said that the only real evil is ignorance.
Effective:	The only real evil, Diogenes said, is ignorance.
Ineffective:	For us time was brief and money was a problem.
Effective:	We had little time; we had little money.

28b   Use an occasional short sentence.

A very short sentence contrasting with longer sentences stops the flow and catches the reader's attention. You can use such a short sentence to emphasize an especially important point. Notice how effective the short sentences are in the following passages:

| **Effective:** | With the jingle and flash of innumerable necklaces, the native woman walked proudly, her head held high, her hair festooned with flowers, her bronze arms glittering. She was magnificent. |
| **Effective:** | If we read of one man robbed, or murdered, or killed by accident, or one house burned, or one vessel wrecked, or one steamboat blown up, or one cow run over on the Western Railroad, or one mad dog killed, or one lot of grasshoppers in the winter, we never need read of another. One is enough. |

—Henry David Thoreau

If you have written three or four long sentences, use a short one for variety. If you find that every sentence begins the same way, following the subject-verb-object pattern, for example, vary the word order and use subordination to express the relation among ideas.

Weak:	We Americans hate to say "no" to refugees from poverty-stricken countries. We seem selfish if we set limits for those seeking freedom. But we cannot continue to absorb increasing numbers of immigrants. Our first duty is to our own needy.
Improved:	Although we Americans hate to say "no" to refugees from poverty-stricken countries and to set limits for those seeking freedom, we cannot continue to absorb increasing numbers of immigrants. Our first duty is to our own needy.

28c Use an occasional balanced or periodic sentence.

Most English sentences are *loose* or *cumulative* sentences; that is, the main clause comes first, followed by details supporting the main idea. The order is reversed in a *periodic* sentence, in which the main idea follows the subordinate details. Because it saves the most important idea for last and because it is less commonly used, the periodic sentence is more emphatic. Do not overuse it, however; save it for those ideas you especially want to emphasize.

Loose:	*The public school is a beleaguered institution,* criticized by parents for failing to educate their children, by teachers for failing to be academically innovative, and by the community for failing to produce educated citizens.
Periodic:	Criticized by parents for failing to educate their children, by teachers for failing to be academically innovative, and by the community for failing to produce educated citizens, *the public school is a beleaguered institution.*

In a balanced sentence, coordinate structures are enough alike that the reader notices the similarity. You can use a balanced sentence to emphasize a comparison or contrast:

28

Balanced: Many of us resent shoddiness in cars, food, and services; few of us resent shoddiness in language.

Balanced: We do not ride on the railroad; it rides upon us.
—Henry David Thoreau

28d   Use a climactic word order.

By arranging a series of ideas in order of importance, you can gradually build emphasis:

Climactic: Like all great leaders, Lincoln was hated by many; like all strong presidents, he was embattled by Congress; and, like many heroes, he was popular only after death.

28e   Write primarily in the active voice.

In most active-voice sentences, the subject does something:

Jim ⟶ hit ⟶ the ball.

In passive voice sentences, the subject receives the action of the verb:

The ball ⟵ was hit ⟵ by Jim.

The active voice is usually more direct, natural, and economical:

Passive: Parental discretion is often advised by the networks.
Active: The networks often advise parental discretion.

Passive: The block committee meeting was held on Tuesday afternoon. The rising crime rate was discussed and a resolution was drawn up to be sent to the mayor. It was also decided that the block picnic should be held on July 20. A proposal was made by two members that a fund be set up for replacing dead trees, but not much enthusiasm for the idea was shown by other members.

Active: The block committee met on Tuesday afternoon. It discussed the rising crime rate in the neighborhood and drew up a resolution to send to the mayor. It also decided to hold the block picnic on July 20. Two members proposed that the committee set up a fund to replace dead trees, but other members showed little enthusiasm for the idea.

There are appropriate uses for the passive, as in these examples:

Passive: Franklin D. Roosevelt was elected to an unprecedented fourth term.

Passive: Bill White's article will be published next month.

In each case, to rewrite the sentence in the active voice, one has to reconstruct the subject:

Active: American voters elected Franklin D. Roosevelt to an unprecedented fourth term.

Active: *Current Anthropology* will publish Bill White's article next month.

If the writer is discussing Roosevelt or the article (or its author), not voters or *Current Anthropology,* the passive voice is more logical. But in general, it is best to write in the active voice. Passive-voice sentences tend to be artificial, wordy, and dull. They are less emphatic, especially when they obscure the doer of the action:

A tax increase was announced yesterday.

Passive-voice sentences can also lead to dangling modifiers (see **30f**):

To be an engineer, a college education is needed.
By doing a few simple tests, the biochemical structure can be isolated.

Finally, the passive is not an effective way to vary your style. Unnecessary shifts from active to passive can be distracting for the reader (see **46a**).

A. Study the following sentences. Mark X for those that need rephrasing for emphasis, E for those that are effective.

x 1. It was suggested that an income tax increase be deferred.

x 2. Adolescent behavior can be affected by junk food, which is commonly eaten by teenagers.

x 3. Whereas for most people the future is uncertain, the past is a time of uncertainty for the Chinese.

x 4. Millet and Corot were leading members of the Barbizon School of painters, who lived near Fontainebleau forest outside Paris, where tourists and art lovers now visit.

x 5. To be an architect, a six-year curriculum must often be followed.

x 6. Johnny Unitas was a great quarterback, Bob Griese was good, and Fran Tarkenton was outstanding.

x 7. Children of working mothers learn that a woman is capable of working and taking care of the home, which has been noted in one study.

E 8. Over half of all American mothers now work outside the home, as compared with twenty years ago when only 10 percent worked.

x 9. One reason for this increase is the growing need for

28

a second income, while the mother's desire to establish a career of her own is another.

x 10. Years ago, many husbands disapproved of their wives' working, but now wives are often encouraged to work by their spouses.

B. *Rephrase the sentences above marked* X.

---

29 awk   Avoid awkward repetitions and omitted words.

Awkward sentences are difficult to read. They may or may not be clear, but they always require extra effort and usually interrupt the flow of thought. In this section we discuss two common causes of awkwardness. But many awkward sentences do not fit into neat categories; they often result from the ineffective choice or arrangement of words, as described in this chapter and in Chapter 10. If awkwardness is a problem for you, try reading your sentences aloud: an awkward sentence usually does not *sound* right.

29a Repeat words only for emphasis or transition.

Repeating a prominent word or expression can provide an effective transition between sentences or paragraphs (see **23b**). Occasional repetition of a key word can emphasize an idea. But use repetition sparingly: too much can create awkward sentences:

Awkward repetition: A sculptor who sculpts abstract or stylized works must first learn to work with realistic subjects.

Improved:	A sculptor doing abstract or stylized works must first learn to treat realistic subjects.
Effective repetition:	Rewriting is valuable because it allows us to see what our words really mean, to see if they make sense, to see if they will be understood by someone else.
Effective repetition:	Social justice is not a moral burden but a moral obligation.

One especially confusing type of repetition is the use of the same word in two different senses in the same or adjoining sentences. Find a synonym for one instance of the word.

| **Awkward repetition:** | No one knew the principal reason for the principal's dismissal. |
| **Improved:** | No one knew the major reason for the principal's dismissal. |

29b Include all necessary words.

Many sentences are awkward because they use unnecessary words, but many others are awkward or confusing because they omit words. Below are some of the more common types of omissions:

Awkward omission:	I could see almost everyone in the room was talking and laughing excitedly. (*That* has been omitted after *see*. Omitting *that* is often confusing and awkward.)
Improved:	I could see that almost everyone in the room was talking and laughing excitedly.
Awkward omission:	The contestants were beautiful and wearing evening gowns. (*Were* has been omitted before *wearing*. *Beautiful* and *wearing* are not parallel.)

Improved:	The contestants were beautiful and were wearing evening gowns.
Awkward omission:	The senior class expressed its appreciation to Mr. Taylor, the principal; Mrs. Jackson, the senior class advisor; and Mrs. Baker, the college counselor. (*To* omitted before *Mrs. Jackson* and *Mrs. Baker.* Repeating the preposition shows the parallel elements more clearly.)
Improved:	The senior class expressed its appreciation to Mr. Taylor, the principal; to Mrs. Jackson, the senior class advisor; and to Mrs. Baker, the college counselor.

When you use two verbs that require different prepositions, be sure to include both prepositions:

Awkward omission:	He could neither comply nor agree to the proposal. (*With* has been omitted after *comply.*)
Improved:	He could neither comply with nor agree to the proposal.

EXERCISE

Mark X *for sentences that are awkward and* E *for those that are effective. Rewrite the awkward sentences.*

29

x 1. Ralph sensed his presence was unwelcome.

x 2. The mayor read a report that treated in detail the water treatment problem.

x 3. The swimmers were tired but wearing big grins.

x 4. In the summers we nibbled wild strawberries and champagne.

x 5. Many colleges eagerly search and recruit minority students.

x 6. A higher degree of promotion is evident in higher education than ever before.

x 7. The dean could neither concur nor approve of the decision.

x 8. Mrs. Johnson is known for her interest in her students' work and her concern about their problems.

E 9. I do not wish to interfere with or alter your plans.

x 10. This year's contest is different, yet in some ways similar to, last year's.

Place all modifiers so that they clearly modify the intended word.

The meaning of English sentences depends largely on word order; if you move words and expressions around, you will often change what a sentence means:

> Nancy Ruiz recently published the poem she wrote.
>
> Nancy Ruiz published the poem she wrote recently.

The rule of thumb is to place modifiers as near as possible to the words they modify.

30a *Place an adjective phrase or clause as near as possible to the noun or pronoun it modifies.*

Single adjectives usually come immediately before the noun or pronoun they modify, adjective phrases and clauses immediately after. When other words come between an adjective and the word it modifies, the sentence may sound awkward, and its meaning may be obscured:

Misplaced: The customer returned the VCR to the store with the broken rewind.

Improved: The customer returned the VCR with the broken rewind to the store.

Often you have to do more than move the modifier; you have to revise the whole sentence:

Misplaced: Unless well fertilized, people cannot grow orchids successfully.

Revised: People can only grow orchids successfully that have been well fertilized.

Misplaced: The sick plant was placed in a new building, which needed all the help it could get.

Revised: The sick plant, which needed all the help it could get, was placed in a new building.

30b Place a limiting adverb, such as only or just, immediately before the word it modifies.

In speech, most of us are casual about where we place such adverbs as *only, almost, hardly, just,* and *scarcely.* But writing should be more precise:

Misplaced: Jan almost completed all of her math problems.

Revised: Jan completed almost all of her math problems.

Notice how moving the modifier can change the meaning of a sentence:

I hit him in the eye only yesterday.

I only hit him in the eye yesterday.

I hit him only in the eye yesterday.

30c Make certain that each adverb phrase or clause modifies the word or words you intend it to modify.

An adverb phrase or clause can appear at the beginning of a sentence, inside a sentence, or at the end:

> After the census, New York lost two congressional seats.
>
> New York, after the census, lost two congressional seats.
>
> New York lost two congressional seats after the census.

Be careful, though, that the adverb modifies only what you intend it to modify:

Misplaced: A man missing in Biscayne Bay was presumed drowned by the Coast Guard.

Revised: According to the Coast Guard, a man missing in Biscayne Bay was presumed drowned.

Misplaced: The ex-convict vowed to kill Terranova at least twice.

Improved: The ex-convict vowed at least twice to kill Terranova.

30d Move ambiguous (squinting) modifiers.

If you find that you have placed a modifier so that it refers ambiguously to more than one word, move it to avoid the ambiguity:

Ambiguous: Conrad enjoyed working for a short time.

Clear: For a short time, Conrad enjoyed working.
Or: Conrad enjoyed short periods of work.

Ambiguous: The student Mr. Guthrie criticized angrily left the room.

Revised: The student Mr. Guthrie angrily criticized left the room.

Or: The student Mr. Guthrie criticized left the room angrily.

30e   Avoid awkwardly split infinitives.

Conventional usage requires that you avoid inserting an adverb between *to*—called the sign of the infinitive—and its verb form *(to quickly run)*. In some instances, splitting the infinitive is natural; many writers would prefer the following sentence to an alternative: "To suddenly stop offering trading stamps might upset our customers." But the following example is awkward:

> The chairman proposed *to,* if no one had any objections, *defer* discussion of the budget.

Revised: The chairman proposed to defer discussion of the budget, if no one had any objections.

30f   Make certain that introductory verbal phrases relate clearly to the subject of the sentence.

Modifiers are said to *dangle* when they do not logically modify a word or expression in the sentence. Most often, a *dangling modifier* does not correctly refer to the subject of the sentence:

Dangling: Driving to the old house, the family cat got loose.

In this sentence, the reader will mistakenly assume that the subject of the sentence *(cat)* is also the understood subject of the verbal *(driving)*. The result is absurd: did the cat drive? The writer should have written:

Improved: *While the family was* driving to the old house, the cat got loose.

The improved sentence illustrates one way of correcting a dangling modifier: supply the necessary words to make the phrase into a complete dependent clause. It is relatively easy to supply missing words when the dangling modifier is an *elliptical phrase* (a predicate with the subject and part of the verb implied but not expressed):

Dangling: While watching the performance, their jewels were stolen.

Corrected: While *they were* watching the performance, their jewels were stolen.

At other times, the best way to correct a dangling modifier may be to revise the main sentence, as in the following examples:

Dangling: *Driving recklessly,* Allen's Corvette crashed into a light pole. (dangling participial phrase)

Corrected: Driving recklessly, Allen crashed his Corvette into a light pole.

Dangling: *To succeed,* a great deal of determination and luck are needed. (dangling infinitive)

Corrected: To succeed, one needs a great deal of determination and luck.

These examples illustrate two common causes of dangling modifiers. In the first sentence, the word that the phrase is intended to modify is not the subject of the sentence but a possessive modifying the subject *(Allen's)*. In the second sentence, the main clause is in the passive voice (see **28e**). Note that the revisions are not only logical but also more direct.

Note: Some verbal phrases (often known as *absolute constructions)* refer not to a single word but to the whole idea of a sentence; hence, they do not dangle.

Acceptable: *Generally speaking,* most books contain errors.

Acceptable: *Considering the cost of gasoline,* the bus fare looks quite reasonable.

30g Be certain that concluding clauses and phrases modify the word intended.

Illogical: Jack Nicholson won an Oscar for *One Flew over the Cuckoo's Nest,* his greatest role. (Was the movie his role?)

Corrected: Jack Nicholson won an Oscar for his greatest role, McMurphy, in *One Flew over the Cuckoo's Nest.*

EXERCISE

Rewrite the following sentences, correcting any dangling or other misplaced modifiers.

1. Without a friend in the world, ~~her problems seemed~~ she felt that her problems were insoluble. ~~insoluble.~~

2. As I was Lying in the hospital bed, my mind began to develop fearful fantasies.

3. "Eleanor Rigby" is only accompanied by string instruments.

4. Bill nearly finished the entire meal in five minutes.

5. Whether it be good or bad the audience has the right to the truth.

6. The speaker tried to get~~across/~~ what he earnestly believed.

7. To win at poker, a cool head ~~is needed.~~ a player needs.

8. Looking out over the river, moss-draped trees ~~could be seen.~~ I could see.

9. At birth Jason ~~only~~ weighed five pounds.

10. ~~Homeowners often complain about property taxes~~ in letters to their elected representatives, Homeowners often complain about property taxes.

---

31 pred	**Make subject and predicate relate to each other logically.**

As a main verb, *to be* links a subject with a complement: The *piano is* an old *Steinway;* The *news is good.* A common error called *faulty predication* occurs when the subject and complement cannot be logically joined:

Faulty: His job was a reporter for the *Sun Times.*

Correct: He worked as a reporter for the *Sun Times.*
(he = reporter)

Faulty: The pentathlon is a chance to prove what an athlete can do.

Correct: The pentathlon provides a chance to prove what an athlete can do.
Or: The pentathlon is an event that proves what an athlete can do. (pentathlon = event)

In general, avoid following a form of *to be* with adverb clauses beginning with *where, when,* and *because:*

Faulty: Someone said that diplomacy is when one lies gracefully for his country.

Correct: Someone said that diplomacy is lying gracefully for one's country.

Faulty: The reason Hubert was fired was because he was rude to many customers.

Correct: The reason Hubert was fired was that he was rude to many customers.

Faulty predication can occur with verbs other than *to be* whenever the subject and predicate do not fit together logically:

Faulty: Abused spouses must be dealt with severely.

Correct: Spouse abuse must be dealt with severely.

EXERCISE

A. Mark E for those sentences in which the subject and complement are compatible, X for those with faulty predication.

x   1. A **Receiving** bad check is an irritating and costly experience

for a retailer.

E   2. Writing bad checks is as illegal as any other crime,

but it is treated less severely than other offenses.

x   3. The reason is ~~because~~ **that** the courts do not take it se-

riously.

x   4. ~~Retail stores are where~~ the problem is most serious, _∧ ^{in retail stores.}

E   5. They must absorb the costs of bad checks and pass them on to their customers in the form of higher prices.

x   6. Another part of the problem is when banks fail to check out new account applicants thoroughly enough. ^{occurs}

x   7. Dale's new position is much better ~~paid~~ than his old one. ^{pays}

x   8. ^{Seeing} A movie is one way to spend an evening.

x   9. ~~College is when~~ many young people grow up, _∧ ^{in college.}

x   10. Juan believes that medicine is the best means of becoming rich. ^{practicing}

32

32 comp Compare only things that are logically comparable.

A common fault is to compare a characteristic of one thing with another thing instead of with its corresponding characteristic:

Faulty:	Shakespeare's plays are studied and performed more widely than any other playwright. (comparing *plays* to *playwright*)
Correct:	Shakespeare's plays are studied and performed more widely than *those of* any other playwright.
Faulty:	A teacher's income is generally lower than a doctor. (*income* compared to *doctor*)
Correct:	A teacher's income is generally lower than a doctor's. *Or:* A teacher's income is generally lower than that of a doctor.

Many comparisons are faulty because the word *other* has been omitted:

Faulty:	New York is larger than any American city.
Correct:	New York is larger than any other American city.

Many faulty comparisons are ambiguous:

Faulty:	Lately I've been calling Maria much more often than George. (Who calls whom?)
Correct:	Lately I've been calling Maria much more often than George has. *Or:* Lately I've been calling Maria much more often than I have called George.
Faulty:	Pensacola is farther from Chicago than Miami.
Correct:	Pensacola is farther from Chicago than it is from Miami.

Many comparisons are incomplete because words such as *as* and *that* are omitted.

Faulty:	Jefferson is as good if not better than other community colleges.
Correct:	Jefferson is as good as, if not better than, other community colleges. *Or:* Jefferson is as good as other community colleges, if not better.

32

Faulty: The poetic style of Vaughan is much like Traherne.

Correct: The poetic style of Vaughan is much like *that* of Traherne.

Or: . . . is much like Traherne's.

EXERCISE

A. Mark E *for those sentences with effective comparisons and* X *for those with ineffective comparisons.*

x 1. When I was a teenager, I vowed to trust my father
more than any _^**other** man.

x 2. Marion loves music more than Sam_^**does.**

x 3. Drunk driving is as serious _^**as,** if not more so than _^any other traffic problem.

x 4. Drunk drivers kill more innocent people than any
_^**other** careless drivers do.

x 5. American families move more often than any _^**other** families.

E 6. The sonnet is more common in English than any other fixed form of poetry.

x 7. The dancer's movements in *Giselle* were like _^**those of** a cat.

x 8. Tom could never tell Bob Seeger's raspy baritone from Rod Stewart_^**'s.**

32

E   9. The temperature is higher in Dallas this year than

        it has been for over thirty years.

x 10. The waves are much higher than _{they were} yesterday.

    B. Reword the sentences marked X.

---

33 comp   **Use parallel structures effectively.**

When you express two or more ideas that are equal in emphasis, use parallel grammatical structures: nouns with nouns,
infinitives with infinitives, adverb clauses with adverb
clauses. The parallel structures clearly and emphatically indicate parallel ideas:

33

Effective: The hero is destroyed by his own strength,
              devoured by his own hunger, and impoverished by
              his own wealth. (verb phrases)

Effective: It may be better, Eliot said, to do evil than to do
              nothing. (infinitive phrases)

Effective: Because of its acute hearing, because of its playful
              imagination, and most of all because of its amazing
              intelligence, the dolphin is a rare creature of the
              sea. (introductory phrases)

33a In parallel structures, use only equal grammatical constructions.

A common error among inexperienced writers is faulty parallelism—treating unlike grammatical structures as if they were parallel. This practice upsets the balance that the reader expects in a coordinate structure. Below are some of the more common types of faulty parallelism:

Faulty: Denise has two great ambitions: to act and becoming a director.

Correct: Denise has two great ambitions: to act and to direct.
Or: . . . acting and directing.

Faulty: Myron is intelligent, charming, and knows how to dress.

Correct: Myron is intelligent, charming, and well dressed.

33b Repeat necessary words to make all parallels clear to the reader.

Awkward, confusing sentences often result if you do not repeat needed prepositions, signs of infinitives *(to)*, auxiliary verbs, or other words needed to make a parallel clear:

Faulty: Central Florida is well known for its family-oriented attractions, such as Disney World, and its beaches, citrus groves, and retirement centers.

Correct: Central Florida is well known for its family-oriented attractions, such as Disney World, and *for* its beaches, citrus groves, and retirement centers.

Faulty: Mr. Simmons, the counselor, told Carmelita that she should be more realistic and dropping one course would not ruin her record.

Correct: Mr. Simmons, the counselor, told Carmelita that she should be more realistic and *that* dropping one course would not ruin her record.

33

33c Always use parallel structures with correlative conjunctions such as both . . . and or neither . . . nor.

Use the *correlative conjunctions* to connect two closely related ideas; use the same grammatical form for both ideas. The most common correlatives are *both . . . and, either . . . or, not only . . . but also, neither . . . nor, whether . . . or.*

Faulty: Gene Burns is well respected both for his mellow, authoritative voice and as a shrewd analyst of local politics.

Correct: Gene Burns is well respected both for his mellow, authoritative voice and for his shrewd analysis of local politics.

Faulty: He is admired not only by those who share his liberal views, but also conservatives respect his integrity.

Correct: He is admired not only by those who share his liberal views but also by conservatives, who respect his integrity.

EXERCISE

A. Mark with E *those sentences that are effective and with* X *those containing faulty parallelism.*

E 1. I cannot decide whether to play my guitar or to read some science fiction.

X 2. To write simply is not as difficult as ~~being~~ to be good.

X 3. Three stars were drafted from the baseball team: ~~one was~~ a pitcher, ~~one played~~ a shortstop, and ~~one as~~ a designated hitter.

x 4. Using a video display terminal can lead to fatigue,

                                        irritation.

      headaches, and ~~is irritating to the~~ eye~~s~~‸

x 5. The English courses are interesting, enjoyable, and

                              ous to the student.

      ~~to the student's~~ advantage‸

x 6. Many women do not mind having their chairs

                          their tab picked up by   **.**

      pulled out for them, their doors opened, or ‸a man‸

      ~~picking up the tab.~~

x 7. During my freshman year, I received much helpful

                 made

      advice and ‸many new friends.

x 8. I believe that everyone should study and ~~be~~ opposed

      ~~to~~ the proposed ordinance.

                           to

x 9. Jeff plans to be an engineer and ‸develop his skills

      as a novelist.

                                     expensive.

x 10. The apartment is convenient, spacious, but ‸~~costs a~~

      ~~lot of money.~~

    B. Reword the sentences above marked X.

PART

II

A GUIDE

TO

STYLE

Basic

Grammar

The principles of grammar are means to an end: effective communication. They express the conventional practices followed by experienced speakers and writers of Standard English. Not following these conventions often results in writing that is not only technically incorrect but also confusing or misleading. Most of the time we follow the conventions of English without thinking about them. But some errors are almost inevitable, and knowing the rules makes correcting those errors much easier.

The parts of speech are the classifications of English words according to their forms and their uses in sentences: verbs, nouns, pronouns, adjectives, adverbs, prepositions, conjunctions, and interjections. Many words can serve as more than one part of speech. *Round,* for example, can be a noun (we won the round), a verb (they rounded the corner), or an adjective (they have a round table). Being able to recognize parts of speech will help you analyze and discuss the sentences you write.

34a Verbs show action, process, or existence.

The **verb** is an essential part of every sentence. Most verbs show some kind of action or process:

> Barry *resigned.*   The lady *screamed.*   The water *boiled.*

Other verbs, known as **linking verbs,** express a state or condition. They link the subject with the noun, pronoun, or adjective that describes or identifies it. (The word linked to the subject is the **subject complement.**) Linking verbs include *be (am, is, are, was, were, being, been), become, remain, grow, seem, appear, look, sound, feel, taste,* and *smell:*

34

> Rosa *is* a brilliant attorney.   The meat *smelled* rancid.

Tense. Tense refers to the time indicated in the sentence. The form of the verb indicates the time of the action or statement:

> Sam *writes.* Sam *wrote.* Sam *will write.* (see **43**)

Voice. If the subject of the sentence does the action, its verb is in the active voice. If the subject receives the action, the verb is in the passive voice (see **28e, 45**):

Active voice: The reviewer condemned the film's violence.
(subject [reviewer] *acts)*

Passive voice: The film's violence was condemned by the
reviewer. *(subject* [violence] *receives action)*

Forms. The English verb has a limited number of forms. Verbs may be regular *(walk, walked, walked)* or irregular *(see, saw, seen)*.

> *Infinitive:* to walk, to see
> *Present:* walk, walks; see, sees
> *Past:* walked, saw
> *Past participle:* walked, seen
> *Present participle:* walking, seeing

The infinitive, the past, and the past participle are known as the *principal parts* of a verb. Most verbs are regular: they just add *-ed* to form the past and past participle. Irregular verbs may change spelling: *go, went, gone; see, saw, seen.* The present participle always ends in *-ing.* For the addition of *-s* in the present tense, see **43**.

Predicates. The main verb in a sentence is called the **simple predicate.** The main verb with all the words that belong to it or qualify it is called the **complete predicate** because it completes the subject (see **35b**).

Verb phrases. A **verb phrase** is made up of a **main verb** preceded by one or more **auxiliary verbs:** I *will have left* by Friday. The most commonly used auxiliaries are *have (has, had), be (am, is, are, was, were, been), do (does, did), will, would, shall, should, can, could, may, might, must,* and *ought.*
    The first word in a verb phrase shows tense and agrees

with the subject: she *has* gone; she *had* gone; they *have* gone; they *had* gone. In identifying verb phrases, note that other words may come between the first auxiliary word and the rest of the phrase:

> His writing *has* never *made* sense to me.
>
> Most children *have*, at least once in their lives, *dreamed* of riding on a fire engine.

Verbals. Forms of the verb may function as nouns, adjectives, or adverbs. When they do, they are called **verbals,** and they may combine with other words in **verbal phrases:** *Waiting for the train every day* is not my idea of happiness.

Gerunds are verbals ending in *-ing* that are used as nouns: *Jogging* is popular. Sometimes a gerund has an object and/or modifiers: *Paying bills promptly* is not easy. The gerund phrase *(paying bills promptly)* also functions as a noun.

> *Laughing* is good for one's health. (gerund as subject)
>
> I would enjoy *laughing all the way to the bank.* (gerund phrase as direct object)

Present participles have the same form as gerunds but are used as adjectives, not as nouns:

> The man *laughing* too loudly annoyed us. (*laughing* is present participle modifying *man*)

34b Nouns name things.

Nouns are the names given to things real or imagined, tangible or intangible:

> trees   endurance   Colorado   woman   physics

In sentences, nouns can be used as subjects, objects of active verbs, complements of linking verbs, and appositives:

Subject	Appositive		Object of preposition	
John Nolan,	*assistant*	to the	*mayor,*	gave

Indirect object		Direct object
reporters	a written	*statement.*

Nouns can also function as modifiers, as in *stone* wall and *television* news.

Almost all nouns take an *-s* or *-es* ending or change spelling to form plurals (see **66**). They also take an apostrophe and *s* or apostrophe alone to show possession: *women's* rights, *prospectors'* hunches (see **60**).

34c Pronouns take the place of nouns.

The noun that a pronoun refers to is called the antecedent:

> The men rushed in. *They* were angry. (The antecedent of *they* is *men.*)

There are five different kinds of pronouns:

Personal pronouns (*I, he, she, it, they, we,* etc.) take different forms according to their function in a sentence. See **39.**

Relative pronouns (*who, whom, whose, which, that*) join a dependent clause to a noun. See **34h.**

Interrogative pronouns (*who, whom, whose, which, what*) are used in questions.

Demonstrative pronouns (*this, that, these, those*) point to

34

nouns: *This* is better than *that.* (When used with nouns, they are called demonstrative adjectives: *This* VCR is cheaper than *that* VCR.)

Indefinite pronouns refer to indefinite persons or things. Examples are *someone, everyone, anything, another.* For verb agreement with indefinite pronouns as subjects, see **38.**

34d   Adjectives and adverbs are modifiers.

To modify is to describe, qualify, or limit the meaning of a word. **Adjectives** modify nouns and pronouns; **adverbs** modify verbs, adjectives, and other adverbs:

> The salesman approached the *reluctant* customer. (adjective modifying noun *customer*)
>
> The program progressed *quite rapidly.* (adverb *quite* modifying adverb *rapidly,* which modifies verb *progressed*)
>
> We faced *extremely* serious problems. (adverb modifying adjective *serious*)

Most adjectives and adverbs can be compared, that is, arranged in order of intensity: *happy, happier, happiest; angrily, more angrily, most angrily.* See **42.**

34e   Prepositions and conjunctions are structural words that work with the major parts of speech.

Verbs, nouns, adjectives, and adverbs express most of the information in sentences, but the meaning of a whole sentence also depends on structural words that show relationships among those major words. Two main groups of structural words are prepositions and conjunctions.

Prepositions relate and link one word with another; examples are *of, in, on, into, at, to, for, after, with, with regard to, aside from.* They are followed by nouns and pronouns that form the **object of a preposition.**

After the long wait, we enjoyed the concert.

   ↑   ↑

(preposition)   (object of preposition)

A preposition and its object together are called a **prepositional phrase:**

The old tree *in the center of town* stood *near the condemned building.*

Prepositional phrases can function as adjectives or as adverbs. See **34g.**

Conjunctions connect words or word groups. The **coordinating conjunctions** *and, but, or, nor,* and *yet* join words, phrases, or clauses of the same grammatical type:

The *camera* and the *lens* must be purchased separately. (*and* joins two nouns)

He *lied* and *stole.* (*and* joins two verbs)

The hunter was *old* yet *strong.* (*yet* joins two adjectives)

Neither *on land* nor *on sea* did they meet any resistance. (*nor* joins two prepositional phrases)

For and *so* are used only between word groups that express complete thoughts:

He used the wrong film, *so* the pictures did not turn out.

The conjunctions *since, because, after, while, when, if, as soon as,* etc., are called **subordinating conjunctions** be-

34

cause the word groups they introduce are subordinate: they depend on other word groups for their completion (see **25**).

> *Since Jamie moved to Dallas* [subordinate], she has matured.

> I feel weak *because I have not eaten* [subordinate].

34f   Interjections express emotion.

Interjections such as *oh* and *ah* show emotion. They may be punctuated as sentences (Oh!) or included in sentences (Oh, I wish you would say something), but they are not grammatically related to other words in the sentence.

34g   A phrase is a group of related words without a complete subject and verb.

The function of a single word can be filled by a group of words. Such a group of words that work together, but lack a subject and verb, is called a **phrase:**

Noun:	I enjoy *art.*
Phrase as noun:	I enjoy *visiting museums.*
Verb:	He *went.*
Verb phrase:	He *should have been going.*
Adjective:	The *tall* man is my uncle.
Phrase as adjective:	The man *towering over the others* is my uncle.
Adverb:	She tried *hard.*
Phrase as adverb:	She tried *with all her strength.*

There are four other common types of phrases:

Prepositional phrase:

Adjective: The clock *on the mantel* belonged to my grandfather.

Adverb: He drove the truck *around the block.*

Infinitive phrase:

Noun: He wants *to fight with everyone.*

Adjective: There must be another way *to settle this problem.*

Adverb: The plumber came *to fix the sink.*

Gerund phrase:

Noun: *Playing on a winning team* adds to the fun of baseball.

Participial phrase:

Adjective: The smoke *rising from the house* alerted the neighbors.
A house *built on a rock* will endure.

34h A clause is a group of words with a subject and verb used as part of a sentence.

If a clause expresses a complete thought and can stand alone as a sentence, it is called an **independent clause** (or *main clause*). If it does not express a complete thought, it is called a **dependent clause** (or *subordinate clause*) and cannot stand alone as a sentence.

34

> The mayor spoke last night. (independent clause properly punctuated as a sentence)
>
> When the mayor spoke last night. (dependent clause improperly punctuated as a sentence)

Dependent clauses are introduced (and made dependent or

subordinate) by subordinating conjunctions (such as *because, when, after, although*). Such clauses cannot stand alone; they modify the main part of the sentence.

When the mayor spoke last night, reporters were strangely absent.

    ↑   ↑
   (dependent/subordinate   (independent/main clause)
     clause)

A subordinate clause functions as a noun, adjective, or adverb:

Noun: They do not know *who wrote the threatening letter.*
      (clause as object of *know*)

Adjective: People *who exercise* live longer than those *who do not.*

Adverb: I ate the cake *because I was hungry.*

EXERCISE

A. Underline and identify the nouns (N), pronouns (P), and verbs (V) in the following sentences.

1. People may dream in the spring, but birds work hard.

2. They must feed their nestlings, who clamor for food.

3. The parents, constantly flying from the ground to the nest, bring a steady supply of worms and insects.

4. Ponds swarm with a multitude of tadpoles, which are the natural prey of ducks and other water birds.

34

5. Conscientious <u>bees</u> <u>clean</u> their <u>hives</u> until <u>they</u> virtu-

       V

ally <u>sparkle</u>.

B. Underline and identify the adjectives (ADJ), adverbs (ADV), and prepositional phrases (PP) in these sentences.

1. <u>In the past,</u> <u>many</u> people had a <u>casual</u> attitude to-

      PP

<u>ward excessive drinking</u>.

2. They saw it as an <u>embarrassing</u> problem <u>for the</u>

   PP

<u>drinker</u>.

3. They <u>often</u> overlooked the fact that alcohol can <u>seri-</u>

<u>ously</u> hurt a <u>productive</u> person.

4. Only <u>dirty</u>, <u>unshaven</u> men, <u>unconscious</u> <u>in the gut-</u>

<u>ter</u>, were assumed to be <u>alcoholic</u>.

5. <u>Now</u> <u>more</u> people are <u>aware</u> that <u>most</u> alcoholics live

in houses and hold jobs until their disease kills

them, <u>quickly</u> or <u>slowly</u>.

C. Underline and identify infinitive phrases (I) and participial phrases (P) in these sentences.

1. Couples go to malls <u>to watch other people</u> as well as

<u>to shop</u>.

2. It's easier <u>to drink coffee</u> and <u>observe faces</u> <u>passing in a</u>

<u>crowd</u> than <u>to jostle through stores</u> <u>looking for bargains</u>.

3. Shoppers return home $\overset{\text{P}}{\underline{\text{feeling tired}}}$, $\overset{\text{P}}{\underline{\text{their feet and}}}$

   $\underline{\text{heads hurting}}$.

4. Non-shoppers, however, come home $\overset{\text{P}}{\underline{\text{congratulating}}}$

   $\underline{\text{themselves}}$ that they are able $\overset{\text{I}}{\underline{\text{to walk}}}$ and have no

   bills $\overset{\text{I}}{\underline{\text{to pay}}}$.

5. $\overset{\text{P}}{\underline{\text{Shopping for new clothes}}}$ is for some people an ex-

   pensive form of therapy.

D. Underline and identify the gerunds (G), gerund phrases (GP), and present participles (P) in these sentences.

1. $\overset{\text{G}}{\underline{\text{Eating}}}$ is more fun than $\overset{\text{G}}{\underline{\text{dieting}}}$, yet many people give

   up the pleasures of $\overset{\text{GP}}{\underline{\text{eating their favorite foods}}}$.

2. $\overset{\text{GP}}{\underline{\text{Drenching popcorn}}}$ with butter is more appealing

   then $\overset{\text{GP}}{\underline{\text{broiling fish}}}$ or $\overset{\text{GP}}{\underline{\text{peeling carrots}}}$.

3. How can chocolates, $\overset{\text{P}}{\underline{\text{lying}}}$ innocently on shelves and

   $\overset{\text{P}}{\underline{\text{smelling}}}$ so delicious, ever threaten anyone?

4. Yet many people are $\overset{\text{P}}{\underline{\text{protesting}}}$, "Chocolate is my

   addiction!"

5. $\overset{\text{GP}}{\underline{\text{Using butter}}}$, $\overset{\text{GP}}{\underline{\text{drinking cocoa}}}$, and $\overset{\text{GP}}{\underline{\text{munching choco-}}}$

   $\underline{\text{late candy}}$ have become subversive activities.

E. Underline and identify the independent clauses (I), and mark subordinate clauses (S) in these sentences.

1. <u>Janet</u>, who is an experienced cashier, <u>works twice as</u>
   s   **I**

   <u>fast as the newer employees</u> because she knows the

   price of everything.

2. Until she became familiar with the routine, however,

   <u>she rarely spoke to customers.</u>

3. <u>Now she can talk about the weather, the cost of liv-</u>

   <u>ing, in-store specials, and any other topic</u>, although

   she always keeps the conversation general.

4. <u>She knows that</u>, no matter how accustomed she is to

   the computer, <u>she still needs to keep her mind on</u>

   <u>her job.</u>

5. Since a number of customers are not honest with

   money or coupons, <u>they have to be watched.</u>

35a   Subject

When a noun, pronoun, or verbal is doing something or is being described by a verb in a sentence, it is a **subject.**

I [subject] saw the game Tuesday night.

Joan's *portrait* [subject] was painted.

Walking [subject] is excellent exercise.

Hearts and minds [compound subject] can easily change.

35b   Predicate

The main verb in a sentence is called the **predicate.** It can be one word: I *saw* the game Tuesday night. More often, the predicate will consist of several words, constituting the complete verb:

He never *wants to leave.*

She *has* always *been able to learn* languages easily.

The complete verb or predicate includes all the words related to the predicate; likewise, the complete subject includes all the words related to the subject.

The first person who comes to the party [complete subject] never wants to leave [complete predicate].

35c   Compound Subject

When a subject consists of more than one noun, pronoun, or verbal, it is a **compound subject:**

Bushes and shrubs obscure our rusty old back door.

35d Compound Predicate

When a predicate has more than one main verb, it is a **compound predicate:**

Every fall, we *prune and fertilize* our azalea bushes.

35e Objects

A noun, pronoun, or verbal which directly receives the action of a verb is called a **direct object.**

Jennifer despises *housekeeping.*
(*Housekeeping* is the direct object of *despises:* what does she despise?)

The library discarded forty-eight *books.*
(*Books* is the direct object of *discarded:* what did the library discard?)

A noun, pronoun, or verbal which is related to the action but which is not the direct receiver of that action is called an **indirect object.** It states to whom (or to what) or for whom (or for what) something is done.

Mystery writers usually give *readers* a few clues.
Writers give clues (direct object) to readers (indirect object).

The teacher told *Jay* some sad news about his grades.
Teacher told news (direct object) to Jay (indirect object).

35f Complements

Although action verbs may have direct objects, linking verbs—forms of the verb *be* such as *is, are, was, were, been*—as well as those verbs that describe a condition or position—such as *feel, look, seem, become, taste, smell*—take a **complement.** Subject complements complete the meaning of a subject:

> Cocoa in its natural state is *bitter.*
> (*Bitter* describes *cocoa,* the subject.)

Object complements complete the meaning of verbs such as *call, elect, find, make, name;* they identify or qualify the direct object:

> She called the proposal   *foolish.*
>   ↑   ↑   ↑
>   (verb)   (direct (object complement)
>   object)

35g *Compound Sentences*

When two independent clauses are joined by a coordinating conjunction *(and, but, or, nor, for, so, yet)* or by a semicolon, the sentence is a **compound sentence:**

> Word processors have much to offer a student writer; they greatly simplify revising and editing.

> Working while being a full-time student is difficult, yet many students manage to do both.

35h *Complex Sentences*

When a dependent or subordinate clause is joined to an independent clause, the sentence is a **complex sentence:**

> When the snow stopped, the ground was white.
>   (dependent)   (independent)

Identify the underlined part of each of the following sentences:

Compound predicate

1. Nicotine <u>can stimulate and relax</u> a smoker's body.

Direct object

2. It can reach the <u>brain</u> within seven seconds.

3. The U.S. Surgeon General <u>has issued reports on the</u>

Complete predicate

<u>addictive nature of tobacco.</u>

Dependent clause

4. <u>Although forty-three million Americans have man-</u>

<u>aged to quit smoking</u>, there are still more than fifty

million smokers.

Indirect object

5. It is sometimes awkward to tell a <u>smoker</u> the facts

about smoking.

Compound subject

6. <u>Biting a pretzel or chewing into an apple</u> may cause

some people pain in the head or neck.

Subject complement

7. This symptom may be <u>long-lasting.</u>

Complete subject

8. <u>This problem, TMJ or temporomandibular joint syn-</u>

<u>drome</u>, may have several causes.

Direct object

9. Some physicians have recommended <u>surgery</u> to

their patients with this disorder.

35

10. Some patients <u>wear corrective appliances fitted over</u>

<u>their teeth.</u>

---

36 frag   Use grammatically complete sentences.

A group of words that is punctuated as a sentence, but that is not a grammatically complete sentence, is called a *fragment* or a *sentence fragment.* Although experienced writers sometimes use fragments intentionally, fragments are usually unacceptable in college writing. Unintentional fragments can create misunderstanding and distract your readers. A fragment is usually either a *phrase* or a *subordinate clause.*

Complete sentence: David is a talented artist.
                       (independent clause)

Fragment: Because David is a talented artist.
                       (subordinate clause)

Fragment: Like a talented artist.
                       (prepositional phrase)

36

Most fragments result from chopping a phrase or clause from the end of an adjoining sentence. It is usually a simple matter to correct them. You can reconnect the fragment to the previous or following sentence, or you can add the necessary elements to make the fragment a grammatically complete sentence. Subordinating conjunctions such as *although, because, if,* and *when* introduce subordinate (dependent) clauses, and such clauses cannot stand alone as sentences. The following examples show the most common types of clauses or phrases used incorrectly as fragments:

Incorrect: Although being left-handed has been seen as a minor misfortune. Many great athletes, artists, and political leaders have succeeded in adjusting to a right-handed world.
(subordinate clause introduced by *although* is not a sentence)

Correct: Although being left-handed has been seen as a minor misfortune, many successful people have adjusted to a right-handed world.
(subordinate clause is connected to independent clause)

Incorrect: Science owes its system of plant classification and its double Latin names for flora and fauna to Linnaeus. The eighteenth-century Swedish botanist.
(final noun phrase is not a sentence)

Correct: Science owes its system of plant classification and its double Latin names for flora and fauna to Linnaeus, the eighteenth-century Swedish botanist.
(noun phrase is an appositive connected to preceding sentence)

Incorrect: The Delta Sigs were disappointed once more. Having finished second in the Greek sing for the fifth year in a row.
(participial phrase as fragment)

Correct: The Delta Sigs were disappointed once more, having finished second in the Greek sing for the fifth year in a row.
(phrase connected to preceding sentence)

Correct: The Delta Sigs were disappointed once more. This was the fifth year in a row that they had finished second in the Greek sing.
(phrase expanded to independent clause)

Incorrect: Collectively they vowed to combine their efforts toward one goal. To win first place next year.
(infinitive phrase as fragment)

36

Correct: Collectively they vowed to combine their efforts toward one goal: to win first place next year.
(infinitive phrase connected to previous sentence)

Incorrect: Practice sessions will begin immediately and will be held weekly for the whole year. After each business meeting.
(prepositional phrase as fragment)

Correct: Practice sessions will begin immediately and will be held after each weekly business meeting for the whole year.
(prepositional phrase inserted in previous sentence)

EXERCISE

A. Mark with S *any word group that is a grammatical sentence; mark with* X *those that are sentence fragments. Explain why those marked* X *are fragments.*

x 1. Memories ~~that~~ flood my mind as soon as I close my eyes.

x 2. ~~Because~~ we could not wait any longer.

x 3. Old-world elegance ^is^ combined with modern convenience.

x 4. ^Please^ ~~If you would only~~ tell me when you want help.

x 5. ~~Although~~ television can offer more excitement for young children than most teachers.

x 6. Although oil supplies kept increasing ^,^ ~~while~~ prices stayed high.

36

s 7. Although oil supplies kept increasing, prices stayed

high.

s 8. Oil supplies kept increasing while prices stayed

high.

x 9. His department's attempts to determine the extent

of damage.

s 10. His department attempts to determine the extent of

damage.

     I hope
x 11. ~~Hoping~~ to write more skillfully.

     I have been
x 12. Getting up thirty minutes earlier than normal so I

can eat in the cafeteria.

s 13. A new feeling of hope was present among the vic-

tims of the hijacking.

     This is
x 14. Absolutely the best course I have ever taken.

          deals
x 15. The first chapter ~~dealing~~ with freedom, the second

        both
with poverty, ~~and~~ described in an unforgettably

moving way.

*B. Rewrite as sentences the fragments that you identified
above.*

36

Separate two independent clauses with a period, semicolon, or comma and coordinating conjunction.

If you fail to separate independent clauses properly, you will create one of two structural problems: a *fused sentence* (or *run-on*) or a *comma splice.*

An independent clause is a group of words that can be punctuated as a complete sentence. Whenever a sentence contains two independent clauses, those clauses must be separated by a semicolon or by one of the coordinating conjunctions *(and, or, nor, for, but, yet,* or *so)* plus a comma. A comma alone is not adequate punctuation, even if it is followed by a conjunctive adverb such as *furthermore, however,* or *moreover.*

Fused sentence: The prosecution could not present reliable witnesses the case was dismissed.

Comma splice: The prosecution could not present reliable witnesses, the case was dismissed.

Once you learn to identify fused sentences and comma splices, you can easily avoid them. Some of the most common ways are shown here:

1. Make each clause a separate sentence:

   The prosecution could not present reliable witnesses. The case was dismissed.

2. Place a semicolon between the clauses:

   The prosecution could not present reliable witnesses; the case was dismissed.

3. Insert a conjunctive adverb between the clauses. The

37

adverb should be preceded by a semicolon and followed by a comma:

> The prosecution could not present reliable witnesses;
> **therefore,** the case was dismissed.

4. Place a comma and coordinating conjunction between the clauses:

> The prosecution could not present reliable witnesses, **so**
> the case was dismissed.

5. Convert one clause into a dependent clause by beginning it with a relative pronoun *(who, whom, whose, that, which, whoever, whomever, whichever, whatever)* or with a subordinating conjunction such as *because, after, since,* or *while:*

> **Because** the prosecution could not present reliable
> witnesses, the case was dismissed.

6. Recast the entire sentence into another pattern:

> The case was dismissed for lack of reliable witnesses.

All of these revisions are grammatically correct. Choosing the best correction is a matter of style. Each of the following fused sentences and comma splices can be corrected in ways other than the one shown:

37

Faulty:	My neighbors across the hall are too noisy, next week I am moving out. (comma splice)
Corrected:	My neighbors across the hall are too noisy; next week I am moving out. (semicolon)
Faulty:	The legislature sensed the mood of the people it passed a law limiting tax increases. (run-on)
Corrected:	The legislature sensed the mood of the people, so

it passed a law limiting tax increases. (comma plus coordinating conjunction)

Faulty: There is one major difference between men and boys, it is the cost of their toys. (comma splice)

Corrected: There is one major difference between men and boys; it is the cost of their toys. (semicolon)

Faulty: Ninety-three-year-old Mr. Kozelko has fallen out of bed three times while trying to climb over the rail, he will have to be restrained for his own protection. (comma splice)

Corrected: Ninety-three-year-old Mr. Kozelko has fallen out of bed three times trying to climb over the rail, so he will have to be restrained for his own protection. (comma plus coordinating conjunction)

Faulty: Many citizens believe that they should not become involved in others' problems this attitude contributes to the crime increase. (fused sentence)

Corrected: Many citizens believe that they should not become involved in others' problems, a belief that contributes to the crime increase. (sentence recast)

EXERCISE

In the following sentences, mark C for those that are correct and X for those containing run-ons and comma splices. Then correct those marked X.

37

x 1. Japanese gardens are quite different from informal

English gardens ; they are also different from formal
                 ∧

Italian and French gardens.

c 2. Stones and water are essential elements in a Japanese garden, and stones are often grouped to create

a specific effect.

x 3. Stones are not left where they occur in nature **;** they

are often shifted.

x 4. Small flat stones may form a path **;** large upright

ones may carry lines of poetry.

x 5. Ponds can induce a sense of restfulness, **and** streams

can gently stimulate the soul.

x 6. The prevailing color in a Japanese garden is green **;**

Western gardens are, by contrast, often filled with

pinks, yellows, and whites.

x 7. But the greens are used in a wide range of shades **;**

there is nothing monotonous about them.

c 8. Another feature of the Japanese garden is the tea-

house, a simple, elegant structure with uncluttered

lines.

x 9. Eating, drinking, and smoking are prohibited in

such gardens **;** therefore, the grounds remain im-

maculate.

x 10. The only sounds are those of birds and running

water, everything contributes to the sense of peace

and spiritual refreshment.

---

38 agr Make each verb and its subject agree in number.

Use the singular form of a verb with a singular subject and the plural form of a verb with a plural subject:

Singular	Plural
She watches.	They watch.
The watch runs fast.	The watches run fast.
The team is playing.	The teams are playing.
The plan has changed.	The plans have changed.
He was especially kind.	They were especially kind.

Notice that the -s or -es ending makes nouns plural but makes present-tense verbs singular.

Making subjects and verbs agree is usually easy in short sentences, but it can be more difficult in longer, more complicated sentences. Be careful to identify the subjects so that your verbs agree with the correct words:

Incorrect: Felix's attention to time, efficiency, and savings deserve favorable consideration.

Correct: Felix's attention [subject] to time, efficiency, and savings *deserves* favorable consideration.

Incorrect: My supervisor's first priority in cutting departmental expenses are reducing overtime and sick pay.

Correct: My supervisor's first priority [subject] in cutting departmental expenses *is* reducing overtime and sick pay.

In a sentence beginning with *there,* the subject follows the verb:

Correct: There *is* an extra *pair* [subject] of shoes in the hall closet.

Correct: There *are* no good *concerts* [subject] at the Sports Stadium anymore.

Forms of the verb *to be* agree with the subject of the sentence, not the complement, even when the subject is plural and the complement is singular, or vice versa:

Correct: Unsafe working conditions [subject] *were* the primary cause [complement] of the wildcat strike.

Correct: Earning extra money is her only reason for babysitting.

38a   *With compound subjects joined by* and, *use a plural verb.*

Incorrect: The movement of the girl's dress and the tossing of her hair captivates the boy.

Correct: The movement of the girl's dress and the tossing of her hair *captivate* the boy.

But when *each* or *every* precedes the compound subject, use a singular verb:

Incorrect: Every boy and girl are required to have parental permission.

Correct: Every boy and girl *is* required to have parental permission.

38

Note: The phrase "as well as" is used as a preposition, not as a conjunction. It does not create compound subjects.

> The Indian diplomat as well as the Pakistani *was* upset by the U.N. vote.

38b With compound subjects joined by *or* *or* nor, make the verb agree with the subject nearer to the verb.

Use a singular verb when two singular subjects are joined by *or* or *nor:*

Incorrect: Either *Hamlet* or *Othello,* rather than the usual *Macbeth,* are going to be performed this year.

Correct: Either *Hamlet* or *Othello,* rather than the usual *Macbeth,* is going to be performed this year.

Use a plural verb when two plural subjects are joined by *or* or *nor:*

Incorrect: Neither Stephen King's novels nor Danielle Steel's seems to lose popularity.

Correct: Neither Stephen King's novels nor Danielle Steel's *seem* to lose popularity.

When *or* or *nor* joins a singular subject and a plural subject, the verb usually agrees with the subject nearer to the verb:

Incorrect: Maria could not decide whether her math class or her two science classes was harder.

Correct: Maria could not decide whether her math class or her two science classes *were* harder.

Also correct: Maria could not decide whether her two science classes or her math class *was* harder.

38

Incorrect:	Neither the clerks nor the assistant manager were watching the register.
Correct:	Neither the clerks nor the assistant manager *was* watching the register.
Also correct:	Neither the assistant manager nor the clerks *were* watching the register.

38c Each, either, neither, one, everybody, somebody, nobody, *and* anyone *require singular verbs.*

Incorrect:	Each of the team's twelve members were given a small replica of the championship trophy.
Correct:	Each of the team's twelve members *was* given a small replica of the championship trophy.
Incorrect:	Nobody from inside the company are ever given serious consideration for the top positions.
Correct:	Nobody from inside the company *is* ever given serious consideration for the top positions.

38d *Quantitative words such as* some, half, all, part, most, *and* more *are singular or plural depending on the nouns they refer to.*

Correct:	All of the members *were* notified, and most *have* arrived.
Correct:	Most of the committee's time *was* wasted in senseless wrangling.
Correct:	One third of all meals eaten in this country *are* purchased in restaurants and fast-food stops.
Correct:	Two thirds of his diet *is* starch.

None usually obeys the same rule, though some writers con-

38

sider the word's origin ("not one") and treat it consistently as singular: I left messages for all of the members, but none *has* returned my call.

38e A collective noun that refers to a group as a unit takes a singular verb.

Nouns such as *class, committee, team, family, crew, jury, faculty, majority,* and *company* take singular verbs when they refer to a group acting as a unit:

Correct: The company *has* tried to diversify its investments.

Correct: If a majority *votes* in favor of adjournment, no further motions are allowed.

Occasionally you may need a plural verb to show that members of a group are acting as individuals:

Incorrect: If a majority votes according to their consciences, these amendments will be defeated.

Correct: If a majority *vote* according to their consciences, these amendments will be defeated.

In the incorrect sentence, the writer has been forced to shift from a singular verb *(votes)* to a plural pronoun *(their)*. Once you have decided whether a collective noun is singular or plural, treat it consistently as one or the other. Another example:

Correct: The jury votes by secret ballot, with twelve votes required for indictment. (*jury* treated as a whole)

Correct: The jury have taken their seats. (*jury* treated as individuals)

Incorrect: The jury has taken their seats.

Many writers of American English avoid using collective nouns in the plural. They say "members of the jury" when they treat the jury as individuals acting separately, or they use the singular: The jury *is* seated.

38f Some singular subjects may look like plurals.

Certain nouns look like plurals but function as singulars and require singular verbs. *News, economics, politics, physics,* and *mathematics* are common examples of words that cannot be made singular because they already are.

Correct: Politics, unfortunately, often *enters* into decisions of campus committees. (not plural verb *enter*)

EXERCISE

A. Study the sentences below for verb-subject agreement. Mark those that are correct with C and those that have faulty agreement with X.

x   1. Even with modern medicine, measles are still a seri-
       ous problem in many countries.

x   2. Neither weight lifting nor isometrics are as good for
       building up injured muscles as is the Nautilus.

x   3. Everybody who attended the grand opening were
       given free souvenirs.

c   4. Neither the food nor the souvenirs were any good.

x   5. The newspaper staff $\overset{is}{\underset{\wedge}{are}}$ composed almost entirely of

journalism students.

x   6. Every city and town in the county $\overset{is}{\underset{\wedge}{are}}$ required to

comply with the new state law.

x   7. In its recent report, the faculty committee $\overset{was}{\underset{\wedge}{were}}$ crit-

ical of the administration.

c   8. Half of the members of the committee were unwill-

ing to endorse the report.

x   9. Either Mark or Roberto $\overset{is}{\underset{\wedge}{are}}$ going to be cast as the

lead in the next play.

c   10. A wide variety of petroleum products is derived from

shale oil.

B. *Correct the sentences above that you marked with* X.

39

39 agr

Use singular pronouns to refer to singular nouns, plural pronouns to refer to plural nouns.

Make each pronoun agree in number—singular or plural—with the noun or pronoun to which it refers. (This noun or pronoun is called the **antecedent.**)

The flight instructor [singular antecedent] finished his [singular pronoun] lecture, but the pilots [plural antecedent] remained in their [plural pronoun] seats.

It is usually easy to recognize an antecedent as singular or plural and to decide whether the pronoun should be singular or plural, but some sentences are complicated. The antecedent may be compound, or it may be a collective noun or an indefinite pronoun.

39a   *Collective nouns such as* team, committee, chorus, *and* class *can be either singular or plural depending on how they are used.*

Avoid treating a collective noun as both singular and plural:

Incorrect: The interview committee *is* going to finish *their* deliberations tomorrow.

Correct: The interview committee *is* going to finish *its* deliberations tomorrow.

Incorrect: Our soccer team *has* not won yet, but Saturday *they* will be doing *their* best.

Correct: Our soccer team *has* not won yet, but Saturday *it* will be doing *its* best.

See **38e** for a fuller discussion of collective nouns.

39b   *Indefinite antecedents such as* a person, each, neither, either, someone, anyone, no one, one, *and* everybody *almost always take singular pronouns.*

Incorrect: There are too many animals for officials to give each one the attention they deserve.

Correct: There are too many animals for officials to give each one the attention *it* deserves.

Incorrect: When a person is confused, they should ask questions.

Correct: When people are confused, *they* should ask questions.

See **72a** on sexist language. See **38c** and **38d** for more on indefinite pronouns.

39c Compound antecedents with and take plural pronouns.

Correct: Beth and Eileen won *their* awards in tennis and swimming.

39d If a compound antecedent is joined by or or nor, the pronoun usually agrees with the antecedent nearer to the pronoun.

If the antecedents are singular, use a singular pronoun:

Incorrect: Neither the television station nor its radio affiliate ever had their license revoked.

Correct: Neither the television station nor its radio affiliate ever had *its* license revoked.

39

If both antecedents are plural, use a plural pronoun:

Correct: It was impossible to blame either the reporters or the editors. *They* did all *they* could to verify the story.

If one antecedent is singular and one plural, make the pronoun agree with the antecedent nearer to the pronoun:

Correct: Either the teacher or the students are responsible for turning off *their* classroom lights and air conditioner.

Do not waste time puzzling over intricate agreement problems with subjects or antecedents joined by *or* or *nor*. If following the rules in this section and in **38b** results in an absurd or awkward sentence, simply rewrite. You may be able to join the subjects or antecedents with *and:*

Awkward: Neither Amanda nor Bob will be in [his? her? their?] office this afternoon.

Rewritten: Both Amanda and Bob will be out of their offices this afternoon.

EXERCISE

A. Mark with X those sentences with pronoun errors. If the sentence is correct, mark C.

x 1. In the past decade either Colonial High School or
       Washington High School has won an award for ~~their~~ [its]
       service clubs.

x 2. Their areas border one another, but each has a
       style of ~~their~~ [its] own.

x 3. Almost every student is proud of ~~their~~ [his or her] alma mater.

x 4. Football fans cannot agree whether Colonial's team
       or Washington's ~~are~~ [is] on top.

x 5. Naturally, each of the coaches favors ~~their~~ [his] own
       team.

                                        it plays
x 6. Industry has become aware of the part ~~they play~~ in
      causing pollution.

x 7. Every great pitcher spends endless hours perfecting
      his
      ~~their~~ delivery.
                                    its
x 8. The Phil Jones Combo will have ~~their~~ first concert
      here next Saturday night.

x 9. Either the management or the workers will have to
          their
      change ~~its~~ position.

x 10. Either the coach or one of the assistants is always
                                    his
      in the weight room working on ~~their~~ own condi-
      tioning.

B. Correct the sentences above that you marked with X.

Make each pronoun point clearly to one antecedent.

40 ref

40

Since a pronoun refers to a noun (its *antecedent*), a pronoun's meaning is clear only when it points clearly to that
noun. Two or more plausible antecedents will confuse your
reader:

Ambiguous: Alex told Waldo that he should be earning more
               money.

Clear:	Alex told Waldo, "You should be earning more money." *Or:* Alex told Waldo, "I should be earning more money." *Or:* Alex complained to Waldo about being underpaid.
Ambiguous:	As soon as Mrs. Kennedy christened the ship, she was set afloat in the Thames.
Clear:	As soon as Mrs. Kennedy christened her, the ship was set afloat in the Thames.

In the second pair of examples, sensible readers will know that the ship, not Mrs. Kennedy, was set afloat; but since they will notice the comical ambiguity, the sentence is still ineffective.

40a Make each pronoun refer to a noun or to an earlier pronoun.

To keep references clear, make each pronoun refer to a noun used as a subject, object, or complement, not as a modifier or possessive:

Ineffective:	Morris questioned the newspaper's honesty even though it had helped him.
Effective:	Even though the newspaper had helped him, Morris questioned its honesty.

Ineffective:	At Sybil's office, she is the manager.
Effective:	Sybil is the manager of her office.

Also be sure that a pronoun can logically refer to its antecedent:

Ineffective:	I had tonsilitis when I was eight, so my doctor removed them.
Effective:	I had tonsilitis when I was eight, so my doctor removed my tonsils.

40

Or: When I was eight, my doctor removed my tonsils because they were continually inflamed.

40b Make each pronoun refer to one word or to a specific group of words rather than to an implied idea.

Except in informal writing, use *you* when referring directly to your reader, not when referring to any person in general. Substitute *one* or an appropriate noun:

Ineffective: Many people believe that college should help you earn a better living.

Effective: Many people believe that college should help a person earn a better living.
Or: Many people believe that college should help one earn a better living.

Except in expressions such as "It is cold," use *it* and *they* only to refer to specific nouns:

Ineffective: On page 381 of our text, it says that Henry Clay was "the great compromiser."

Effective: On page 381 of our text, the author says that Henry Clay was "the great compromiser."
Or: On page 381, our text says that Henry Clay was "the great compromiser."

Ineffective: They do not have many Catholics in Iran.

Effective: Iran does not have many Catholics.
Or: There are few Catholics in Iran.

40c Insert nouns to clarify the reference of *this, that,* and *which*.

This, that, and *which* are often vague when they refer broadly to an idea expressed or implied in a preceding clause. To avoid confusion, change the pronoun to a noun or add a noun.

Vague: The young residents did the actual cutting even though the surgeon received credit and payment for the operation. This is common in many hospitals.

Clear: The young residents did the actual cutting even though the surgeon received credit and payment for the operation. This practice is common in many hospitals.

Vague: The professor lectured while his teaching assistants worked with individual students, which is quite common.

Clear: The professor lectured while his teaching assistants worked with individual students, a common arrangement.

EXERCISE

Underline all pronouns used inappropriately in the following sentences.

1. They drink more wine in Europe than we do in America.

2. After Max's apartment was robbed for the sixth time, he moved.

3. Cicero once told a friend that he could have written him a shorter letter if he had had more time.

4. The population is aging, which is why health care costs have been increasing.

5. It says in the newspaper that you can expect a tax increase next year.

6. Politicians use fancy words because it impresses voters.

7. I watched Cassandra sneak out early, but no one else noticed this.

40

8. The nurse was unsympathetic; <u>this</u> is indicative of much apathy in our society.

9. After Sam finally removed the leg from the desk, he was ready to paint <u>it</u>.

10. Dr. Gonzales gave her the news that <u>she</u> would soon be moving her office.

<table>
<tr><td></td><td>Determine the correct case of a pronoun by the word's function in the sentence.</td></tr>
<tr><td>41 ca</td><td></td></tr>
</table>

The personal pronouns *(I, we, you, he, she, it, they)* appear in different case forms depending on their function in the sentence: *I* liked *her*, but *she* hated *me*.

	Nominative	*Objective*	*Possessive**
First Person	I, we	me, us	my, mine our, ours
Second Person	you	you	your, yours
Third Person	he, she it, they	him, her, it, them	his, her, hers, its, their, theirs

*Note that no apostrophe is used for the possessives.

41

The **nominative** (also called **subjective**) case forms are used for the subject and predicate nominative functions:

> *We* were turned away. (subject)
> This is *she*. (predicate nominative)

The **objective** case forms are used for direct objects, indirect objects, and objects of prepositions:

The sound system gave *us* trouble all night. (indirect object)

The Cougars beat *us* badly in both games. (direct object)

Next year we will be ready for *them*. (object of preposition)

The **possessive** case forms are used to show possession:

Their system was no better than *ours*. (possessives)

Be especially careful of the pronoun case in compound structures. Note the following:

Incorrect: Him and his older brothers learned to play "Duelling Banjos."

Correct: He and his older brothers learned to play "Duelling Banjos." (compound subject)

Incorrect: She may try to get you and I in trouble.

Correct: She may try to get you and me in trouble. (object of *get*)

Incorrect: The nurse was unsympathetic to my mother and I.

Correct: The nurse was unsympathetic to my mother and me. (object of *to*)

A pronoun used as an appositive (an explanatory word, phrase, or clause that clarifies a noun) should be in the same case as the noun or pronoun it refers to:

Correct: The culprits, Harvey and I, were caught at midnight.

Correct: The police quickly apprehended the culprits, Harvey and me.

Incorrect: Three contestants won prizes at the finale: Karen Turner, Kris Bercov, and me.

Correct: Three contestants won prizes at the finale: Karen Turner, Kris Bercov, and I.

Use the possessive form immediately before a gerund:

41

Incorrect:	My parents are concerned about me working while carrying fifteen credit hours.
Correct:	My parents are concerned about *my working* while carrying fifteen credit hours.

But you can generally use a nonpossessive common noun before a gerund, especially if the noun is plural:

Correct:	The officials attributed the rise in unemployment to *women entering* the job market.

Use the nominative case for the subject of an implied verb form:

Incorrect:	No one on their team is as tall as me.
Correct:	No one on their team is as tall as *I*. (understood "am tall")

Use the nominative form as the subject of a clause regardless of the function of the clause:

Incorrect:	Most Americans still show great respect for whomever is President.
Correct:	Most Americans still show great respect for whoever is President. (*Whoever* is the subject of *is* in the final clause.)

In formal writing, such as theses and research papers, always use *whom* as you would *me* or any other objective form. Many people have stopped using *whom*, especially in speech and informal writing; but in most college writing it is best to use *whom* whenever it is called for.

Incorrect:	Whom did you say was calling?
Correct:	Who did you say was calling? (*Who* is the subject of *was*.)

Correct: Whom did you call? (*Whom* is the object of *call.*)

Correct: To whom was that call made? (*Whom* is the object of the preposition *to.*)

A quick way to determine the case is to rephrase such questions as statements: "You did call whom."

As a relative pronoun, *whom* is often dropped from the sentence:

Correct: Alderman Fischer is the only one [whom] we should reelect. (*Whom* is the direct object of *reelect.*)

EXERCISE

A. Study the following sentences. Mark X for those with improper pronoun case and C for those sentences that are correct.

x   1. Macintosh thought he would get the manager's job
                                                                  he
      because nobody else had sold as much as ~~him~~.

c   2. Few of the other salespeople were as conscientious

      or as popular as he.
                                              his
x   3. My friend's parents are upset over ~~him~~ seeing me so

      much.

c   4. The credit manager is the one to whom Stan com-

      plained.
                                                      me
x   5. The odds makers are listing you and ~~I~~ as the team

      to beat.

41

c   6. Last year's champions, Bill and I, were not allowed

to play together this year.

x   7. Jackson does not remember ^{**my**} ~~me~~ paying the rent.

c   8. Who did Mr. Gold think the manager was?

c   9. Few could believe that the only victims were Josie

and she.

x 10. ^{**Who**} ~~Whom~~ did you say was playing at the rap concert

next week?

B. Correct the sentences above that you marked with X.

Use adjectives to modify nouns; and use adverbs to modify verbs, adjectives, or other adverbs.

42 adj/adv

Both adjectives and adverbs are modifiers; they limit or describe other words.

Adjectives: The *radical* changes of personnel were *unpleasant* but *necessary.*

Adverbs: The *highly* complex steering mechanism turned the glider *smoothly.*

Adverbs are usually distinguished by their *-ly* endings *(rapidly, formally),* but many adjectives, such as *ghastly* and *heavenly,* also end in *-ly,* and many adverbs, such as *often* and *well*, do not. If you are in doubt whether a word is an adjective or adverb, check your dictionary.

In very informal writing and speaking, certain adjectives—such as *sure, real,* and *good*—are often used in place of the adverbs *surely, really,* and *well;* but in more formal writing, the safer practice is to use the adverb forms to modify verbs, adjectives, and other adverbs and to use adjectives to modify only nouns or pronouns:

Very informal: I did so *bad* on my first calculus test that I never regained my confidence.

More formal: I did so *badly* on my first calculus test that I never regained my confidence.

Use adjectives for subjective complements after verbs such as *feel, look, smell, sound,* and *taste,* which function like forms of the verb *to be;* use adverbs to modify these verbs. A quick test to make sure that the complement is correct is to substitute *is, was,* or other appropriate forms of the verb *to be.*

Predicate adjective: He was obviously upset, but he did not look *angry.* (Substitute *was* for *did look.*)

Adverb modifying verb: He looked *angrily* at us, then stalked off.

Predicate adjective: I felt *nervous* as I approached the dark building. (Substitute *was* for *felt.*)

Adverb modifying verb: I felt *nervously* in my pocket for a match.

42a Use the correct comparative and superlative forms for adverbs and adjectives.

Most short adjectives add *-er* for the comparative and *-est* for the superlative. Longer adjectives and most adverbs use *more* and *most*. A few have irregular comparative and superlative forms. Check your dictionary when you are in doubt.

Positive	Comparative	Superlative
strong	stronger	strongest
happy	happier	happiest
surprising	more surprising	most surprising
happily	more happily	most happily
good	better	best
well	better	best
bad	worse	worst

Use the comparative form when comparing two items, the superlative for three or more:

Incorrect: Bill and Kathy were both excellent players, but Bill had the most even temperament.

Correct: Bill and Kathy were both excellent players, but Bill had the more even temperament.

Incorrect: Diamonds are the better sellers among the three stones most often picked for engagement rings.

Correct: Diamonds are the best sellers among the three stones most often picked for engagement rings.

EXERCISE

A. Mark the following sentences with C *if they are correct; mark with* X *those containing incorrectly used adjective or adverb forms.*

x 1. Snow skiing and waterskiing are both great sports,

                more

   but waterskiing is the ~~most~~ popular of the two.

c 2. It is cheaper, and water is more accessible than

   snow.

x 3. Most people can learn to water-ski pretty ~~good~~ in an

   hour or two.

            really badly

x 4. But I did ~~real bad~~ my first time out.

c 5. Fortunately, my coordination improved, and now I

   do well.

c 6. No one could be more happy than I was when I first

   got up on one ski.

                    weakest

x 7. I didn't mind that I was the ~~weaker~~ of the three ski-

   ers on the lake that day.

c 8. Even with practice, I still perform nervously when I

   use only one ski.

                  nervous

x 9. My friends say I even look ~~nervously~~ just waiting to

   begin.

                  good

x 10. Maybe someday I'll actually look ~~well~~ on skis.

   B. *Correct those sentences above marked* X.

42

The word "**well**" is handwritten above "good" in sentence 3.

43 t

Use the verb tense appropriate to the time of an action or situation.

Although English relies heavily on adverbs and adverbial phrases and clauses to refer to time *(now, tomorrow, yesterday morning, after the play had already started)*, it also indicates time by changes in the verb. By using verb tenses accurately, you can help your reader keep track of time relationships in your writing.

English verbs have only two primary tenses, present and past; but by using auxiliary verbs we can create complex verb forms. Thus we can list three simple tenses, three perfect tenses, and progressive forms for all six.

Simple tenses. The **simple present tense** is far from simple in the ways it is used:

> *Present time:* I *hear* you calling. He *looks* anxious.
>
> *Habitual time:* I *hear* the train go by every morning. He *repairs* his old Volkswagen himself.
>
> *Historical present:* Brutus *hears* the mob hailing Caesar.
>
> *Literary present:* In "The Man That Corrupted Hadleyburg," Twain *exposes* the power of money to corrupt us.
>
> *Future action:* The case *goes* to court next week. When the defense attorney *finishes* her remarks, the jury will retire.

43

In the present tense, verbs of third-person singular subjects require an *-s* ending.

The **past tense** is formed by adding *-ed* to regular verbs or by changing the spelling of most irregular verbs. The **future tense** uses the auxiliary *shall* or *will.* Traditionally, *shall* has been reserved for use with first-person subjects *(I shall go),* *will* with second- and third-person subjects *(you will go; she will go),* except when the writer reverses the usage to show strong emphasis: I *will* win; you *shall* obey me. Today, only the most formal writing observes that distinction, and *will* is regularly used with all persons.

The following list shows the forms for a regular verb *(play)* and for the most irregular and often used English verb, *be*:

	Regular verb	To be
Present:	I play	I am
	you play	you are
	he, she, it plays	he, she, it is
	we, you, they play	we, you, they are
Past:	I played	I was
	you played	you were
	he, she, it played	he, she, it was
	we, you, they played	we, you, they were
Future:	I will (shall) play	I will (shall) be
	you will play	you will be
	he, she, it will play	he, she, it will be
	we, you, they will play	we, you, they will be

Perfect tenses. The perfect tenses indicate a relationship between two times. The **present perfect** refers to an indefinite time in the recent past or to a time beginning in the past and continuing to the present:

> Congressman Green *has voted* with the conservatives more often than with the liberals.

> This ten-dollar watch *has kept* perfect time for two years.

The **past perfect** indicates a time before some other specified or implied time in the past:

> The teams *had met* twice before the playoffs.

Similarly, the **future perfect** may be used to indicate a time before some other stated or implied time in the future:

> Before they return, the astronauts *will have broken* the record for time spent in space.

43

Note that *return* in the previous example is a typical case of the present used for future time. This use of the present is very common in dependent clauses.

The perfect tenses combine a form of the auxiliary *have* with the past participle of the main verb:

Present perfect:	I have played	I have been
	you have played	you have been
	he, she, it has played	he, she, it has been
	we, you, they	we, you, they
	have played	have been
Past perfect:	I had played	I had been
	you had played	you had been
	he, she, it had played	he, she, it had been
	we, you, they	we, you, they
	had played	had been
Future perfect:	I will (shall) have	I will (shall) have been
	played	
	you will have played	you will have been
	he, she, it will have	he, she, it will have been
	played	
	we, you, they	we, you, they
	will have played	will have been

Progressive tenses. Progressive forms of verbs indicate continuous actions:

The candidates *are waiting* for the results of the election.

I *was running* toward the stop when the bus pulled away.

I *shall be working* on my tax return all day tomorrow.

Mr. Velkoff told me last week that I *had been using* the wrong forms for at least six months.

There are progressive forms for all six tenses:

Present progressive:	I am playing
	he, she, it is playing
	we, you, they are playing

43

Past progressive:	I was playing
	he, she, it was playing
	we, you, they were playing
Future progressive:	I, he, she, it will (shall) be
	playing
	we, you, they will (shall)
	be playing
Present perfect progressive:	I have been playing
	he, she, it has been playing
	we, you, they have been playing
Past perfect progressive:	I, he, she, it had been playing
	we, you, they had been playing
Future perfect progressive:	I, he, she, it will (shall) have
	been playing
	we, you, they will (shall) have
	been playing

Tenses of verbals. Verbals (infinitives, gerunds, and participles) have present and present-perfect forms. The participle also has a past form:

Present infinitive:	to sink, to be sinking
Perfect infinitive:	to have sunk
Present gerund:	sinking
Perfect gerund:	having sunk
Present participle:	sinking
Perfect participle:	having sunk, having been sinking
Past participle:	sunk

Use the past or perfect form of a verbal to indicate a time before the main verb in the clause:

43

Emily would like [now] *to have played* in last night's concert.

He could not get over *having failed* his teammates.

Having signed all the letters, she went home early.

But: The woman *addressing* the assembly will retire next

month. (The present participle here indicates the same time as the speaking or writing of the sentence.)

Use the past participle to indicate a time before that of the main verb or to describe a condition that began before the time of the main verb:

> *Angered* by the story, the apartment owner sued both the newspaper and the reporter.

In most other cases, use the present forms of verbals:

> Emily decided to *play* Chopin. (The playing follows the deciding.)
>
> Emily enjoys *playing* Chopin. (The playing and the enjoying take place at the same time.)
>
> *Writing* about *Dick Tracy,* Pauline Kael remarked. . . . (The writing and the remarking take place together.)

Voice. English verbs also show active voice (the butler *committed* the crime) or passive voice (the crime *was committed* by the butler). The forms presented in this section have all been in the active voice. Verbs in the passive voice combine a form of *be* with the past participle of the main verb:

	Active	Passive
Present:	I know	I am known
Past:	I knew	I was known
Future:	I will know	I will be known
Present perfect:	I have known	I have been known
Past perfect:	I had known	I had been known
Future perfect:	I will have known	I will have been known

Progressive verbs are sometimes used in the passive voice: *I am being watched.* Careful writers generally avoid the passive voice because it is wordy, indirect, and less natural than the active. For a thorough discussion of voice and style, see **28e.**

A. Mark these sentences with C if they are correct and with X if they contain errors in verb tense.

x 1. In 1993 my sister Sara will h̶a̶v̶e̶ ̶b̶e̶e̶n̶ **be** twelve years old.

x 2. When she was two, she was b̶e̶i̶n̶g̶ diagnosed as having juvenile diabetes.

x 3. She spent a lot of time in the hospital when she h̶a̶d̶ ̶b̶e̶e̶n̶ **was** in the first three grades.

x 4. When she failed her last grade, it seemed that she w̶o̶n̶'̶t̶ **wouldn't** graduate with her class.

x 5. Even by h̶a̶v̶i̶n̶g̶ ̶g̶o̶n̶e̶ **going** to summer school, she c̶a̶n̶'̶t̶ **couldn't** make up that year.

x 6. Now she has put her emphasis on learning and decided not to b̶e̶ ̶w̶o̶r̶r̶i̶e̶d̶ **worry** too much about promotion.

c 7. Two years ago, she wanted to finish at the same time as her best friend, Marianne, but she was forced to reconsider.

43

x   8. The principal ~~had~~ told us that he will work with our

family.

x   9. The major problem at the moment ~~will be~~ **is** getting

the right tutor.

x 10. We are happy that Sara is with us and, for right

now, ~~was~~ **is** not in any pain.

B. *Correct sentences marked* X.

<hr>

44 vb	**Use the correct principal parts of irregular verbs.**

You must know the principal parts of verbs in order to form all the tenses correctly. English verbs have three principal parts: the infinitive (or present stem), the past tense, and the past participle. For regular verbs, the past tense and past participle are formed by adding -*d* or -*ed* to the infinitive: *walk, walked, walked; close, closed, closed.* Other verbs—the irregular verbs—form the past tense and past participle by various means, usually by changing a vowel in the infinitive *(win, won).* The list below includes the principal parts of the most common irregular verbs and a few regular verbs often mistakenly treated as irregular. Your college dictionary also gives the principal parts of irregular verbs. If it does not list the past tense and past participle forms, you can assume that the verb is regular.

INFINITIVE	PAST TENSE	PAST PARTICIPLE
awake	awaked (awoke)	awaked (awoke)
beat	beat	beaten
become	became	become
begin	began	begun
bend	bent	bent
bite	bit	bitten
bleed	bled	bled
blow	blew	blown
break	broke	broken
bring	brought	brought
build	built	built
burst	burst	burst
buy	bought	bought
catch	caught	caught
choose	chose	chosen
come	came	come
cut	cut	cut
deal	dealt	dealt
dig	dug	dug
dive	dived (dove)	dived
do	did	done
drag	dragged	dragged
draw	drew	drawn
drink	drank	drunk
drive	drove	driven
drown	drowned	drowned
eat	ate	eaten
fall	fell	fallen
fight	fought	fought
fly	flew	flown
forget	forgot	forgotten (forgot)
freeze	froze	frozen
get	got	got (gotten)
give	gave	given
go	went	gone
grow	grew	grown
have	had	had
hide	hid	hidden
hold	held	held

44

INFINITIVE	PAST TENSE	PAST PARTICIPLE
keep	kept	kept
know	knew	known
lead	led	led
leave	left	left
lend	lent	lent
let	let	let
lose	lost	lost
mean	meant	meant
prove	proved	proved (proven)
read	read	read
ride	rode	ridden
ring	rang	rung
rise	rose	risen
run	ran	run
say	said	said
see	saw	seen
sell	sold	sold
send	sent	sent
sew	sewed	sewed (sewn)
shake	shook	shaken
shave	shaved	shaved (shaven)
shrink	shrank (shrunk)	shrunk (shrunken)
show	showed	showed (shown)
sink	sank (sunk)	sunk
speak	spoke	spoken
swear	swore	sworn
swim	swam	swum
take	took	taken
teach	taught	taught
tell	told	told
think	thought	thought
throw	threw	thrown
wear	wore	worn
win	won	won
write	wrote	written

A few verbs that have two distinct meanings have different principal parts in each meaning:

44

bid (a price)	bid	bid
bid (an order)	bade (bid)	bidden (bid)
hang (execute)	hanged	hanged
hang (suspend)	hung	hung
shine (emit light)	shone	shone
shine (polish)	shined	shined

Three pairs of verbs are easily confused, especially in their past-tense and past-participle forms. The key distinction is that one of each pair is transitive (it takes an object) but the other is intransitive (no object).

Transitive

lay (place)	laid	laid
set (place)	set	set
raise (lift)	raised	raised

Intransitive

lie (recline)	lay	lain
lie (falsehood)	lied	lied
sit (be seated)	sat	sat
rise (rise up)	rose	risen

He *laid* his head on a rock and *lay* in the sun for an hour.

She *set* her pen on the desk and *sat* waiting for others to finish.

He *rose* from the bed and *raised* the window.

EXERCISE

44

Underline the correct verb forms in the following sentences.

1. Snorkels enable a swimmer to (*lie*, *lay*) just below the surface of the water.

2. Many scuba divers have (*forgot*, *forgotten*) how many times they have (*dived*, *dove*).

3. Some divers have *(swam, swum)* long enough to have *(grown, grew)* careless.

4. We *(rose, rised)* at dawn to *(rise, raise)* our dive flag and start down.

5. The boat has *(broke, broken)* away from her moorings where she *(lay, laid)* at rest.

6. Our friends *(lent, lended)* us the money which otherwise would have *(laid, lain)* idle in the bank.

7. For our last three dives we have *(run, ran)* to the Florida Keys as soon as the last school bell has *(rung, rang)* in early June.

8. I was injured once when I cut my arm on a piece of coral, and the cut *(bleeded, bled)* profusely.

9. My telephone *(rung, rang)* eight times before the caller *(hanged, hung)* up.

10. It was Joe wanting to *(set, sit)* up another dive trip, but he had *(drank, drunk)* too much and couldn't speak plainly.

45 mo Use the mood required by your sentence.

English has three moods: **indicative** for statements of fact and questions about facts, **imperative** for commands, and **subjunctive** for wishes and demands or statements that are contrary to fact.

Indicative: I *know* who he *is.*

Imperative: Be yourself.

Subjunctive: If I *were* you, I would avoid that subject.

The subjunctive is used far less now than earlier in the history of the language, but there are some situations in which the subjunctive is still the usual choice:

Correct: He demanded that Maria *finish* the work. (Desired action. Less formally, this might be expressed, "He told Maria to finish the work.")

Correct: It is essential that I *be seen* at the party.

Correct: Mario drank as if Prohibition *were* being reintroduced. (contrary to fact)

Correct: Eve wishes that she *were* more talented. (contrary to fact)

Only a few forms of the subjunctive are different from the indicative forms given in **43.** Those forms are shown here in bold type:

Present:	that I walk that he, she, it **walk** (no -s) that we, you, they walk	that I **be** that he, she, it **be** that we, you, they **be**
Past:	that I walked that he, she, it walked that we, you, they walked	that I **were** that he, she, it **were** that we, you, they were
Present perfect:	that I have walked that he, she, it **have** walked that we, you, they have walked	that I have been that he, she, it **have** been that we, you, they have been

Study the sentences below. Mark with C those that are correct and with X those that have errors in mood. Correct the sentences marked X.

x 1. A cat lover looks at a cat as though it ~~was~~ **were** a harm-

less, domestic creature.

c 2. He or she may insist that a cat be respected for its

independence and self-sufficiency.

x 3. If a cat ~~go~~ **goes** by carrying a bird or a mouse, the cat

lover looks the other way.

x 4. If every feline victim ~~was~~ **were** entered on a list—an impos-

sible task—and the entries counted up, we might be

surprised at the total.

c 5. Two British biologists insisted that this situation be

studied.

46

46 shift

Be consistent in using verbs and pronouns.

To present your information smoothly and clearly, be consis-tent in the tense, voice, and mood of verbs and in the person and number of nouns and pronouns. Unnecessary shifts—

from past to present or from singular to plural, for instance—make awkward reading and can confuse meaning. Some shifts are necessary—to indicate passing time, for example—but it is best to make such shifts only when you feel they are necessary.

46a Avoid unnecessary shifts in tense, voice, and mood.

A change in **tense** usually signals a change in time, so be sure not to give your reader a false signal by switching tenses unnecessarily. A shift such as the following is often just the result of carelessness:

Shift in tense: As he *turned* the corner, he *became* aware that someone *is* following him.

Corrected: As he *turned* the corner, he *became* aware that someone *was* following him.

Be careful not to shift time when you are using one of the perfect tenses:

Shift in tense: We had paid our dues and are ready to begin attending meetings. (past perfect with present)

Corrected: We have paid our dues and are ready to begin attending meetings. (present perfect with present)
Or: We had paid our dues and were ready to begin attending meetings. (past perfect with past)

See **43** for a discussion of verb tenses. Active and passive **voice** can be mixed in one sentence (she *ran* twice and *was defeated* twice), but an unnecessary shift in voice can spoil the focus of a sentence:

Shift in voice: Electrolysis is used by Dr. DeKleva, and he also performs minor surgery.

46

Improved:	Dr. DeKleva uses electrolysis and performs minor surgery.
Shift in voice:	The report showed that white-collar criminals almost never serve hard time, while long sentences are served by petty burglars.
Improved:	The report showed that white-collar criminals almost never serve hard time, while petty burglars serve long sentences.

Active voice is usually more direct and natural than passive voice (see **28e**).

A change in mood should reflect a change in the way the writer views the action or situation being described: "If I *were* willing to lie, I *would tell* you I enjoyed the story; but I *am* not willing to lie." Unmotivated shifts are distracting:

Shift in mood:	If I were the President, I would take action, not act as if I was still in Congress.
Corrected:	If I were the President, I would take action, not act as if I were still in Congress.

See **45**.

46b   Be consistent in the number and person of your nouns and pronouns.

Shift number (singular or plural) only to show a valid change: I wanted to go to Europe, but *we* could not afford the trip.

Faulty:	The class of 1990 was academically outstanding, but they were unusual.
Improved:	The class of 1990 was academically outstanding, but it was unusual.
Faulty:	The staff was given a brief explanation of the new medical policy as part of our orientation program.

46

Improved: The staff was given a brief explanation of the new medical policy as part of its orientation program.

Similarly, keep the person of your pronouns consistent. Be especially careful to avoid slipping into the universal *you* (second person) when you are writing in the third person *(she, he, it)*:

Faulty: Deer hunters in the Ocala National Forest must wear bright clothing so you will not get shot.

Improved: Deer hunters in the Ocala National Forest must wear bright clothing so they will not get shot.

Faulty: Other hunters will shoot at you if they see movement in the brush.

Improved: Often other hunters will shoot carelessly if they see movement in the brush.

EXERCISE

A. Mark C for sentences without awkward shifts and X for those with awkward shifts.

x 1. Up until fifty years ago, a small town in Scotland
                                      married
    was world famous because people ~~marry~~ quickly

    there.
                            is

x 2. The name of the town ~~was~~ Gretna Green, and it is

    right over the English border.
                               could

x 3. If a couple were fleeing from irate parents, they ~~can~~

    head for Gretna Green and be wed without awk-

    ward questions.

46

x 4. Scotland had no residency requirement nor any law

                 required

       that ~~requires~~ a clergyman to officiate.

x 5. The names of Latin-American and European heir-

       esses ~~will~~ appear on the old wedding registers.

                Jeff had mastered physics, he

x 6. After ~~physics had been mastered, Jeff~~ had little

       trouble with engineering.

x 7. Our summer in Europe should be a bargain, but

       we

       ~~you~~ have to plan on unexpected expenses.

c 8. A person should always be careful about what he

       signs his name to.

       All teachers use   **approaches,**

x 9. ~~Each teacher uses a~~ different ~~approach,~~ but they ~~all~~

       get their presentations across.

       She purchased

x 10. The emerald ring ~~was purchased~~ for two hundred

       dollars, but ~~she~~ sold it for four hundred.

B. Reword those sentences above marked X.

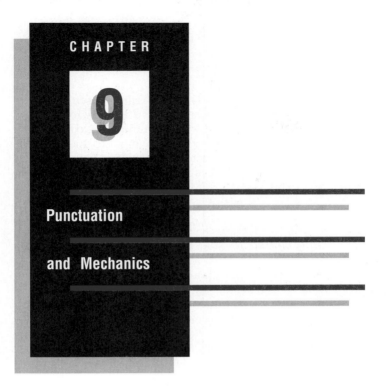

CHAPTER

9

Punctuation

and Mechanics

Punctuation marks represent much of the information we convey in speaking when we pause and raise or lower our voices, information such as where a sentence ends and whether the sentence is a question or a statement. They also signal things that we cannot communicate easily in speech, such as quoting someone directly, for example. Although we can often "hear" when we need a punctuation mark, such as when we hear where we need commas in this sentence, we cannot always tell which mark to use. The only sure way to punctuate correctly is to know the conventions.

47 , Use commas to separate certain elements of a sentence.

The comma is the most widely used—and misused—mark of punctuation. One of its most common uses is to separate clauses and phrases. Use it with a coordinating conjunction (*and, but, for, nor, or, so,* or *yet*) to join two independent clauses, to separate introductory clauses and long introductory phrases from the rest of the sentence, and to separate items in a series.

47a Place a comma before a coordinating conjunction joining two independent clauses.

Use a comma before coordinating conjunctions (*and, but, or, nor, for, yet,* or *so*) when they join two independent clauses. A comma without a coordinating conjunction between such clauses is not enough (see comma splice, **37**).

Incorrect: The poor are legally first-class citizens but they can afford only second-class protection.

Correct: The poor are legally first-class citizens, but they can afford only second-class protection.

Incorrect: Jack read innumerable warnings about smoking so he gave up reading.

Correct: Jack read innumerable warnings about smoking, so he gave up reading.

If the clauses are very short and closely related, you may omit the comma, but it is generally safer to include it.

Correct: It is dark and I am alone.

Correct: The facts are important, but the truth is essential.

Note the difference between a compound sentence (one with two independent clauses) and a sentence containing a compound predicate (double verb):

Correct: Ministers *write and preach* many sermons each year. (No comma is used before this *and* since it does not join two independent clauses.)

47b   Place a comma after an introductory subordinate clause or a long introductory phrase.

Incorrect: Although there are many trial marriages there is no such thing as a trial child. (introductory subordinate clause)
Correct: Although there are many trial marriages, there is no such thing as a trial child.
—Garry Wills

Incorrect: Fixing his eyes soulfully on the guests the little dog begged his way around the table. (long introductory phrase)
Correct: Fixing his eyes soulfully on the guests, the little dog begged his way around the table.

Incorrect: When the teacher refused to mark the tests on a curve the students became indignant. (introductory subordinate clause)
Correct: When the teacher refused to mark the tests on a curve, the students became indignant.

Incorrect: Although it was hard to believe the story was true.
Correct: Although it was hard to believe, the story was true.

Commas are optional after brief introductory modifiers:

Correct: After this month, all my bills will be paid.

Correct: After this month all my bills will be paid.

Correct: In 1989, the Berlin Wall became an anachronism.
Correct: In 1989 the Berlin Wall became an anachronism.

There is usually no pause and no need for a comma when an adverb clause *follows* the main clause:

No comma: He walked as if he owned the whole town.

A comma may be needed before clauses that follow the main clause when they add a contrasting idea or when they are loosely connected to the main clause. There is a pause because the subordinating conjunction (*although, whereas*) functions as a coordinating conjunction:

Comma needed: The supervisor decided to use the new C.P.M. calculator in determining next year's budget, although she had never tried it on a small job.

Comma needed: Jealousy is the fear of being deprived of someone or something, whereas envy is the desire to deprive others of what they have.

47c Place commas between items in a series.

Place a comma after each item except the last in a series of words, phrases, or clauses unless all items are joined by conjunctions. In a series with the last two items joined by a conjunction (a, b, *and* c), place a comma before the conjunction to prevent a possible misreading. Some writers omit this comma, but the safer practice is to use it.

Incorrect: A traditional spice cake requires a good amount of cinnamon nutmeg cloves and allspice.
Correct: A traditional spice cake requires a good amount of cinnamon, nutmeg, cloves, and allspice.

47

Incorrect:	Many dieters try to eliminate potatoes cut down on bread and restrict themselves to one sweet a day.
Correct:	Many dieters try to eliminate potatoes, cut down on bread, and restrict themselves to one sweet a day.

Incorrect:	Consider the feeding habits of the following mammals: bears wolves wildcats rabbits foxes and cats and dogs.
Correct:	Consider the feeding habits of the following mammals: bears, wolves, wildcats, rabbits, foxes, and cats and dogs.
	(Since the *and* before *cats* makes *cats and dogs* a single item, no comma is placed after *cats*.)

47d Use commas to separate coordinate adjectives.

Coordinate adjectives modify a noun equally:

long, windy speech   cold, dark, muddy waters

You can identify coordinate adjectives by placing *and* between them or by reversing their order:

long and windy speech   muddy, dark, cold waters

Do not place commas between cumulative adjectives, those in which one adjective modifies the rest of the expression:

severe economic difficulties

In the above example, *severe* modifies not just *difficulties* but *economic difficulties. And* could not be inserted between *se-*

vere and *economic*, nor could the adjectives be reversed. Therefore, no comma is used.

Incorrect: The author lives in one of the quaint, colorful,
              fishing, villages along the rugged, Cornish coast.
Correct: The author lives in one of the quaint, colorful
              fishing villages along the rugged Cornish coast.

Incorrect: We replaced our old, color television.
Correct: We replaced our old color television.

In the example above, *old* and *color* are not coordinate adjectives.

EXERCISE

Mark unnecessary commas and add commas where necessary in the following sentences. If the sentence is correct, mark C.

1. Many people use *horns* and *antlers* interchangeably,

   but the words represent two very different things.

2. Animals with antlers grow and shed them every

   year,but animals with horns keep them for life.

c 3. Although Mount St. Helens' eruption destroyed

   Spirit Lake, very few people were hurt.

4. The eruption occurred on Sunday morning,so there

   were no loggers on the mountain.

5. Even though hurricanes can be fiercely destructive,

   they give us more warnings than earthquakes do.

47

6. After an earthquake, survivors may have bad dreams,sudden tremors,and fears about driving over bridges.

7. Because the movie provoked so much criticism and controversy,many theaters refused to show it.

8. Despite the fact that the *Springfield Sentinel* did not support the proposal,it passed with a large majority.

9. Mary was hurt/ and ran away.

10. Space explorers look for ways to escape Earth,to search for intelligent life elsewhere,to seek some assurance that they are not alone in the universe.

---

48 , Use commas to set interrupting elements apart from the rest of the sentence.

48

Commas set apart groups of words that interrupt the normal flow of a sentence. Four such interrupters are especially common: nonrestrictive modifiers, appositives, parenthetical expressions, and transitional adverbs or phrases.

48a Use commas to separate a nonrestrictive modifier from the rest of the sentence.

A **restrictive modifier** limits or restricts the noun or pronoun it modifies. The noun *candidate,* for example, can refer to any of those people seeking office, but *candidate who supports higher taxes* refers to someone from a much more limited group. In the sentence, "A candidate who supports higher taxes cannot get elected in this state," the modifier *(who supports higher taxes)* is needed to restrict the noun *(candidate)* so that it refers to someone in the smaller group. Take out the modifier and the sentence is no longer accurate: "A candidate cannot get elected in this state."

A **nonrestrictive modifier,** on the other hand, is not needed to restrict the noun or pronoun it modifies: "Phil Spender, *who supports higher taxes,* cannot get elected in this state." Here the subject already refers to just one person, and the modifier simply adds information. Thus the modifier is nonrestrictive.

Enclose a nonrestrictive modifier in commas:

Incorrect: The Roman Empire which had endured for five hundred years fell to invaders in 476 A.D.

Correct: The Roman Empire, which had endured for five hundred years, fell to invaders in 476 A.D.

Do not set off a restrictive modifier with commas:

Incorrect: Men, who are over 55, should have annual medical checkups.

Correct: Men who are over 55 should have annual medical checkups.

Incorrect: Stores, which honor credit cards, have noticed an increase in sales.

48

Correct: Stores which honor credit cards have noticed an increase in sales. (restrictive)

Correct: Fairway Stores, which honor all major credit cards, have noticed an increase in sales. (nonrestrictive)

It is often difficult to determine whether a modifier is restrictive or nonrestrictive. Study the sentence both with and without the modifier. If the meanings are substantially different, the expression is restrictive and no commas are needed. You can also read it aloud: if you pause noticeably before and after the expression, you probably need commas.

Correct: For many disturbed patients who cannot care for themselves, the hospital has a separate wing.

Also correct: For many disturbed patients, who cannot care for themselves, the hospital has a separate wing.

Note: Relative clauses beginning with *that* are almost always restrictive:

The car *that Lee bought last year* is a Volvo.

Many stylists recommend that writers use *that* for restrictive modifiers and *which* for nonrestrictive modifiers:

Correct: Houses *that* include pools are popular in Florida. (restrictive)

Correct: Houses, *which* may or may not include pools, are more popular than condos. (nonrestrictive)

Note: Be careful to place a comma at both ends of a nonrestrictive element (unless, of course, the clause ends the sentence).

48

48b Use commas to separate an appositive from the rest of the sentence.

An appositive is a noun or a noun phrase that restates, explains, or supplements a preceding noun:

> The newcomer, *a friend of Rita's,* is from Venezuela.

Most appositives are nonrestrictive (see **48a**) and can be dropped from the sentence without changing its meaning. Enclose them in commas:

Incorrect: Flannery O'Connor the great American writer who lived in Georgia died at age thirty-nine in 1964.

Correct: Flannery O'Connor, the great American writer who lived in Georgia, died at age thirty-nine in 1964.

Incorrect: When I need extra money, I wait on tables at Ruby's a local restaurant.

Correct: When I need extra money, I wait on tables at Ruby's, a local restaurant.

A restrictive appositive, like a restrictive modifier, is essential to the meaning of the sentence and so should not be set off with commas:

Correct: My friend *Jamie* always avoids using the word *dumb.*

48c Use commas to separate a parenthetical element from the rest of the sentence.

Parenthetical elements are words, phrases, or clauses inserted into a sentence to clarify or emphasize a point or to give extra information. They interrupt the basic sentence structure and so should be set off with commas:

Correct: Mr. Johnson, as Jane predicted, refused to attend the meeting.

48

Correct: Their wedding, of course, was no surprise to those who knew them.

Correct: Sixty percent of Civil War battles, major and minor, took place in Virginia.

Use commas to set off nouns that name the reader or listener in direct address.

Correct: I've told you that before, Fernando.

Correct: Any of you who think I'm joking, just think again!

Use commas, too, for mild interjections:

Correct: Well, I guess I have no choice in the matter.

Commas also prevent misreadings:

Incorrect: Unless Joe calls his grandmother will not be expecting him.

Correct: Unless Joe calls, his grandmother will not be expecting him.

While they eat, the tourists watch the show.

48d Use commas to set off transitional expressions.

Words like *however, moreover,* and *nevertheless* are often used as parenthetical expressions to provide transition between sentences or paragraphs. (See **23b** for a brief list.) Set them off with commas:

Correct: Hemingway's Americans sound more like Hemingway than Americans. *On the other hand,* they could not be anything other than Hemingway Americans.

Correct: *Therefore,* many readers find Hemingway's style American in a special way.

48

The comma in the last sentence is optional, and many writers would omit it. The best way to tell whether to use a comma with a short transitional expression is to read the sentence aloud. If you pause between the transition and the rest of the sentence, use a comma.

Mark any unneeded commas in the following sentences, and add commas where needed. If a sentence is correct, mark C.

1. One thing Mr. Fitweiler would not tolerate,however, was an interruption.

c 2. People like George who work eighty hours a week are likely to get ill.

3. Those parents/ who don't support their children/ are being unfair.

4. On the other hand,children have to do their fair share too.

c 5. Everything, Sandy said, will work out for the best.

6. Many men/ with an extra Y-chromosome/ have problems with aggression.

7. Clubs/ that rely on bake sales/ rarely make much money.

48

8. Leslie's friend,the exchange student from Holland, speaks excellent English.

9. The lover, the poet, and the lunatic,Shakespeare's Theseus says,are alike.

10. Pregnant women/ who smoke cigarettes/ endanger the health of their unborn children.

---

49 , Use commas in numbers, addresses, titles, and quotations.

Separate the day of the month from the year with commas:

October 24, 1957   December 23, 1990

When only a month and year are given, the comma is optional:

February, 1941   *or*   February 1941

The inverted form, 1 December 1990, requires no commas.

Commas also separate numbers into thousands, millions, and so on:

3,916   *or*   3916   4,816,317,212

49

Within sentences (not on envelopes), items in addresses are separated by commas. Notice that no comma appears between the state name and the ZIP code.

Toledo, Ohio
400 7th Street, New Kensington, PA 15068
121 87th Street, Brooklyn, NY 11209

In sentences, the final item of an address or a date is also followed by a comma:

Working in Palm Springs, California, has many compensations.
March 12, 1922, was a day he never forgot.

Use commas to separate titles and degrees from proper names:

Ronald B. Nelson, Ed.D.   Joseph Hernandez, M.D.
Robert Pew, Ph.D., C.D.P., C.D.E.
Albert M. Johnston, Jr., took over as chief clerk.

Use commas to introduce direct quotations and to separate quoted material from non-quoted material:

Dr. Guber asked, "When is her test scheduled?"
"I'm not sure," I answered, "that I really want to go."

Use commas to set off expressions such as *he said* and *she replied*.

"The future," she wrote, "is just the past getting younger."
He said, "I pull habits out of rats."
"No, you don't," she replied.

If the original quotation ends with a period, change the period to a comma when the quotation is followed by non-quoted material. In all cases, place the comma inside quotation marks. Omit the comma if the quotation ends with an exclamation point or question mark:

"Do you want to register?" [*no comma*] Mr. LaPorte asked.

EXERCISE

Supply needed commas in the following sentences; if a sentence is correct, mark C.

1. Bernhard Drick,Ph.D.,assistant professor of French, was born in Antwerp,Belgium.

2. We expected that this bill would be paid by December 15,1990.

c 3. In 1961, John F. Kennedy thrilled Berliners by saying, "*Ich bin ein Berliner,*" even though his German was incorrect.

4. The President meant to say,"I am a Berliner," but he said,"I am a jelly donut."

5. Ralph W. Mitchell, Jr.,moved from St. Louis, Missouri,to Orlando, Florida,on August 1,1970.

6. After she received the Nobel peace prize, Mother Teresa said,"I am not trying to be successful. I am only trying to be faithful."

7. Josephine Canteras was born on May 26, 1934, in New Kensington, Pennsylvania.

c 8. She was married in Quantico, Virginia, in September 1955.

9. Pearl Harbor was attacked on 7 December/ 1941.

10. The twenty-first century will begin on January 1, 2001, not on January 1,2000.

---

50 no, Omit all unnecessary commas.

Unnecessary commas will make your reader pause needlessly or look for relationships that are not there. Use a comma only when any of the guidelines above calls for one or when you are certain that a comma is necessary to prevent misreading.

Do not separate a subject from its verb:

Incorrect: The cholesterol problem caused by eating too many eggs, involves the yolk more than the white.

Correct: The cholesterol problem caused by eating too many eggs involves the yolk more than the white.

Do not separate a verb from its object:

Incorrect: Mother always says, that Tom will be late for his own funeral.

50

Correct: Mother always says that Tom will be late for his own funeral.

Do not use a comma before a coordinating conjunction *(and, but, for, or, yet)* except when the conjunction precedes the last item in a series or joins two independent clauses:

Incorrect: Eating a bountiful dinner, and taking a long walk afterward are my favorite evening activities.

Correct: Eating a bountiful dinner and taking a long walk afterward are my favorite evening activities.

Do not separate a restrictive modifier from the rest of the sentence (see **48a**):

Incorrect: The two bills, that had the greatest popular support, failed in the Senate.

Correct: The two bills that had the greatest popular support failed in the Senate.

Do not use a comma before the first item or after the last item of a series:

Incorrect: History, language, and culture, are prized possessions of all peoples.

Correct: History, language, and culture are prized possessions of all peoples.

EXERCISE

A. Mark any unnecessary commas in the following sentences.

1. A man is not honest/ merely because he does not steal.

2. I would remind you/ that Plato was the first censor.

3. Everyone, Kierkegaard said, is an exception.

4. Rollo May's *Love and Will* includes chapters entitled "Love and Death," "The Will in Crisis," and "Communion of Consciousness."

5. Frances FitzGerald wrote a book/ on twentieth-century history textbooks entitled *America Revised*.

6. Professor Skoglund/ likes to say/ that students don't spend nearly enough time studying.

7. Father Smith both knows/ and respects my beliefs.

8. Roads/ that were built in 1970/ are no longer adequate.

9. The daily task of getting my car started/ bothered the entire neighborhood.

10. Dr. Kaiser says/ that reading poems/ and writing about them are valuable activities.

---

51 . Use periods after statements or commands and in abbreviations and decimals.

The period ranks second to the comma as the most common mark of punctuation. It is also one of the easiest to use properly, serving three basic functions: to end sentences, to end abbreviations, and to separate decimals.

51a Use a period after a sentence that is not a direct question or exclamation.

The examples below show three types of sentences ended by periods:

Direct statement: The occult sciences are alive and flourishing.

Indirect question: I wonder why Chris walks so slowly.

Instruction or command: Turn it down, please.

51b Use periods according to conventions in abbreviations and decimals.

Periods are required after most abbreviations, as shown below. See **63** for help in using abbreviations.

Ms.   Mrs.   Mr.   Jr.   Dec.   a. m.   e.g.

Do not use periods in acronyms (abbreviations pronounced as words) and abbreviations of company names and governmental agencies:

NATO   CORE   ITT   FBI   CIA   NOW

Many writers omit periods from capitalized abbreviations:

FDR   USSR   NJ

Use a period as a decimal point preceding a decimal fraction, between a whole number and decimals, and between dollars and cents:

.007   .95   98.6°   3.1416 $ .19 $36,500.00

Include the period *inside* quotation marks (see **58c**). See Exercise on page 260.

52 ? Use a question mark to indicate a direct question.

52

Question marks are end stops for direct questions; they can also be used within sentences, as shown here:

Correct: Why has Tolkien's *The Hobbit* remained so popular through the years**?**

Correct: I want to go, but how can I**?**

Correct: "When will we get there**?**" she asked.

Correct: Mr. Walsh called in three backup units (who knows why**?**) when none were needed.

Correct: You actually like Sean**?** (Notice that the question mark here shows the reader how to read the sentence; a period would produce an entirely different meaning.)

Use a period after an indirect question:

Correct: Brad asked if he could be seated without a tie**.**

53 ! Use an exclamation point to show extreme emphasis.

An exclamation point shows extreme emotion or disbelief and can end a sentence, an interjection, or a clause or phrase. Do not overuse the exclamation point. Try to achieve emphasis through your choice of appropriate words. Do not use a comma or period following an exclamation point.

Correct: What a night we've had**!**

Correct: Get out of my way**!** Now**!**

Correct: No, you can't be serious**!**

Mark any punctuation errors and provide correct usage in the following sentences. If a sentence is correct, mark C.

1. Why! Many local jails are worse than state penitentiaries!.

2. You might ask why people being held for trial are often treated like convicts?.

3. "Why do you always procrastinate," I inquired?.

C 4. Would you please pay attention?

5. Oh! how clear the stars are tonight.

6. Susan cried out—or was it Sandra—"Get me out of here!"?

7. "It's alive," she screamed from the dank, cavernous hole.

8. That certainly is a strange choice of words!.

C 9. Did he really tell her to shut up?

C 10. I have long wondered why he didn't do it sooner.

The semicolon is an intermediate mark, stronger than a comma but weaker than a period. It is used only between grammatically equal units—two or more independent clauses or two or more items in a series.

54a Use a semicolon to connect two independent clauses not joined by a coordinating conjunction.

In compound sentences (two or more independent clauses that could stand alone as sentences), join the clauses with a semicolon unless you use a coordinating conjunction (*and, or, nor, for, but, yet,* and *so*) and a comma (see **37**):

Incorrect: Our courts need a better definition of insanity, the standard definitions are inadequate. (comma splice)

Correct: Our courts need a better definition of insanity; the standard definitions are inadequate.

Incorrect: The student parking lot is half empty at 3:15 p.m. this must be a commuter campus. (fused sentence)

Correct: The student parking lot is half empty at 3:15 p.m.; this must be a commuter campus.

Use a semicolon before a conjunctive adverb (*however, hence, therefore,* etc.) or transitional phrase (*on the contrary,* etc.) that introduces an independent clause:

Incorrect: The skill of big-name athletes is indisputable, however, their greed is threatening to destroy professional sports.

54

Correct: The skill of big-name athletes is indisputable; however, their greed is threatening to destroy professional sports.

Incorrect: Their music is not a chaotic mishmash, as the casual listener often thinks, on the contrary, it is as carefully contrived as the work of any so-called serious composer.

Correct: Their music is not a chaotic mishmash, as the casual listener often thinks; on the contrary, it is as carefully contrived as the work of any so-called serious composer.

Before a coordinating conjunction joining two long independent clauses that already contain internal punctuation, use a semicolon rather than a comma:

Preferred: My father never mentioned Louis Armstrong, except to forbid us to play his records; but there was a picture of him on our wall for a long time.
       —James Baldwin, *Notes of a Native Son*

Do *not* use semicolons between a main clause and a subordinate clause:

Incorrect: Although the skies looked threatening; the game began on time. (dependent clause with independent clause)

Correct: The skies looked threatening; the game nevertheless began on time. (both independent clauses)

54b Use semicolons to separate the items in a series when the items themselves contain commas.

When punctuating a series of items that contains commas, such as dates or cities and states, use semicolons between the items to avoid confusion with the internal commas:

Incorrect:	Bonnie has already attended colleges in Fort Collins, Colorado, Tempe, Arizona, and Galesburg, Illinois.
Correct:	Bonnie has already attended colleges in Fort Collins, Colorado **;** Tempe, Arizona **;** and Galesburg, Illinois.
Incorrect:	Murray met several uninvited guests at the door: Bruno, his older brother, Max, his former roommate, and Maria, his secretary.
Correct:	Murray met several uninvited guests at the door: Bruno, his older brother **;** Max, his former roommate **;** and Maria, his secretary.

EXERCISE

In the following sentences, replace incorrectly used commas with semicolons and replace incorrectly used semicolons with commas. If a sentence is correct, mark C.

1. Socrates accepted the hemlock courteously; drink-

   ing it without any fuss.

2. His friends wept; he, however, did not shed a tear.

3. Although almost twenty-five centuries have passed

   since his death; his memory is still green.

4. Orlando, Florida; Phoenix, Arizona; and Seattle,

   Washington, are among the fastest-growing cities in

   the nation.

5. Many people suffer from a fear of cats; called ailuro-

   phobia.

54

6. Last week our secretary began to scream$\overset{;}{_\wedge}$ a kitten had strolled in the back door.

7. Jacqueline Still, the principal$\overset{;}{_\wedge}$ Murray Schenkman, the assistant principal$\overset{;}{_\wedge}$ and Janice McCormick, the secretary, were honored by the graduating class.

8. There are millions of stars we cannot find without a telescope$\overset{;}{_\wedge}$ they don't shed enough light for us to see them.

9. Everyone thought that the storm would delay the game$\overset{;}{_\wedge}$ on the contrary, it made the game more exciting.

c 10. In Oregon rain is called "Oregon mist"; in Florida it is called "liquid sunshine."

c 11. He recognizes the problems of the disadvantaged; he just does not care about them.

c 12. Milton's style has been accused of being grand; this is exactly what it is supposed to be.

13. Mr. Chubb reluctantly left the board$\overset{;}{_\wedge}$ however, as he made clear, he would be available as a consultant.

54

14. Despite the endless street noises; we slept soundly.

15. We slept through the din of fire engines, trucks,

    and trains; in fact, silence would have startled us.

---

55 : Use a colon to call attention to what comes next or to follow certain mechanical conventions.

The colon is a formal mark that calls attention to words that follow it. It also has special uses in titles, scriptural references, time references, and formal letters. Do not confuse it with the semicolon, which separates grammatically equal elements.

55a *Use a colon to introduce a list, an explanation or intensification, an example, or (in certain cases) a quotation.*

Place a colon at the end of an otherwise grammatically complete sentence to introduce a list of items, an explanation of the first part of the sentence, or an example. A complete sentence following a colon may begin with either a capital or a lowercase letter:

Correct: As project coordinator, my boss always followed the same policy: Do what is right today; justify it later.

Correct: In my old neighborhood we lived lives of plenty: plenty of relatives, boarders, landlords, cats, fights, and cockroaches.

Do not place a colon before a list unless the list is introduced by an independent clause. A colon is unnecessary after *such as* and should not be used immediately following the verb:

Incorrect: I enjoy a variety of sports, such as: baseball, swimming, tennis, and soccer.

Correct: I enjoy a variety of sports, such as baseball, swimming, tennis, and soccer.

Incorrect: The students who applied for the job were: Thomas, Sims, and Allen.

Correct: The students who applied for the job were Thomas, Sims, and Allen.

Incorrect: Peter is interested only in: his stereo outfit, his motorcycle, and his girlfriend.
(The words before the colon are not a grammatically complete sentence.)

Correct: Peter is interested only in his stereo outfit, his motorcycle, and his girlfriend.

Colons may separate two independent clauses when the clauses are very closely related and the second explains or intensifies the first:

Correct: Miguel couldn't decide what to do or where to turn: he was stymied.

Correct: Yesterday I realized my age: my son asked if I remembered an old-time singer named Bob Dylan.
(The second part of the sentence explains the first part; the colon = *that is.*)

Use a colon to introduce a long quotation (more than one sentence) or a shorter quotation not introduced by a word such as *said, remarked,* or *replied:*

Correct: I remember my reaction to a typically luminous observation of Kierkegaard's: "Such a relation which relates itself to its own self (that is to say, a self)

must either have constituted itself or have been
constituted by another."

> —Woody Allen,
> "My Philosophy"

Correct: Consider the words of John Donne**:** "No man is an
island entire of itself. . . ."

55b *Use a colon between title and subtitle, between Bible chapter and verse, between hours and minutes, and after the salutation of a formal letter.*

Scripture:	Genesis 1 **:** 7 John 3 **:** 16
Time references:	3 **:** 00 1 **:** 17 p.m.
Salutations:	Dear Ms. Jones **:** Dear Sir or Madam **:**
Subtitles:	*Greek Tragedy* **:** *A Literary Study*
	The Fields of Light **:** *An Experiment in Critical Reading*

EXERCISE

*In the following sentences, mark any incorrectly used
punctuation and insert colons where necessary.*

1. She and Travis have one characteristic in common͜ꞁ

   they are both alone.

2. The old proverb still has value͜ "He who hesitates is lost."

3. He read from Proverbs 3͜17.

4. The tour took us to̷ Paris, Avignon, Arles, and

   Cannes.

5. My report was entitled; "Music to Our Ears—the Ef-

   fect of High-Volume Sound on Human Hearing."

---

56 -- Use dashes to signal sharp changes or to set apart emphatic parenthetical elements.

The dash is a strong, dramatic mark that has several important uses. Unfortunately, it is often misused and overused. In
college- and job-related writing, it should be used sparingly,
not overused as a substitute for other punctuation.

56a Use a dash to signal a sharp change in thought or tone.

Correct: "There is a simple solution to every complex
               problem—the wrong one."
                                                    —H.L. Mencken

Correct: Kendricks' treatment of urban health problems is
               poorly researched, inaccurately documented, badly
               written—but why go on?

56b Use dashes to separate and emphasize a parenthetical element or to set off a parenthetical element that contains commas.

As a stronger mark than the comma, indicating a longer
pause in reading, the dash gives extra emphasis to parenthetical elements. It is also useful when parenthetical elements themselves contain commas:

Correct: Invertebrates——creatures without backbones——thrive on coral reefs.

Correct: The real Lawrence of Arabia——vain, secretive, obsessive, manipulative——remains both fascinating and infuriating.

In printed material, the dash is shown as a continuous line. In typing, however, form a dash by using two hyphens together with no space before or after. For hyphens, see **61**.

57 ( ) Use parentheses to set off parenthetical material that is long or strictly supplementary.

Unlike dashes, which *emphasize* parenthetical material, and commas, which relate the material closely to the rest of the sentence, parentheses set such material apart from the rest of the sentence and *deemphasize* it. Use parentheses for material that is not essential to the meaning of the sentence, material that could as well appear in footnotes. Notice in the first example below that the period is inside the parentheses: The parenthetical material is a complete sentence and is not included in another sentence. Otherwise, put end punctuation after the final parenthesis.

Correct: Milton lived well into the Restoration period. (He died in 1674.)

Correct: Only one of the thirteen tests (see Appendix A) showed even minor irregularities.

Correct: Cajun (from the word *Acadian*) refers to Louisiana culture and cuisine.

57

In the following sentences, mark any incorrectly used parentheses or dashes and insert proper punctuation. If a sentence is correct, mark C.

c 1. Jose is using his new IBM PC (personal computer).

2. My brother-in-law ˍ the wild one I told you about ˍ finally got a job last week.

3. My wife ˍ Dan's baby sister ˍ thinks he is just misunderstood and mistreated.

c 4. The other sisters (Beth, Darlene, and Wanda) all recognize him for the lazy person he is.

5. Dan can be completely charming (if he stays sober).

58 " " Use quotation marks to indicate direct quotations.

Quotation marks enclose words quoted directly from another source. Use them only when you quote the exact words of your source. Indirect quotations, which report only the gist of a message but not the exact words, do not need quotation marks.

58a Enclose direct quotations in double quotation marks.

Put double quotation marks around the exact words spoken or written by your source; do not enclose introductory or interrupting information, such as *she said.*

Correct: According to Samuel Kaplan, "The social and economic segregation of suburbs also is resulting in the political segregation of suburbs."

Also correct: Samuel Kaplan said that "the social and economic segregation of suburbs also is resulting in the political segregation of suburbs."

Correct: "I'll bet you can't catch me," Martha retorted, jumping back quickly.

Do not enclose an indirect quotation in quotation marks:

Direct: According to *Robert's Rules of Order,* "The subsidiary motion to Amend . . . requires only a majority vote, even in cases where the question to be amended takes a two-thirds vote for adoption."

Indirect: *Robert's Rules of Order* says that an amendment needs only a simple majority, even when the main motion needs a two-thirds vote.

Combined: *Robert's Rules of Order* says that an amendment needs only a simple majority, "even in cases where the question to be amended takes a two-thirds vote for adoption."

58

For quotations of four or more typed lines, double-space, indent ten spaces from the left margin, and omit quotation marks:

Correct:

Roger Taylor comments on women writers:

> The Equal Rights Amendment has stimulated community interest in the issues of women's rights. Both men and women are taking a second look at the roles and expectations of women in society. The subject of women and "women writers," therefore, moves to the forefront of what should be offered to the community (21).

In quoting poetry of more than three lines, indent each line ten spaces from the left margin, double-space, and do not add quotation marks (shorter quotations of poetry can be included within the text):

Correct: But at my back I always hear

Time's wingèd chariot hurrying near;

And yonder all before us lie

Deserts of vast eternity.

—Andrew Marvell

58b Use single quotation marks to enclose a quotation within a quotation.

Correct: As John Ehrlichman wrote, "Nixon is the 'Man of a Thousand Facets' to me."

58c Place other punctuation marks inside or outside closing quotation marks, according to standard conventions.

Place all periods and commas *inside* closing quotation marks.

Correct: "No," she replied, "I'm not interested in your proposition in the least."

Correct: His favorite poem is Matthew Arnold's "Dover Beach."

Exception: The hero asserted, "Patience conquers all" (Joyce 21). (The period follows the source of the direct quotation; see **85**.)

Place question marks, exclamation points, and dashes inside quotation marks when they apply only to the quoted material:

Correct: My mother asked her favorite question, "Where do you think you're going, young lady?"

Correct: My only response was, "Oh, no!"

When a question mark, exclamation point, or dash is not part of a direct quotation, place it outside quotation marks. (If both an entire sentence and the quoted material are questions or exclamations, place the question mark or exclamation point inside the quotation marks.)

Correct: Was it Pete Seeger or Woody Guthrie who wrote, "This Land Is Your Land"?

Correct: It was Guthrie, but wasn't Seeger the one who wrote "Where Have All the Flowers Gone?"

58

Correct: Why did Jim Hubbard submit a theme with the title, **"**An Immodest Proposal**"?**

Place all colons and semicolons outside closing quotation marks.

Correct: In his first conference he stated emphatically, **"**We will finish by July 30**";** in the second conference he hedged a bit.

Correct: His first pronouncement was, **"**I am not yet ready to quit**";** he resigned the next day.

58d Use an ellipsis (. . .) to indicate material omitted from a quotation.

An ellipsis consists of three spaced periods. Use a full line of periods, though, when a full paragraph or more has been omitted. It is usually unnecessary to use an ellipsis at the beginning or end of a quotation. However, if you omit material at the end of a sentence within a quotation, use four dots (period plus ellipsis), with no space before the first:

Correct: According to Dr. Peter LeWitt, **"**the brain may record short-term and long-term memory differently. . . . Long-term memory might be recorded more permanently.**"**

Correct: **"**As soon as sensible birth control devices became widely available, women . . . began to use the new methods—when the front office allowed them to.**"**
  —Richard Cornuelle, *De-Managing America*

58e   Use brackets ([ ]) to mark an insertion into a quotation.

Brackets have only one commonly accepted function in prose: to enclose editorial comments or other information inserted into a direct quotation. Do not confuse parentheses with brackets. Parentheses appear within quotations only when they are part of the quotation itself.

Correct: His response was a mild, "Well, I do the best I can [debatable], but sometimes that isn't good enough."

Correct: "They [the staff] are all conscientious, honest people."

Always quote your original exactly, including errors. Insert *sic*—meaning *thus*—in brackets [*sic*] after the error to indicate that the error appears in the original:

Correct: "The civil rights movement picked up steam after President Kennedy's assassination in 1964 [*sic*]."

EXERCISE

Mark any errors in punctuation in the following sentences, and provide correct usage. Mark C if the sentence is correct.

C   1. "Architecture has its political uses. . . . It estab-

lishes a nation, draws people and commerce, and

makes the people love their country."

2. Christman defines general aviation as "all flying

done other than by scheduled carriers [airlines] and defense agencies [military]".

3. Oscar Wilde said that "life is too important to be taken seriously".

4. The guests shouted, "Congratulations!" and "Good luck!"

5. Jacobson said, "yes;" Johanson said, "no."

6. "President Nixon was inaugurated in 1968 [*sic*] and reelected in 1972."

7. When did you say, "I do"?

c 8. We said the words right after the minister asked, "Who objects?"

9. T. S. Eliot wrote that "the greatest treason [is] to do the right deed for the wrong reason".

10. "Art is a lie," Picasso said, "which makes us realize the truth."

58

Use underlining (italics) or quotation marks to designate titles and certain types of words.

Enclose titles of articles, chapters, poems, short stories, musical compositions, or paintings in quotation marks:

Correct: Stanley thinks that Updike's best short story is "A&P."

Correct: I just read a helpful article entitled "Theftproof Your Car Radio."

Correct: The best poem in the magazine is "The Sandpiper."

Use underlining (italics) to designate the title of a book, newspaper, periodical, play, motion picture, or television series. In handwritten or typed materials, use underlining to indicate italic print.

Correct: Reston's column was featured in such papers as the *St. Louis Post-Dispatch.*

Correct: He always kept *The American Heritage Dictionary* and the *Information Please Almanac* close at hand.

Correct: After becoming popular in the television series *Rawhide,* Clint Eastwood starred in such movies as *Dirty Harry* and *A Fistful of Dollars.*

Never use both italics and quotation marks to indicate a title:

Incorrect: One of my favorite paintings is *"The Naked Maja."*

Correct: One of my favorite paintings is "The Naked Maja."

Do not use italics or quotation marks to refer to the Bible or parts of the Bible:

Correct: Genesis is the first book of the Bible, Revelation the last.

Use underlining (italics) to indicate a foreign word that is not yet a standard part of English; a scientific name of a plant, animal, disease, etc.; a word mentioned as a word; or letters or numbers used as examples:

Correct: The word *liberal* comes from Latin *liber,* meaning free.

Correct: *Gauge* is now spelled *gage* in some professional journals.

Correct: *Dracaena marginata* is an easy plant to propagate by mound layering.

Correct: Social security numbers beginning with *3* come generally from the Midwest.

Some writers use underlining or quotation marks to give a word or phrase special emphasis, but you should do so very sparingly. Avoid enclosing slang in quotation marks as a form of apology. Emphatic wording is much more effective.

EXERCISE

Correct any sentences in which italics or quotation marks are improperly used. If correct, mark C.

1. My oldest brother always carries a copy of the ⸢New Testament.⸣

2. Joel's capital F̲'s and T̲'s are almost impossible to distinguish.

3. *Apocalypse Now* is a film based on Conrad's novel ⸢Heart of Darkness.⸣

59

4. ~~Preludes~~ is one of the initial poems in the volume ⸌The Complete Poetry of T. S. Eliot.⸍

5. Ricardo enjoys baseball biographies such as ⸌Mr. Cub,⸍ the story of Ernie Banks.

6. The new coach called his fast-moving attack a <u>blitz-krieg</u>.

7. The medium told Pierre that his lucky number was <u>2</u>.

c 8. "The Celebrated Jumping Frog of Calaveras County," one of Twain's earliest short stories, features a dog with no hind legs and a frog loaded with buckshot.

9. Was it a <u>faux pas</u> to ask for a legal conference ⸌<u>in camera</u>⸍?

10. Some writers use ⸌<u>per se</u>⸍ and ⸌<u>ipso facto</u>⸍ unnecessarily.

Use apostrophes to form contractions, certain plurals, and the possessive form of nouns and indefinite pronouns.

60a Use an apostrophe to indicate the possessive of nouns and indefinite pronouns.

Add an apostrophe and *s* to form the possessive of indefinite pronouns (*everyone, someone, somebody,* etc.) and of most singular nouns:

Sally's coat   Ms. Cullom's office
anybody's game   one's chances
a day's pay   a cat's life

The same rule applies if a one-syllable singular noun ends with an -*s* sound:

boss's relatives   class's performance

But in words of more than one syllable, the -*s* following the apostrophe is optional when it might not be pronounced:

Sophocles' *or* Sophocles's   Countess' *or* Countess's

Add only the apostrophe to plurals ending in -*s*. Add an apostrophe and *s* to plurals not ending in -*s*:

girls' jumpers   cats' lives
ladies' shoes   two months' work
children's clothes   mice's cages

Add an apostrophe and *s* to the last word of a word group or compound:

the editor-in-chief's office   the chief of staff's car

Add an apostrophe and *s* to each name to indicate individual ownership; add the apostrophe and *s* only to the last name to show joint ownership:

Jo's and Arnie's cars   David and Linda's apartment

60b Use an apostrophe to indicate the omitted letters in a contraction. Use it also to indicate omitted parts of dates or other numerals.

they'll (they will)   it's (it is)   can't (cannot)   class of '65

Note that the apostrophe goes where letters are left out, not necessarily between words joined in a contraction:

wouldn't

60c Use an apostrophe to form the plural of lowercase letters and of abbreviations followed by periods. Use it also to prevent confusion in forming plurals of other abbreviations, of capital letters, of symbols, and of words used or singled out as words:

M.S.'s	*j*'s	*miss*'s
J's or Js	UFO's or UFOs	@'s or @s

Note that the *s* is not italicized.
Never use an apostrophe to form a simple plural:

Incorrect: Three dog's barked. Broiled steak's were served.

EXERCISE

Where needed, correct the use of apostrophes in the following sentences. If correct, mark C.

1. Its function is to cool the room whenever ~~its~~ **it's** too

   humid.

C 2. Mississippi contains four *s*'s, four *i*'s, two *p*'s, and

   one *M*.

3. The pet store has cats\in cages piled three deep.

   cat's
4. Each ~~cats'~~ cage is kept immaculately clean, though.

C 5. The Secretary of State's job is one of the most cru-

   cial in the world.

C 6. My mother-in-law's taste in art is provincial.

7. The Johnson/s always send Christmas cards.

   Men's
8. ~~Mens'~~ clothes are sold on the sixth floor of Boyd's.

   It's
9. ~~Its~~ true that many good books are unread.

10. The lives of the Adamses\were uneventful.

Use a hyphen to join two words into a single adjective, to join a root word to a prefix or suffix, and to write out a fraction or compound number.

Compound words are sometimes written separately, sometimes hyphenated, and sometimes written together as one word. When in doubt, consult your college dictionary.

61a Use a hyphen to join two or more words serving as a single adjective before a noun.

up-to-date information   energy-related problems
seventeen-year-old son   late-night meeting
well-intentioned actions   claw-like arms

But do not hyphenate such adjectives following the noun:

The information was clearly not up to date.

His son was seventeen years old.

The agency's actions were well intentioned.

Do not use a hyphen between an adverb ending in -*ly* and an adjective:

unusually fine wine

carefully developed plot

61b Use hyphens to write out fractions and compound numbers between twenty and one hundred.

But do not hyphenate a fraction used as a noun:

61

twenty-two	three hundred sixty-one
a two-thirds majority	two thirds of the members
one-fourth complete	one fourth of a cup

61c Use hyphens to join root words to certain prefixes and suffixes.

The suffix -*elect* and the prefixes *pro-*, *anti-*, *ex-*, *self-*, and *great-* are normally joined with hyphens to root words. Check your dictionary when you are uncertain whether to use a hyphen with a prefix or suffix.

ex-convict	self-confessed	great-grandmother
anti-abortionist	pro-abolitionist	congressman-elect

61d Use a hyphen to avoid a confusing combination of letters or syllables.

re-creation (*not* recreation)
steel-like (*but* froglike, etc.)

61e Use a hyphen to divide a word at the end of a line.

Do not divide a one-syllable word:

dined	tenth	strength

Divide only between syllables. Consult your dictionary. Most dictionaries indicate syllabication with dots:

in · ti · mi · date	wis · dom	a · ni · mal

Do not put a single letter at the beginning or ending of a line; do not put a two-letter ending at the beginning of a line:

61

Improper: thick- ly   ax- es   a- brupt   fox-y

EXERCISE

Correct any misuses or omissions of hyphens in the following sentences. If correct, mark C.

1. Twenty-one freedom seeking refugees crossed the

   border.

c 2. Her dress was a light rosy-beige.

3. Oakwood Village's recreation of the Nativity scene is a

   tradition.

c 4. Mr. Stevenson, ex-district attorney and self-made

   man, is our new judge-elect.

5. Thirty-seven units were completed in one/half the

   usual time.

62 cap

Always capitalize the first word of a sentence and the word *I*; capitalize proper nouns and important words in titles according to conventional practice.

62

Appropriate capitalization is a matter of convention. This section will show you basic conventions, but conventions vary, and careful writers often disagree on what should be capitalized. Consult your college dictionary for specific problems;

words commonly capitalized will be capitalized in the dictionary entry.

62a Capitalize the first word of a sentence and I.

Correct: He advised our club on energy-saving devices.

Incorrect: I would go if i could.

Correct: I do not know whether I should use styrofoam or vermiculite insulation in the exterior walls.

62b Capitalize the names of persons, races, and nationalities.

Also capitalize derivatives of such words:

English	Maxwell R. Folger	Ms. Tucker
Chicano	Americanize	Cuban
Caucasian	Russian	Michigander

Neither *black* (African-American) nor *white* (Caucasian) is capitalized; however, *Hispanic* is capitalized.

62c Capitalize place names.

Puerto Rico	Amazon River	Orange County
Zaire	Nile Valley	North Carolina

62d Capitalize the names of organizations, historical events, holidays, days of the week, and months.

62

World War II	Xerox	Thursday
Chrysler Corporation	Yom Kippur	Thanksgiving
Easter	NAACP	July

62e Capitalize titles preceding a name.

These same titles following a name are capitalized in addresses and typed signatures of letters, but not in sentences:

Professor Elizabeth Kirk   Elizabeth Kirk,
                                     Professor of Chemistry
Chairman Dick Fisher   Dick Fisher,
                                     Chairman of the Board

The chairman of the board called the meeting to order.

I wrote a letter to Professor Miller.

Elizabeth Kirk is a professor of chemistry.

62f Capitalize common nouns such as street, company, river, or aunt only when they are part of a proper noun. Capitalize north, south, east, and west only when they refer to specific regions.

Huskey Company   my brother's company
Kirkman Road   on the road
Roosevelt University   at a university
Atlantic Ocean   at the ocean
American Airlines   a major airline
Uncle George   my favorite uncle
Oak Ridge High School   my old high school
The Midwest   go west
East Texas   toward the east

62g Capitalize the first word and all important words of the title of a book, periodical, article, report, or other document. Also capitalize the titles of chapters and other major divisions.

The Scarlet Letter   *Macbeth*

A, an, the, conjunctions, and prepositions of fewer than five letters should not be capitalized unless they are the first or last word in a title or subtitle.

EXERCISE

Correct any errors in capitalization in the following sentences. If a sentence is correct, mark C.

  1. After graduating from Shimer College, Scott went to work for the Devex corporation in Chicago.

  2. Jon is not going home for the Holidays.

c 3. Cyril's Welsh ancestry was not apparent in his singing voice.

  4. The Colorado river flows through much of the west.

  5. Awilda Orta is director of New York city's office of bilingual education.

  6. Bilingual Education is offered in seventy languages, including Chinese, Russian, and Vietnamese.

  7. Hugo graduated from Newark Community high school in Newark, Illinois, a small town southwest of Chicago.

62

8. For cultural reasons, many people consider south Florida as Northern and North Florida as southern.

9. When Peter the Great died in 1725, he had moved Russia out of the oriental middle ages and into the mainstream of modern western civilization.

10. The poet Milton was an official in the government of Cromwell, the English puritan leader who overthrew the monarchy of king Charles I in 1642.

---

63 ab Capitalize and punctuate abbreviations according to conventional practice.

Abbreviations and figures are widely used in technical reports, tables, footnotes, and bibliographies; but only a few abbreviations and figures are commonly used in the text of college writing.

63a Use only conventionally accepted abbreviations in college and general writing.

The following abbreviations are recommended:

Mr.	M.D.	Rev. (Rev. Jane Smith or
Mrs.	M.S.	the Rev. Mr. Jones)
Ms.	S.P.A.	Col. and other military
Dr.	A.D. or B.C.	titles

St. (Saint)	a.m. or p.m.	Ph.D. and other degrees
Jr.	no.	CIA, IBM, NAACP, and
Sr.	D.C.	other groups commonly
		known by initials

63b Spell out the following in college writing:

Check your college dictionary for the proper spelling, punctuation, and capitalization of abbreviations.

Units of measure: pounds, feet

Place names: Arkansas, New York

Parts of addresses: Street, Avenue, Road

Corporate identities: Company   Incorporated
(except in official titles)

Parts of written works: page 3   chapter seven   volume 14

Personal names: Charles (not Chas.)

Names of courses: English 101 (not Eng. 101)

EXERCISE

Correct any improper abbreviations or supply abbreviations as needed in the following sentences. If correct, mark C.

Colonel
1. The ~~Col.~~ came by this afternoon.

Arkansas,   Tuesday morning.
2. She was born in Texarkana, ~~Ark.~~, on a ~~Tues. morn.~~

page   Volume
3. India is described on ~~p.~~ 367 of ~~Vol.~~ 12.

c 4. The package weighed three pounds.

5. Washington, ~~District of Columbia,~~ is our nation's

   capital.

   > D.C.,

6. We took David Anthony to his ~~Dr.,~~ Kenneth Dutt,

   for his annual physical.

   > doctor,

7. ~~Geo.'s~~ new ~~co.~~ is Steinberger Enterprises, Inc.

   > George's   company

8. Oscar had wanted to be ~~an R.N.~~ ever since he could

   remember.

   > a registered nurse

9. Terry moved from ~~Chi.~~ to ~~L.A.~~ and then to ~~N.Y.~~

   > Chicago   Los Angeles   New York.

10. ~~Robt.~~ Louis Stevenson is best known for his chil-

    dren's classic, *Treasure Island.*

    > Robert

---

64   Spell out one- and two-word numbers except to follow certain conventions.

Use figures for page numbers, numbers with units of measure, time followed by *a.m.* or *p.m.*, percentages, decimals, identification numbers, and numbers that cannot be written in one or two words. Otherwise write out numbers in the text of your papers.

Use figures		Write out
428	5,687,414	eleven twenty-two
		seventeen thousand
3¾		three-quarters
		one third of the population
East 181st Street		East Eighty-first Street

Use figures	Write out
channel 3	
page 17	seventeen-page report
85°F 12 meters	eighty-five cadets
6:30 p.m.	six-thirty that afternoon
38% 10 percent	
3.1416 .005	
U.S. 66 I-84	
4 B.C. 1986	

It is best to avoid beginning a sentence with a number, but if it is unavoidable, write out the number:

Four hundred twenty-eight people attended the opening ceremonies.

In a series, if one number must be written in figures, write all the numbers in figures:

Incorrect: Of the students who responded to the questionnaire, thirty had never used the pass-fail option, twelve had used it once, and 123 had used it more than once.

Correct: Of the students who responded to the questionnaire, 30 had never used the pass-fail option, 12 had used it once, and 123 had used it more than once.

EXERCISE

Correct any errors in number usage in the following sentences. If correct, mark C.

c   1. The 30,000 BTU model needs 220 volt wiring, but

the smaller models can use ordinary 110 voltage.

64

2. My ex-boyfriend lives on ~~81st~~ **Eighty-first** Street near Interstate

   ~~seventy-five.~~ **75.**

3. ~~351~~ **Three hundred fifty-one** people attended the first performance.

4. Only ~~twenty~~ **20** percent of my serves were good, by far

   my worst performance ever.

c 5. Pierre's lucky number is *2.*

6. Sue counted 456 words on page ~~seventy-five~~ **75** of vol-

   ume 3.

7. Only a third of my high school graduation class

   entered college immediately, but another $\frac{1}{4}$ **fourth** entered

   within a year.

8. Cable Channel ~~Thirteen~~ **13** picks up many shows not

   shown by the local network affiliates, channels 2, 6,

   and 9.

9. Temperatures in West Texas averaged over ~~one hun-~~

   ~~dred~~ **100** degrees throughout much of July 1985.

c 10. His 16-page term paper was thirteen days late.

64

Use proper materials and follow conventional manuscript form in preparing a final draft.

In both college and general writing, correct manuscript form and appearance contribute to the effectiveness of your work. If your instructor, department, or organization has formal guidelines, follow them carefully; otherwise use the guidelines below.

Materials. Submit typed papers on standard $8\frac{1}{2}$- × 11-inch paper. Use good-quality paper, not onionskin. Type with a good ribbon and clean keys. Submit handwritten papers on wide-lined notebook paper, not on sheets torn from spiral notebooks or legal pads. Write on one side of the paper only and on every other line. Use blue or black ink for handwritten papers.

Margins and spacings. For typed papers, use a $1\frac{1}{2}$-inch margin at the top and left side, a 1-inch margin at the right and the bottom. Double-space college papers and reports. For handwritten work, leave blank the top and left margins on notebook paper and allow approximately an inch at the right and bottom. Indent each paragraph five spaces in typed papers and approximately one inch in handwritten papers. Double-space footnotes, headings, and long quotations. Center the title on the top line or an inch and a half from the top. Leave an extra space between the title and the first line.

Pagination. Use ordinary arabic numerals (2, 3, etc.) without the word *page* or parentheses in the upper righthand corner of all pages beyond the first.

General appearance. Endorse or head the paper as your instructor suggests; this usually includes your name, the name of the course, the date, and the title or number of the assignment.

Correct your final draft carefully so that your typed copy is as neat as possible with minimal last-minute corrections. Make such corrections unobtrusively, using a caret (∧) for insertions and a single line to cross out words. Most instructors do not mind a few neatly inked-in corrections on typed papers (see editing, **15**).

66 sp Proofread for proper spelling, and work on your spelling weaknesses.

Unfortunately, there is no easy shortcut to effective spelling. Some writers who are otherwise very skillful struggle all their careers with poor spelling. If you are a poor speller and cannot seem to improve much, allow extra time to look up spellings. If you frequently misspell the same words, make a list of them. The suggestions below should help you with some of the more common spelling problems; however, for many words, only memorization or reference lists will help.

ie or ei: Place *i* before *e*, except after *c* and in words pronounced with other than the long *e* sound:

Correct:	field	ceiling	sleigh	height
	grief	conceit	vein	stein
	niece	deceive	weigh	foreign
	relief	conceive	neighbor	heir

Exceptions: fiery, seize, species, weird, neither

Final e: Drop a silent final *e* before suffixes beginning with a vowel; keep it before suffixes beginning with a consonant:

Correct:	writ*ing*	hope*ful*	guid*ance*
	love*ly*	nine*teen*	sincere*ly*

Exceptions: dye*ing* (clothes), nin*th*, tru*ly*, courag*eous*

66

Changing y to i: When adding a suffix, change a final *y* to *i* except before a suffix beginning with *i:*

Correct: fly, flying, flier
                   rely, reliance
                   forty, fortieth

Plurals: Most plurals add -*s* to the singular; plurals of nouns ending in *s*, *ch*, *sh*, or *x* add -*es*.

Correct: girls   tables   typists   spoonfuls
                   dishes   taxes   churches   bosses

Singular nouns ending in *y* preceded by a consonant change the *y* to *i* and add -*es*.

Correct: cities, tragedies, replies, supplies

Singular nouns ending in *o* preceded by a consonant usually add -*es*, but note the exceptions:

Correct: potatoes, tomatoes, heroes, zeroes, hypos, pros,
                 jumbos
                 ghettos or ghettoes, mosquitos or mosquitoes

The Glossary of Usage at the back of this handbook (page 430) lists some words easily confused because of similar spelling; a few others are:

advice, advise
ascent, assent
censor, censure
decent, descent, dissent
definite, definitive
device, devise
idea, ideal

inequity, iniquity
paradox, parody
passed, past
prophecy, prophesy
stationary, stationery
to, too
weather, whether

Here is a list of one hundred commonly misspelled words:

66

absence
accommodate
acquaintance
adequately
aggravate
alleviate
all right
altogether
amateur
analysis
apparatus
apparent
argument
athletic
becoming
bureaucracy
calendar
category
cemetery
committee
competition
condemn
conscientious
conscious
consistent
continuous
criticize
definitely
description
desirable
desperate
develop
disappoint
disastrous

dissatisfied
eighth
embarrass
environment
existence
exaggerate
familiar
feasible
February
forth
gauge
government
grammar
harass
hindrance
hurriedly
hypocrisy
imitation
incredibly
independent
intelligence
irrelevant
irresistible
knowledge
leisure
license
loneliness
maintenance
maneuver
mischievous
necessary
noticeable
occasionally

occurred
omitted
parallel
permissible
personnel
possess
preceding
predominant
prejudice
prevalent
privilege
procedure
proceed
prominent
psychology
questionnaire
receive
recommend
repetition
rhythm
ridiculous
schedule
separate
sergeant
succeed
supersede
susceptible
temperament
thorough
unanimous
undoubtedly
vacuum
villain

EXERCISE

Underline the correctly spelled words.

1. <u>independent</u>

2. resistence

3. evidentally

4. larnyx

5. indispensable
6. heighth
7. occurrance
8. mispell
9. preceed
10. procede
11. compatible
12. chastise
13. futiley
14. column
15. incidently
16. reciept
17. accidently
18. develope
19. pursute
20. hurriedly

10

Appropriate

Diction

Diction refers to selecting and using appropriate language,
putting the right word in the right place to say just what
you intend. Effective writing requires a respect for words,
an awareness of their various uses and the various effects
they can have on readers. It requires using words that are
specific and concrete, precise and forceful, vivid and clear.
Finding such words is perhaps your greatest challenge as
a writer. To meet that challenge, you must know what
words mean and how to use them. As you become more
sensitive to words—to their ability to clarify or obscure
and to their suitability for your purposes and audiences—
you will use them with increasing confidence.

Words are "right" only when they have an appropriate effect in your sentence; choosing words, then, always means considering the context in which they are used. We speak and write in various "languages": one for friends, one for family members, one for employers and instructors. Though you may speak of an "*awesome* evening," you will generally write "*enjoyable* evening" unless your reader would expect informality, as in many narrative essays. The writing context will usually require you to *submit* a report (not *hand it in*) or to provide *abundant* (not *a lot of*) facts.

A good dictionary will help you decide whether the word you think is the right one actually expresses what you intend. It will also warn you if a word is considered slang or obsolete or in some other way inappropriate for college writing. The following sections will help you use your dictionary more efficiently and will offer other advice about choosing words wisely.

67 lev — Write at a level appropriate to your subject and audience.

A writer's choice of words involves basic questions of style: How should I sound? Does my subject require a relaxed or a dignified tone? Should I talk directly to the reader? You can achieve an effective style by avoiding stilted, impersonal language and by using the appropriate person (see **46b**), the active voice whenever possible (see **28e**), and sentences that are properly emphatic (see **28**). In addition, effective writers are aware of various levels of usage, in keeping with their audience's expectations.

Dictionaries generally classify words according to these four types—formal, standard, informal, or slang—reflecting different levels of usage:

Formal or learned words are more common in reading than

in speaking and are serious and scholarly, sometimes affected, in tone. Some examples are *prevaricate* (to lie), *ameliorate* (to improve), and *altercation* (quarrel).

Standard or popular words are familiar to the widest group of educated speakers and writers. *Truth* is the standard counterpart of the more formal *veracity.*

Informal or **colloquial** words are appropriate to spoken language and to writing that aims for a conversational effect. Many good writers use colloquial terms for humor or for a casual, relaxed tone.

Informal	*Standard*
flunk	fail
mad	angry
guy	man
TV show	television program
job	position
to kid	to tease
to cook up	to invent, concoct

Slang is highly informal language, widely used to add color and novelty to speech. Because it often does not last long enough to have a clearly established meaning, slang is inappropriate in most college writing.

Slang	*Standard*
split	leave
neat	wonderful
trashed	vilified
laid-back	relaxed
uptight	very nervous

The English language includes many dialects—different ways of speaking or writing in particular geographic areas or among particular groups of people. The predominant dialect used by educated writers and speakers of American English

67

is called Standard English. It is the variety of English expected in college papers, business reports, and books like this one. Most dictionaries mark the words not usually used in Standard English as *nonstandard, substandard,* or *dialect. Nowheres,* for example, is labeled *Dial.* in *Webster's New Collegiate Dictionary.* (*Note:* Some words may be standard in one sense but not in another. *Learn* is nonstandard when used to mean "teach.") The abbreviations for these labels vary; your dictionary will have a section at the front or back explaining its labels and abbreviations.

Standard English is written and spoken in many styles, which we can arbitrarily divide into three "levels": formal, informal, and general. Each level is appropriate in some situations but not in others.

Formal English is found in technical reports, scholarly books and articles, and many types of professional or academic writing. It uses an extensive, elevated vocabulary and sentences more complex than those found in other levels of writing. It avoids contractions and colloquial expressions and therefore sounds different from the way people speak:

> Money and the habitual resort to its use are conceived to be simply the ways and means by which consumable goods are acquired, and therefore simply a convenient method by which to procure the pleasurable sensations of consumption; these latter being in hedonistic theory the sole and overt end of all economic endeavor. Money values have therefore no other significance than that of purchasing power over consumable goods, and money is simply an expedient of computation.
>
> —Thorstein Veblen

Informal English, on the other hand, has a more conversational tone. Writers of Informal English regularly use contractions, colloquial expressions (*a couple of* instead of *two, really* instead of *very*), and slang. They usually write in loose sentences with more *and*'s and fewer subordinate clauses than are used in other levels of writing. Informal English is gaining popularity in journalism but is generally not considered appropriate for college papers.

> Diana's mother's kitchen was full of the most colossal assortment of junk food I have ever been exposed to. My house was full of apples and peaches and milk and home-made chocolate-chip cookies—which were nice, and good for you, but-not-right-before-dinner-or-you'll-spoil-your-appetite. Diana's house had nothing in it that was good for you, and what's more, you could stuff it in right up until dinner and nobody cared.
>
> —Nora Ephron

General English follows a middle course between formal and informal. Most of its sentences are less complex than those of Formal English but tighter than those of Informal English. In the right circumstances, General English might use relatively formal words like *haughty* and *attire* or informal words like *stuck-up* and *threads,* but most of the time it uses words like *proud* and *clothes.* General English is usually the best choice for college or business writing.

> Beginnings are apt to be shadowy, and so it is with the beginnings of that great mother of life, the sea. Many people have debated how and when the earth got its ocean, and it is not surprising that their explanations do not always agree. For the plain and inescapable truth is that no one was there to see, and in the absence of eyewitness accounts there is bound to be a certain amount of disagreement.
>
> —Rachel Carson

EXERCISE

A. Label each of the following paragraphs F for Formal, I for Informal, or G for General English. Be prepared to discuss the circumstances in which each paragraph would be appropriate.

67

Appropriate Diction

G 1. In general, two types of fiction deal with the past: historical fiction and fictional history. The more common of the two is historical fiction, in which fictional characters and events are placed in a more or less authentic background. Examples include *Gone with the Wind* and *War and Peace*. In a sense, since nearly all novelists place their characters in some period, most fiction can be thought of as historical to a degree; but the term is applied only to novels in which historical events are prominent. Fictional history, on the other hand, uses real historical figures and events but with the novelist's imagination free to invent and imagine non-historical episodes. Gore Vidal and E. L. Doctorow are prominent writers of fictional history.

F 2. It can be maintained that all symbolization proceeds by indirection and to this extent demands a lack of contact with reality. It is of the essence of symbolization that the symbol stands for a reality other than itself. To the extent that he uses symbols to represent actuality to himself, and especially in his use of impermanent vocal symbols to achieve contact with truth which he knows to be extratemporal and permanent, man ineluctably resorts to pretense. The pretense in oral verbalization, however, is less contrived than in alphabetic writing.

I 3. Our dinner at Chez Louis was a pretty good deal if you consider the incredible number of courses they served. But the fish was a tad overcooked, and the baked potato was wrapped in foil, like in some cheap roadside diner, and the service was the pits. I guess the waiter thought that guys who work in classy joints should be snooty, which he was.

B. Complete the following exercises using a current English dictionary.

67

1. Check your dictionary to see if the following words are considered slang, colloquial (informal), or standard: crook, dorky, exam, kid, jock, hacker, klutzy, nutty, sleaze, zany.

2. Look up the word *gimmick* in your dictionary to see how it can be both colloquial (informal) and slang. Find another such example.

3. Determine which of these words is considered formal, informal (colloquial), slang, or standard: hassle (noun), hassle (verb), hang-up, altercation, argument. How do the meanings differ? Under what circumstances would each be appropriate?

4. List five slang terms, and write short, original definitions for each. Then compare your definitions with those in your dictionary.

68 d Keep your level of usage consistent.

Appropriate diction requires a consistent style. Mixing formal and informal language can produce distracting and absurd results:

> It seemed inconceivable that the thieves could hope to penetrate the supposedly impregnable chamber; their rip-off was truly awesome.

Here the slangy conclusion clashes with the standard, if somewhat formal, level of the rest of the sentence. Just as you would not wear blue jeans with a dinner jacket, you do not want to call attention to yourself by mixing styles of writing inappropriately.

Inappropriate:	The professor's inaugural lecture contained several off-the-wall comments.
Appropriate:	The professor's inaugural lecture contained several ridiculous comments.
Inappropriate:	As Orwell observed, the English language is unquestionably hard up.
Appropriate:	As Orwell observed, the English language is unquestionably in difficulty.

EXERCISE

A. Study the levels of usage in the following sentences. Mark with X those that are too informal and with A those that are appropriate. Reword those marked X.

x 1. Shakespeare's characters, though they speak memo-
    rable poetry, are often ~~tough to relate to.~~
    difficult to understand.

A 2. Some people are convinced that, having said nothing,

    they have said a great deal.

x 3. Constance in Chaucer's "Man of Law's Tale" is
    falsely charged with killing
    ~~framed for wasting~~ Hermengyld.

x 4. While some reporters ~~went bananas over~~ the scandal,
    were excited by
    the President stayed ~~cool.~~
    calm.

x 5. My research assistant telephoned to inquire what
    happening
    was ~~going down~~ in the laboratory.

B. Rewrite the following sentences in General English:

Many people get angry

1. ~~A lot of folks really get ticked off~~ at TV commercials.

   commercials suggest
2. TV ~~ads tell you~~ that remedies are instantly available

   problem.
   for every conceivable ~~hang-up.~~

   problem of excessive commercialization.
3. Many viewers opt for the public television network,

   preferring to avoid the ~~hassle of commercial hype.~~

   willing
4. Few parents are ~~hard-nosed enough~~ to eliminate ~~the~~

   television
   ~~tube~~ from the home.

5. Commercial programs are seldom an intellectual

   challenge.
   ~~turn-on.~~

An **idiom** is a customary expression peculiar to a language. Native speakers of English naturally say "with the naked eye," for example, not "with a bare eye," though it is impossible to explain why. You may have difficulty with some of the idiomatic uses of certain prepositions: When do you say *differ from,* when *differ with*? Do you say *to the contrary* or *on the contrary*? If your ear cannot guide you, your college dictionary usually can. Here are some troublesome phrases:

69

Unidiomatic	Idiomatic
absolve of	absolve from
accept to	accept by
accuse with	accuse of
accustom with	accustom to
adhere in (or by)	adhere to
adjacent of	adjacent to
agree in	agree to (a proposal)
	agree on (a course of action)
angry at (a person)	angry with (a person)
apologize about	apologize for
bored of	bored with (or by)
comply to	comply with
concur about	concur with (a person)
	concur in (a decision or action)
conform in	conform to (or with)
derived of	derived from
different than	different from
in accordance to	in accordance with
in search for	in search of
intend on doing	intend to do
interfere about	interfere with (= prevent)
	interfere in (= meddle)
oblivious about	oblivious of (or to)
plan on doing	plan to do
preferable than	preferable to
similar with	similar to
superior than	superior to

EXERCISE

A. *Use your dictionary to determine which of the following sentences are idiomatic.*

1. The decision is one _{in} *about* which few experts would

   concur.

2. Tristan was *infatuated* ~~by~~ Iseult's beauty.
   [with]

3. Minnie is *different* ~~than~~ the other girls in her class.
   [from]

4. Ken is caught in a vicious cycle ~~in~~ *which* he cannot

   escape.
   [from]

5. Given today's *attitudes* ~~of~~ money, upward mobility is
   [toward]

   prevalent ~~with~~ many Americans.
   [among]

6. Nick's *arrival* ~~to~~ the college was unexpected.
   [at]

7. Sara was too *angry* ~~at~~ him to *apologize* ~~about~~ her
   [with]   *[for]*

   own rudeness.

8. Ellen *graduated* high school at sixteen, benefiting
   [from]

   ~~by~~ an accelerated program.
   [from]

9. They could not *acquiesce* ~~to~~ the jury's decision.
   [in]

10. Few students are *capable* ~~to handle~~ both full-time
    [of handling]

    jobs and a full academic load.

B. Correct the sentences that are not idiomatic.

---

70 vague Use specific and concrete words.

Consider the following sentences:

We protected all of the plants in the yard.

We mulched the shrubs, mounded around the rose bushes, and covered the eucalyptus tree.

The second sentence is more specific; it identifies the plants and the ways of protecting them. It is longer, but the extra words give the reader a clearer picture.

Specific terms give more information than general ones. *Surgeon,* for example, implies *doctor,* but *doctor* does not identify a person as a surgeon. If you find yourself writing *people* when you mean *U.S. citizens* or *college students,* you are not asking yourself this important question: Am I identifying what I am referring to as specifically as I should? The following list shows how little effort it takes to become more specific:

General	*Specific*	*More specific*
building	house	duplex
contest	footrace	Boston Marathon
go	run	sprint
go	walk	shuffle
religion	Christianity	Roman Catholicism
officer	Cabinet officer	Secretary of State

The best choice is usually the most specific expression that says what you mean. In the following examples, notice how the specific sentences clarify the general ones:

General: The patient's wound was treated.
Specific: The nurse bandaged the patient's minor wound.
Specific: The intern stitched the patient's four-inch laceration.

General: He studied.
Specific: He read three chapters in his geology text.
Specific: He memorized his French vocabulary list.

Abstract terms often combine with general terms in dull writing. An abstract term names something intangible, like an idea or a quality: *democracy, finance, linguistics*. A concrete term, on the other hand, points to something physically real: *desk, checkbook, motorcycle.* We could not communicate complex ideas without using abstract terms, but dull writing tends to be unnecessarily abstract. Sentences filled with *aspects, cases, factors, circumstances,* and *instances* will deaden your writing. Many writers mistakenly convert verbs *(explain, prefer)* into abstract nouns *(explanation, preference)* and use those nouns with vague verbs like *be, have,* or *make:*

> Jonathan offered no explanation for his preference for California wines.

We can improve the sentence by changing the abstract nouns back to verbs:

> Jonathan did not explain why he preferred California wines.

Notice how the following abstract sentence, taken from a newspaper report, is improved by avoiding the abstract nouns *decline* and *use:*

Abstract: The U.S. Department of Agriculture statistics show a decline in the annual per capita use of eggs during the period 1974 to 1984.

More concrete: According to U.S. Department of Agriculture statistics, the average American ate fewer eggs in 1984 than in 1974.

Often you may not be able to make your writing more concrete simply by changing a few words. If your sentences are filled with abstract and general terms, you may find that you need to explore your subject more deeply in order to find specific examples. Vague language often indicates vague or incomplete thinking.

Vague: Bobby Deerfield has a routine life until love enters his empty world.

Specific: Bobby Deerfield—a man who is emotionally half dead, whose human relationships are as mechanical as the formula 1 car he drives or the commercials he grinds out for extra money—starts coming to life again because of his love for Lillian.

EXERCISE

A. Mark specific or concrete sentences with S *and vaguely worded ones with* X. *Rewrite the latter so that you support abstractions with concrete words and replace general points with specific ones.*

Example: Please try to contact all those who might help.

Please try to telephone all the social committee members who might help.

x   1. Many young people deprived of childhood fantasies turn to various types of escapism.

s   2. Since Sputnik first beeped its way around the world in 1957, the United States has more than caught up with the Russians in space.

x   3. Examination of the plan was carefully done by all the committee members.

x   4. In many cases, consumers are easily misled by advertising.

s   5. Toy commercials on television manipulate children's minds.

x   6. The installation of these parts can be easily achieved by our company.

x   7. A married couple needs many resources.

x   8. Many people tend to think that a college degree is a major factor in achieving success.

x   9. The government official visited the company's new facilities.

70

x   10. Compliance with federal rules results in excessive expenditures of time and energy on the part of college officials.

B. *Expand the following dull sentences by adding specific, concrete words.*

1. The president must be many things to many people.
2. After considerable struggle, we caught some fish.
3. California is not only our largest state but also one of the most varied.
4. Alfred Hitchcock's movies contain a great deal of suspense.
5. Dietetic variations of many foods are now available.

71 ww   Make sure you understand the meanings of words.

A well-chosen word, Eric Sevareid once said, is worth a thousand pictures. If you are to select the word that expresses precisely what you intend to say, you must understand its denotation, what it literally means. If you write *notorious* when you mean *famous*, or *erotic* when you mean *erratic*, you will confuse your readers and cause them to doubt your competence as a writer. The Glossary of Usage (page 430) lists a number of easily confused words.

Imprecise: Chemical research includes effort, time, and efficiency. (Effort, time, and efficiency do not constitute chemical research.)

Precise: Chemical research *requires* effort, time, and efficiency.

71

Imprecise: The President's analyzation of the current economic situation differs from that of his advisers.

Precise: The President's *analysis* of the current economic situation differs from that of his advisers.

EXERCISE

A. Use your dictionary to determine the difference between these paired words:

1. apprehend—comprehend
2. simple—simplistic
3. notable—notorious
4. exceedingly—excessively
5. disinterested—uninterested

6. fortunate—fortuitous
7. feasible—possible
8. forceful—forcible
9. illusion—allusion
10. censor—censure

B. Is the italicized word in each of the following sentences correct? If not, supply the correct word.

1. If inflation is gradually ~~subjugated,~~ overcome, the economy will

   continue to improve.

2. In his speech, the senator gave ~~tacit~~ implicit approval to the

   conference.

3. At the ~~onset~~ beginning of the class, the instructor gave a sur-

   prise quiz.

4. My dad still has ~~a mania~~ an enthusiasm for high school football.

5. Louise's office ~~services~~ serves disabled students.

                                           involved
6. John did not wish to be ~~implicated~~ in his wife's

   problems.
                                     a famous
7. My voice coach was once ~~an infamous~~ tenor at the

   Metropolitan Opera.
                  implies
8. Love ~~infers~~ trust.
          underlying
9. The ~~underlining~~ reason for the novel's melancholy

   tone is the author's unhappy youth.

10. With further education and reading, I hope to be-
                  better informed.
    come ~~more opinionated.~~

Make sure the connotations of your words are appropriate.

We choose words for their literal as well as for their implied
meanings. Whereas **denotations** (literal dictionary definitions) are neutral, **connotations**—the suggested or implied
meanings of words—convey feelings and attitudes and include emotional overtones. The dictionary, for example, defines *politician* as one who actively engages in politics. But if
you call a fellow student "a real politician," you call up not the
literal meaning of *politician*, its denotation, but its connotations: your fellow student is a smooth operator. Consider the
differences in tone in each of these sentences:

The faculty senate *discussed* the proposed grading system.
The faculty senate *debated* the proposed grading system.

Appropriate Diction

The faculty senate *argued about* the proposed grading system.

The faculty senate *quarreled over* the proposed grading system.

After three hours of *questioning,* the *detained protesters* were *released.*

After three hours of *grilling,* the *political prisoners* were *liberated.*

The dictionary can help you distinguish among various synonyms whose meanings overlap yet remain distinct:

> —*rare* is applied to something of which there are not many instances or specimens and usually connotes, therefore, great value [a *rare* gem]; *infrequent* applies to that which occurs only at long intervals [his *infrequent* trips]; *uncommon* and *unusual* refer to that which does not ordinarily occur and is therefore exceptional or remarkable [her *uncommon* generosity, this *unusual* heat]; *scarce* applies to something of which there is, at the moment, an inadequate supply [potatoes are *scarce* these days].
>
> —*Webster's New World Dictionary*

Many words have powerful social and political overtones. Because they may evoke personal, emotional responses in those who hear or read them, you must be conscious of their connotations. *Loaded words,* used especially by propagandists and advertisers, appeal to emotion rather than reason. Such words are imprecise and biased. Words such as *un-American, radical, leftist, subversive,* and *reactionary* indicate prejudicial political stereotyping. Journalists sometimes refer to liberals as "bleeding hearts" or to welfare payments as "government handouts."

72a   Avoid sexist language.

Among the changes occurring in contemporary usage is that writers are trying to avoid sexist language and are using less offensive, more inclusive terminology. Although much of this terminology was once exclusively male, the language preferred today is designed to include women. Good examples are the changes in job titles from *salesman* to *salesperson* and the change from the generic use of *man* or *mankind,* in referring to both men and women, to *human beings* or *humankind.* Other gender-neutral terms that prevent sex-role stereotyping are:

chairperson, chair	*rather than:* chairman
member of the clergy	clergyman
firefighter	fireman
personnel	manpower
member of Congress, legislator	congressman
worker	workman

You can also avoid using singular masculine pronouns *(he, him, his)* to refer to both men and women when you are unsure of the gender of the antecedent or when both sexes are involved (see Agr, **39b**). That is, you can change:

Every writer has *his* own story to tell.

to:

Every writer has *his or her* own story to tell.

But since the use of *his or her* can become awkward, a better strategy is to use the plural:

Writers have *their* own stores to tell.

You can also rewrite sentences so that the issue of gender does not arise:

Before starting his practice, a physician must put in many long, hard years of work.

Before starting a practice, a physician must put in many long, hard years of work.

72

A. Complete the following sentences by selecting the most appropriate words:

1. Under the circumstances, the cashier's attitude toward the robber was surprisingly _____ (lenient, reasonable, temperate).

2. Beginning drivers are often a bit too _____ (wary, cautious, discreet).

3. Because of some low grades, my plans to attend law school do not seem _____ (feasible, possible, practicable, probable).

4. Paloma attended only one of our _____ (scarce, rare, infrequent, unusual) meetings.

5. The new model-Z car is an unbeatable combination of European _____ (skill, genius, artistry, craftsmanship) with the traditionally _____ (courageous, bold, intrepid) American design. This accounts for its _____ (peculiar, distinctive, special) style.

B. Rewrite these sentences, eliminating sexist language.

72

1. The Western civilization course concerns the history

       human

   of ~~man's~~ ingenuity and persistence.

2. A racing-car driver should first attend classes at

       or her

   his local drivers' school.

                         officers

3. The mayor requested two additional police~~men~~ to

   staff

   ~~man~~ the polling place.

               s   **their**

4. Success for a law school student depends on ~~his~~

   command of language skills.

       person

5. A ~~man~~ alone is in bad company.

C. How do the connotations of these paired words differ?

1. cheap—inexpensive
2. design—shape
3. tough–durable
4. invincible—unbeatable
5. distinguished—distinctive
6. startled—shocked
7. spinster—bachelor
8. childish—childlike
9. brilliance—ingenuity
10. smart—elegant

D. Replace any loaded words in the following paragraph:

                        project,

My opponent's latest ~~boondoggle,~~ which has been properly

criticized   **ideas**

~~blasted~~ by the news media, is typical of the ~~schemes and~~

72

            presented to   partner
promises he has ~~foisted on~~ the voters. His ~~accomplice~~ in
   project   well-known friend
this ~~deal~~ is a ~~notorious crony~~ of organized crime who has
                 deceive   manipulate
tried everything to ~~hoodwink~~ and ~~brainwash~~ public

opinion.

---

73 fig Use figures of speech to create vivid images.

Figurative language or imagery is not limited to poetry. Comparisons between the familiar and the less familiar are a basic part of everyday communication. When we talk about a politician playing hardball, we are not speaking literally about sports, but figuratively: we are comparing two unlike things that are similar in some often unexpected way. Figures of speech can clarify a point and make writing come alive by creating vivid pictures for the reader. The most commonly used figures are similes and metaphors.

Similes are direct, explicit comparisons, using *like* or *as:*

> "His arms were too long for his shirt sleeves, and his hands dangled out like big price tags."
>
> —Fred Chappell

> "The oar broke in my hand like a stalk of celery."
>
> —Student

Metaphors are indirect, implied comparisons, without *like* or *as:*

"Churchill mobilized the English language and took it to war."

—John F. Kennedy

"Doreen's white hair stood out in a cotton-candy fluff around her head."

—Student

Personification is a type of metaphor that gives human qualities to inanimate objects or abstractions: Patriotism is a word all dressed up in red, white, and blue.

Compare these statements to see how a dull literal statement can be made more lively with imagery:

Dull: Her face was large, childlike, and blank.

Vivid: "Her face was as broad and innocent as a cabbage."

—Flannery O'Connor

Dull: This movie is empty and pretentious.

Vivid: "This movie is a toupee made up to look like honest baldness."

—Pauline Kael

If, however, you cannot create a fresh metaphor that fits your subject, rely on an accurate literal statement. A dull, over-used metaphor (see **75**) will only demonstrate that you are not original; a wildly inappropriate or strained metaphor will spoil what you have to say.

Strained: Nutrition has long been a poor foster-child in medicine, a Cinderella who must flee before the nation's clock strikes midnight.

Strained: The photographer's lens is riveted to life's passing parade.

73

A. Complete each of the following with an original metaphor or simile.

1. After working for thirty-six hours without stopping,

   Tom was so tired that _____ .

2. The judge listened, as impartial as a _____ .

3. Banks of snow suddenly shifted and then collapsed

   like _____ .

4. The old woman's hair was so thin that _____ .

5. The old charred books _____ in my hands like

   pieces of _____ .

B. List as many figures of speech as you can that are derived from baseball, such as "ballpark figure."

C. Revise the following strained images so that they create clear and consistent pictures.

1. The rising sun, pushing aside the darkness, spit out

   a glowing welcome sign over the horizon.

2. The sun slowly sank in the bosom of the distant hills

   as night made its appearance on the sky's dark

   stage.

3. The idea blossomed, then quickly crept away like a ghost into the cellar of his haunted brain.

4. The empty spaces on the library shelves grinned broadly, like a gap-toothed crone.

5. The poet cuts away at our illusions, like a butcher hacking away at a carcass.

---

74 fig | ## Make your figures of speech consistent with each other and with your subject.

Metaphorical language is so common that writers may be unaware of the comparisons their words evoke. For example, when you speak of "grasping" or "catching" rather than "understanding" what a writer is saying, you are making a simple comparison between the mind and hands. If you speak of being "flooded with memories," you are using another metaphor: the mind is the land, the memories the floodwaters. But if you were to say, "When I grasped what he was saying, it flooded me with memories," you would have a **mixed metaphor,** two images that conflict with each other. Mixed metaphors are a sure sign that you are not thinking about the pictures your words create:

Mixed: The scandal that rained on the presidential parade nearly derailed it.

Mixed: The theater of life is often a valley of tears.

Revise trite figures of speech whether they conflict with other images or not (see **75**), and make sure that your images call up pictures that fit your subject.

EXERCISE

Explain why the figures of speech in the following sentences are ineffective.

1. The senator, fishing in troubled waters, went out on a limb on the abortion issue.

2. If the President keeps the ship of state on an even keel, America will be pulled out of the moral quagmire of recent years.

3. Our language seems to be coming apart at the seams because writers burn themselves out on a diet of clichés.

4. The bottom line on inflation boils down to some tough decisions which Congress may find hard to swallow.

5. Evelyn didn't have a leg to stand on after the judge warned her that she was skating on thin ice.

In conversation, we often use stale expressions without thinking about what they mean. But writers have time to think and so should try to make the most of their words.

Clichés. Many of the figures of speech that come most readily to mind were once fresh images. But through overuse, they have lost their effectiveness. We too easily substitute these trite expressions, or **clichés,** for original thought. No reader will be impressed by such hackneyed images as *fresh as a daisy* or *dead as a doornail.* Here is a brief list of clichés that have lost their value as figures of speech:

acid-test	grind to a halt
beat around the bush	in a nutshell
by leaps and bounds	nipped in the bud
bit the dust	light as a feather
crystal clear	no stone unturned
explore every avenue	playing with fire
frosting on the cake	silver lining

Fillers. Also common are useless phrases such as *in a very real sense, so to speak, as it were, needless to say, it goes without saying,* and *as a matter of fact.* These phrases add words but no meaning. Here are some others to avoid:

all in all	last but not least
better late than never	part and parcel
each and every	point with pride
easier said than done	rain or shine
few and far between	short and sweet
first and foremost	safe and sound
golden opportunity	without rhyme or reason

Using an original metaphor, Richard Altick sums up the point: A writer should provide "traction for the readers' minds rather than allow them to slide and skid on a slippery surface paved with well-worn phrases."

Euphemisms. A **euphemism** refers indirectly to something unpleasant or embarrassing. For example, many people use *pass away* or *expire* to mean *die.* A euphemism is sometimes the best way to avoid hurting someone's feelings; but many euphemisms are trite, many are wordy, and many conceal truths that should be plain.

Members of Congress seldom mention *bribes, graft,* and *expense-paid vacations;* they do mention *honorariums, campaign contributions,* and *travel reimbursement.* The result of such language is a dangerous double-talk that misleads readers and distorts truth.

Trite and wordy: under the influence (drunk)
                     stretch the truth (lie)
                     woman of the streets (prostitute)

Misleading: civil disturbance (riot)
                     protective reaction strikes (bombing)
                     inoperative statement (false, retracted statement)
                     revenue enhancement (tax increase)

EXERCISE

A. *To see how easily clichés come to mind, complete the trite expressions in the following "speech":*

"First and _____foremost_____ as you travel down the

_____road_____ to success, you will face many challenges

_____above_____ and beyond the call of _____duty_____ . If

you persevere, you will pass life's greatest tests with

_____flying_____ colors; and you can then point with

_____pride_____ to your achievement. For you will then be truly in a class __by yourself__. In the _____final_____ analysis, when all is _____said_____ and _____done_____ , it goes without _____saying_____ that each and _____every one_____ of you can succeed only if you _____tow_____ the line and keep your _____shoulder_____ to the wheel as well as your _____nose_____ to the grindstone. Last but not _____least_____ , I must remind you that all of this is _____easier_____ said than _____done_____ ."

B. *Find a euphemism for each of the following:*

1. bossy **assertive**
2. cheap **inexpensive**
3. steal **permanently borrow**
4. spy **intelligence agent**
5. ugly **unattractive**

C. *Find equivalents for the following clichés and euphemisms:*

1. raining cats and dogs
2. life in the fast lane
3. bottom line
4. severe nutritional deficiency
5. electronic surveillance
6. revenue enhancement
7. bite the dust
8. nipped in the bud
9. wedded bliss
10. uphill fight

75

76 flowery   Avoid pretentious and unfamiliar words.

In general, write in plain English. Although you should try to build a rich vocabulary, strive to use it precisely, not just to show it off. "Pomposity," "flowery diction," "overwriting," and "fine writing" are just some of the terms used to describe the common mistake of using big words where more familiar words would be more appropriate to the audience and subject. Use a long formal word only when it expresses your meaning exactly, and avoid falsely poetic, foreign, and artificially formal terms:

Pretentious: The several members of the fraternal organization caroused in a buoyant spirit of nocturnal wassailing.

Improved: Some of the fraternity members had a wild drinking party.

Pretentious: Perspicacious persons who take pen in hand, albeit bewitched by the glitter of polysyllabic utterance, do so with the intent to eschew obfuscation.

Improved: Despite the attraction of fancy words, smart writers avoid obscure language.

EXERCISE

Translate the following pretentious sentences into more direct English.

1. Harvey, albeit inebriated, was not guilty of prevarication when he asserted that his position had been terminated.

76

2. The employment of astrological prognostication can reap a bountiful pecuniary harvest.

3. A not unimportant date is that of our impending nuptials.

4. The novel is replete with the myriad adventures of intrepid characters.

5. The sky's stellar sentinels signaled the termination of the day.

6. Individuals who inhabit domiciles composed of frangible substances containing silicon compounds should be wary of casting hard, non-metallic mineral matter.

7. It is requested that superfluous illumination be extinguished upon exiting the premises.

8. Percipient weather prognosticators indicate that significant amounts of precipitation are anticipated in these United States.

9. The unauthorized ignition of tobacco-containing substances constitutes felonious behavior.

10. It will behoove underachievers to develop dialogues

with their respective learning facilitators.

| **77 jargon** | **When writing for the general reader, avoid jargon and highly technical language.** |

Nearly every specialized field develops its own specialized language: psychologists speak of *syndromes* and *psychoses,* computer operators discuss *core capacity* and *interface,* art critics refer to *texture* and *value contrast.* Among specialists, a specialized vocabulary can convey exact meanings. Among nonspecialists, however, the same vocabulary is only jargon, usually pretentious and confusing. If you want to use a technical term, ask yourself two questions: Do I really need the term? Will my readers understand it? If you do need the term and your readers might not understand it, be sure to define it.

Jargon also refers to the many unnecessarily technical expressions that grow up in most fields. Some of these expressions are euphemisms (see **75**), some just inflated language. Here are a few examples of educational jargon:

learning facilitator (= teacher)
exceptional student (= slow or fast learner)
underachiever (= slow student)
economically deprived (= poor)
learning resources center (= library)
experiential approach (= learn by doing)

Big words such as the following are often misused to give a technical flavor to nontechnical writing:

ameliorate (improve)	exhibit (show)
endeavor (try)	factor (item, point, cause)
inaugurate (begin)	*per se* (in itself)
individual (person)	peruse (read)
initiate (begin)	presently (now)
maximum (most)	utilize (use)
optimum (best)	viable (workable)

Here is President Kennedy's famous statement, "ask not what your country can do for you; ask what you can do for your country" translated into modern jargon:

> It is not deemed appropriate to make inquiry as to those initiatives to be actualized by this nation on behalf of individuals but, contrariwise, to ascertain the methodologies by which said individuals can maximize their optimum contributions to said nation.

Such bloated language prevents communication.

EXERCISE

Rewrite the following sentences, eliminating jargon.

1. ~~A vast majority~~ **Most** of the specimens ~~presently under examination exhibit~~ **being examined show** deteriorative tendencies ~~sugges-tive of~~ a virus as the ~~causal factor.~~ **cause of deterioration.**

2. ~~Within the parameters of~~ **In** the social sciences, ~~the thrust of~~ much research is ~~focused on ameliorating~~ **concerned with improving** conditions which ~~militate against the optimum ad-justment of partners in a marital situation.~~ **prevent happy marriages.**

3. Astrology ~~endeavors to maximize~~ the public's need for
   tries to provide people with
   spiritual meaning.
   ~~nonmaterial reinforcement.~~

   Just when I met with success, my
4. ~~My career had just plateaued when my company de-~~
   company went broke.
   ~~veloped a weakened cash-flow situation.~~

   Capitalism rightly believes that the
5. ~~There is truth in the capitalist belief that the salutary~~
   good fortune of others is also one's own.
   ~~fortune accruing to other individuals is also ulti-~~

   ~~mately one's own.~~

78 wdy rep   Avoid needless repetition and wordiness.

As you revise, look for ways to eliminate anything that does
not add to your meaning. Writers often pad sentences with
clichés (see **75**) and jargon (see **77**):

Wordy: As to the reason for the delay, it was not because
of the inefficiency of the plan in question.

Improved: The reason for the delay was not the inefficiency of
the plan.

Wordy: It is our supposition that the safety device in
question possesses the capability of being used by
the airlines.

Improved: We suppose that airlines can use this safety
device.

Avoid long verb phrases (*give consideration to* or *come to a
conclusion*); instead use simple, concrete verbs (*consider, con-*

78

clude). Avoid unneeded intensives *(indeed, really, quite frankly)*, windy openers *(it is, there are)*, and stock phrases such as these:

> due to the fact that (= because)
> in all probability (= probably)
> in excess of (= more than)
> in many instances (= often)
> in a similar fashion (= similarly)
> in the neighborhood of (= about)
> on a daily basis (= daily)
> in the event that (= if)
> on the part of (= by *or* among)
> a large number of (= many)
> a small number of (= few)
> during the time that (= while)
> small-sized (= small)

EXERCISE

Reduce each phrase to one word:

outside ~~of~~

plan ~~ahead~~

can ~~possibly~~

recur ~~again~~

question ~~as to whether~~

rectangular ~~in shape~~

~~quite~~ exact

cease ~~and desist~~

contain ~~within~~

visible ~~to the eye~~

in the ~~near~~ future

advance ~~forward~~

~~future~~ plans

~~possible~~ likelihood

disappear ~~from view~~

red ~~in color~~

~~absolutely~~ essential

~~most~~ unique

~~complete~~ monopoly

Replace each of these phrases with a single verb:

conduct an investigation   **(investigate)**

undertake the removal of   **(remove)**

result in damage to   **(damage)**

have a necessity for   **(need)**

take a measurement   **(measure)**
place a call to   **(call)**

78a   Eliminate meaningless intensives.

We tend to fill our speech with words such as *very, so, certainly, quite, really,* and *simply.* But in writing, we should eliminate most of these words because they are vague, insincere, or unnecessary. Clear thoughts do not usually need modifiers such as *very (clear), quite (clear),* or *really (clear).* So too it is best to avoid imprecise, extravagant modifiers like *fabulous, fantastic, terribly, awfully.*

78b   Eliminate obvious repetition and redundancy.

Other forms of wordiness include obvious repetition, redundancy (expressing the same idea in different ways, as in *cease and desist, basic essentials,* or *the reason is because*), and unnecessary negatives *(not unlikely).* See the Glossary of Usage (page 430) for some common redundant expressions and **29a** for repetition in sentences.

Obvious repetition:	When any two films are compared, one must consider many aspects. Some of these aspects are readily discernible. These aspects can, in fact, be similarities or differences.
Improved:	When comparing two films, one must consider both similarities and differences.
Redundant:	Throughout the entire story, Young Goodman Brown is tempted by the devil.
Improved:	Throughout the story, Young Goodman Brown is tempted by the devil.

78

Needless Negatives: It is not surprising that Wyatt's autobiography is not unexciting to read.

Improved: As expected, Wyatt's autobiography is exciting.

EXERCISE

A. Improve the following sentences by eliminating unnecessary words. Reword the sentences if necessary.

1. ~~It is~~ the unemployment situation ~~which~~ needs attention.~~at the present time.~~

2. The painter ~~employs the use of~~ **uses** color and light ~~very~~ effectively.

3. ~~There are~~ several statements in the book ~~that are~~ revealing the author's bias.

4. The letter was written by someone ~~whose name~~ **who** must remain ~~absolutely~~ anonymous.

5. **While investigating** ~~In the process of conducting her program of investigating~~ marital brutality, Dr. Steinmetz made some ~~truly~~ unique discoveries.

6. **Many** ~~It is noteworthy that not a few modern-day~~ airports **probably** ~~in all probability~~ serve ~~the needs of~~ a larger number

78

of passengers ~~on a~~ daily ~~basis~~ than they were ~~originally~~ intended to.

7. *The Zoo Story* is a play by Edward Albee. ~~It is a play that is~~ dealing with ~~the subject of~~ alienation.

8. ~~There is truth to the contention that~~ the causes of the Civil War were ~~in a very real sense~~ economic.

9. This ~~particular~~ device is hexagonal ~~in shape~~.

10. One reason for the economic decline is ~~because of~~ the ~~past~~ history of the deficit.

B. Explain the redundancy in each of the following, and reduce it.

1. present incumbent
2. personal friendship
3. advance planning
4. past experience/history
5. period of time

P A R T

A PRACTICAL

GUIDE TO

WRITING

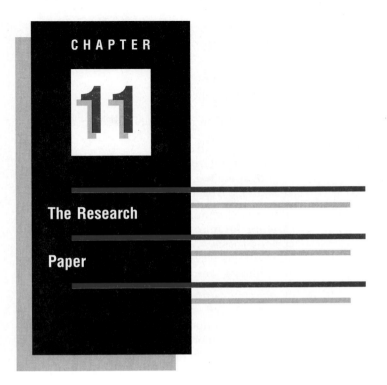

CHAPTER

11

The Research

Paper

The research paper is a documented essay containing citations to the sources you have consulted. It combines your own ideas, experiences, and attitudes with supporting information provided by other sources. These sources allow you to develop your topic with informed opinions, which you support with the evidence you have gathered. Using sources properly will help you write more authoritatively.

The process of research involves these principal activities:

1. Searching for a topic and for library sources
2. Reading to select an appropriate topic and to gather information
3. Evaluating information and ideas
4. Organizing and writing the paper

Or the process might be more fully outlined as follows:

Step 1. Beginning the research
        Choosing an interesting subject
        Selecting a limited topic
        Developing a working thesis

Step 2. Locating and skimming sources
        Searching for information relevant to your working thesis
        Eliminating irrelevant information
        Re-examining your working thesis

Step 3. Reading sources and drawing conclusions
        Reading selected sources carefully
        Taking detailed notes
        Analyzing the information
        Developing a thesis statement

Step 4. Writing the paper
        Composing the first draft
        Revising the paper
        Adding documentation
        Typing and editing the final draft
        Preparing the "Works Cited" (bibliography) page
        Proofreading and submitting the paper

Taking the research paper assignment step by step, as outlined in this chapter, and giving yourself adequate time for each step in the process will make the task more profitable and manageable.

79 Select an interesting, manageable topic.

Research papers too often become long recitations of facts and opinions copied out of library books. The best way to avoid producing anything so unoriginal and to eliminate needless drudgery is to choose a subject you already know something about and want to learn more about. As you read general reference books, consider aspects of the broad subject that experts differ on. And look for a topic that can be covered within the limits of your assignment. Then your research will not only satisfy your curiosity but will also allow you to write with authority about a topic that means something to you. By examining facts, sifting evidence, and comparing opinions, you will be able to arrive at your own conclusions and keep your own contribution at the center of your paper.

If you are free to choose your own subject, do not try to read everything you can find on sports, nature, art, or whatever general field most interests you. You must focus on one small corner of that field: not sports but the problem of violence in hockey; not nature but the causes of weed pollution in certain lakes; not art but the influence of Cézanne on cubist painting. An arguable topic—one that has at least two sides—or one involving a problem will let you approach the question in an interesting way. Your instructor may propose a general subject, such as "television advertising," and challenge you to develop your own topic. Out of that you might develop these:

Types of deception used in television commercials
Sexual stereotyping in television commercials
Government regulation of television advertising
Methods advertisers use to influence programming

You can save yourself time if you avoid certain predictable kinds of unsuitable topics:

Topics too complex or controversial to be handled in anything less than a book: "AIDS research"

Topics so limited that you can find only a few brief sources: "developing Ektachrome"

Topics so new that little has yet been published on them

Topics so cut-and-dried that you can do little more than summarize your sources in a report on your reading: "the life of Benjamin Franklin"

Topics about which you can learn little that is not already known to most people: "cigarettes are harmful"

Topics about which you have such strong feelings that you might not be able to evaluate what you read objectively

---

EXERCISE

A. *Decide which of the following topics would be suitable for a documented paper of eight to ten pages. Mark these with* S. *Mark with* X *those that would be unsuitable. Explain the reasons for your views.*

S   1. How global warming can be stopped

X   2. Animal experimentation is immoral

X   3. Pollution of our resources: one of the chief problems facing America today

S   4. Fairy tales are not harmful to children

S   5. Five reasons that capital punishment should be abolished

X   6. Baseball's long and colorful history

X   7. Football is too violent

X   8. Democracy works better than communism

X   9. How Franklin D. Roosevelt could have prevented war with Japan

X 10. Who really killed John F. Kennedy?

x 11. There *is* intelligent life on other planets!

s 12. Job opportunities for respiratory therapists

s 13. How spin-offs from the space program affect our daily lives

s 14. Alternate food sources for the Third World

x 15. Women in political life

B. *Focus the following subjects more sharply to create topics suitable for a documented paper.*

1. gun control
2. television news
3. science fiction
4. criminal justice
5. teenage alcoholism
6. reggae music
7. word processors
8. photography
9. energy sources
10. noise pollution

80 Explore library resources.

Before you settle on a topic, be sure that you can find enough material to develop that topic. First, decide on a research plan that suits your library resources, your topic, and your available time. A typical procedure is to read general reference books such as encyclopedias to get an overview of the subject and to help you narrow the focus to a manageable topic. You might then search for books (through the card catalog) and magazine and journal articles (through periodical indexes) that you can skim to see how relevant they are for your purposes.

In his paper on year-round schools (see p. 373), Russ Thomas began with the computerized catalog in his college library to see what books were available. Finding nothing under that subject heading, he asked the reference librarian for help and was introduced to a database file on education, ERIC (Educational Resources Information Center), which revealed several possible sources. He then used the *Education Index* for additional articles. He skimmed the material he found before selecting the sources to be read more carefully.

As you develop a basic bibliography—a list of books, articles, and other sources you will investigate—write on a 3″ × 5″ card the call number, author's full name, full title, and other pertinent information for each source. Being complete and using correct form (see **86**) will save you time later when you prepare your final paper.

80a Locating Information

The library catalog. Whether your library is traditional or computerized, its main catalog of books—the card catalog—will be arranged by author, title, and subject. Use subject headings to locate material on your topic. To determine the headings under which books are likely to be cataloged, consult the two-volume *Library of Congress Subject Headings.* When Russ Thomas began his search for material on year-round schools, he found the following in LCSH:

> Schedules, school
> RT school year (= restricted topic)

He then looked up "school year" in the subject index of his college catalog and found these books listed:

1. semester system (1984) LB 2347 .P37
2. annual school plan (1977) LB 3034 .P56
3. issues in year-round education (1977) LB 2347 .R52
4. year-round education (1973) LB 3034 .M32
5. year-round school program (1973) LA 245 .C47 .S47

Bibliography Card: Book

Servetter, Leonard. _Year-Round School Program: A Case Study._ Chula Vista: People Education and Communication Enterprises, 1973.

LA 245
.C 47
.S 47

Bibliography Card: Periodical

Gitlin, Lisa. "Does Year-Round Education Really Make Sense? _The Education Digest_ 54.3 (1988): 16-18.

L 11
.E 265

6. year-round school (1971) LB 3034 .H44
7. the year-round school (1970) LB 3034 .A45

After copying the call numbers of the more recent titles, he went to the shelves to see which of these would be most useful for note taking and copied on bibliography cards the complete information (author, title, publishing data, call number) for those books. He discovered, however, that periodical literature provided more up-to-date facts.

Periodical indexes. Since some of the most current information is available in magazine and journal articles, the various indexes to periodical literature are essential in almost every library research project. Just as the card catalog is the key to books, so the periodical guides are the keys to articles. Do not limit yourself to the best-known and most general of these indexes, the *Readers' Guide to Periodical Literature.*

General indexes:

> *Humanities Index* (1974–   ); formerly the *Social Sciences and Humanities Index* (1965–73) and the *International Index* (1907–65)
> *New York Times Index* (1913–   )
> *National Newspaper Index* (1979–   )
> *Newsbank* (1970–   ), microfiche compilation of articles from more than one hundred newspapers
> *Readers' Guide to Periodical Literature* (1900–   )
> *Social Sciences Index* (1974–   ); formerly the *Social Sciences and Humanities Index* (1965–73) and the *International Index* (1907–65)

Specialized indexes:

> *Applied Science and Technology Index* (1958–   )
> *Art Index* (1929–   )
> *Biography Index* (1946–   )
> *Biological and Agricultural Index* (1964–   )

Business Periodicals Index (1958–   )
Central Index to Journals of Education (1969–   )
Education Index (1929–   )
General Science Index (1978–   )
Index to Legal Periodicals (1908–   )
MLA International Bibliography [literature, language]
    (1921–   )
Music Index (1949–   )
Public Affairs Information Service Bulletin (1915–   )
See also the various abstracts: *Abstracts of English Studies,*
    1958–   ; *Biological Abstracts,* 1927–   ; *Chemical
    Abstracts,* 1907–   ; *Psychological Abstracts,*
    1927–   , etc.

Reference books. Also cited in the card catalog are the
library's encyclopedias, dictionaries, atlases, and many other
basic reference tools. Here are a few:

Special encyclopedias:

Encyclopedia of Education. 10 vols.
Encyclopedia of Philosophy. 8 vols.
Encyclopedia of World Art. 15 vols.
International Encyclopedia of the Social Sciences. 17 vols.
Langer, William L. *An Encyclopedia of World History*
McGraw-Hill Encyclopedia of Science and Technology.
    15 vols.
The New Catholic Encyclopedia. 15 vols.
Van Nostrand's Scientific Encyclopedia

Other:

Britannica Book of the Year (1938–   )
Current Biography (1940–   )
Dictionary of American Biography. 10 vols.
Dictionary of National Biography. (British). 22 vols.
Facts on File (1941–   )
Statistical Abstract of the United States (1878–   )
The Times Atlas of the World.
World Almanac and Book of Facts (1868–   )

Libraries also contain pamphlets, government documents, films, filmstrips, videos, tapes, records, and other non-printed sources. Research can also include information gathered from interviews and questionnaires.

EXERCISE

Compile a bibliography of at least ten sources (both books and articles) on a topic that interests you. Use at least four of the following reference works. After each entry, cite the title of the work that referred you to that book or article.

1. Card catalog—subject index
2. *Readers' Guide to Periodical Literature*
3. *Essay and General Literature Index*
4. *Social Sciences Index, Humanities Index,* or *Applied Science and Technology Index*
5. Either *Public Affairs Information Service* or *The New York Times Index*
6. One of the general or specialized encyclopedias listed above (under "Reference Books")

81 Evaluate your sources of information.

Analyzing the material you find is always important. Not everything in print is reliable, and some sources carry more weight than others. A short article in a popular magazine will seldom be as authoritative as a book or journal article, but even a book may represent just one person's thinking about a subject. Always be careful to distinguish between facts and opinions. As you examine any source, ask yourself these questions:

> Is the writer a recognized authority on the subject, one whose work is cited by other writers?
>
> Does the work seem to be biased? Does the author give sufficient attention to other points of view?
>
> Is the work recent enough to provide up-to-date information?

Aim for a balanced bibliography that reflects as many viewpoints as possible and that includes journal articles as well as books and magazine articles. If half of your sources consist of articles from one periodical, search further. Scholarly journals provide more thoroughly documented material than magazines, which might be general, exaggerated, or slanted to reflect a particular bias. For a paper on acid rain, for example, you would not consult a newspaper article but a journal such as *Nature* or *Science.* Interviews, if they provide information not easily found in published sources, can be useful as long as those interviewed are knowledgeable and objective. Corporations, museums, government agencies, specialized organizations (the Red Cross, for example), as well as your class notes can also provide information not found in libraries.

After researching printed indexes and bibliographies, you may wish to supplement your material by using some of the increasing types of database files available through your library. The use of on-line database computer facilities can help you broaden or limit the scope of a research project. First, check with the librarian to determine if the costs to you will make such a search worthwhile. Next, work with the librarian to formulate the appropriate computer terminology. Developing key terms, or descriptors, for the search requires some new skills and an understanding of information accessing. Then select a specific file, which is accessible to your library through a national network of research files. These include PAIS (Public Affairs Information Service), Newsearch (a daily index of news articles from 1,400 newspapers and periodicals), ERIC (Educational Resources Information Center), and many other specialized databases.

Primary and secondary sources. Primary sources are the actual texts of reports, novels, and documents, as well as interviews, recordings, and other original material. Secondary sources are the critical and historical accounts based on primary materials. For a paper on the space shuttle, for example, your primary sources might include reports from NASA as well as interviews with or letters from space officials. For a paper on educational television for children, reports of experiments in childhood learning as well as the programs themselves would be your primary sources. Clearly, watching the programs would be essential to understanding the topic; you would not wish to get most of your information second-hand. Whatever your topic, locate and use as many primary sources as possible.

Secondary sources may help you find additional primary sources, and they can point out ways of interpreting those sources. By examining a number of secondary sources, you can determine which ones offer the most convincing interpretation of the facts. Since you will probably not have time to read all the available secondary sources in their entirety, check their indexes and tables of contents and skim chapters you think might help you. Also check each secondary source for a bibliography that might direct you to other sources.

EXERCISE

Mark A *if the source is appropriate for the topic cited. Mark* X *for inappropriate sources. What cautions would you have to take in using those marked* X?

x   1. *The Reliability of Public Opinion Polls:* a 1990
       Reader's Digest article

x 2. *Chimpanzees and Human Language:* a 1991 article
      in *People* magazine

A 3. *Religious Symbolism in Popular Music:* a 1991 article
      in *Harper's Magazine*

A 4. *The Greenhouse Effect:* a 1990 article in *Scientific
      American*

x 5. *Gun Control:* a 1981 pamphlet by the National Rifle
      Association

x 6. *Auto Safety:* Ralph Nader's 1965 book, *Unsafe at
      Any Speed*

x 7. *I.Q. Tests:* a 1947 article in the *Harvard Educational
      Review*

x 8. *Future of the Olympics:* a 1990 pamphlet by the U.S.
      Olympic Committee

A 9. *Portrayal of Blacks on TV:* a 1991 *New York Times*
      article

x 10. *Spin-offs from the Space Program in Our Daily Lives:*
      a 1975 NASA report

82 Prepare a preliminary thesis statement and working outline.

As early as possible in your research, formulate a tentative
statement of the main point you expect to make in your paper
(see **6**). You will need to change this preliminary thesis statement if further research gives you a new perspective, but
writing down the thesis early will help you concentrate your
note taking on material that supports, contradicts, or in
some other way bears directly on your main point.

  Next, consider the subpoints you will need to support your

thesis, and arrange these into a rough outline (see **7**). For example, if you are working on the future of the Olympic movement, your preliminary thesis and rough (working) outline might look like this:

Thesis: The Olympic Games are fated to die unless reforms are made.

  I. Ancient ideals need to be studied.

 II. Political rivalries should be abolished.

III. Commercial trends should be curbed.

As you develop the topic further, you will find ways to develop each of the subtopics: what was the original Greek idea, and how do the modern Games differ? How have politics and greed entered into the Games? How can specific solutions be found? You may also find new subtopics or discover that you have to change some of the ones you have. You might also find that you need to sharpen your thesis statement. For example, you could specify how changes in the Olympics would solve the recent problems:

> The Olympics can return to the ideals of peace, fellowship, and sportsmanship by avoiding political nationalism and commercial exploitation.

Think of your working outline as a flexible guide in your search for pertinent information. If you code your note cards to the sections of your rough outline, you will be able to see if you are finding enough information for each section and if you are turning up useful information that calls for changes in your outline.

EXERCISE

Suggest a thesis statement and a working outline of at least three main parts for one of the following topics.

The Research Paper

1. Altering College Admissions Standards for Disadvantaged Applicants
2. Addictive Behavior
3. Training for Mentally Retarded Children
4. The Effects of Vitamin C
5. The Effect of Television on the Popularity of Football

83 Take thorough, accurate notes on your sources.

Your aim in taking notes is to record accurately and concisely the important facts from your sources. A 4″ × 6″ note card will provide room for substantial notes as well as for a subject heading and a key to the corresponding bibliography card. Use one card for each idea you record so that you can later sort the cards as you refine your organization. Each card should contain the following information:

1. *Subject.* In a few words at the top of the card, identify the information the card contains.
2. *Source.* List the author's name or an abbreviated title. Or you might number your bibliography cards and use the appropriate number to identify each note card.
3. *Page number.* If a quotation runs from one page to the next, use a slash line to indicate the page break. You may later want to use just part of the quotation.

The note itself may be a quotation, a paraphrase (rewording) of the original material, a précis, or a summary.

Quotation. Although most note taking should not be word-for-word copying, quote your source directly whenever you think you might want to give your reader the exact wording of your source. When quoting, follow these guidelines:

1. On your note card, place quotation marks around all direct quotations to remind yourself that the wording is not yours. This distinction is essential.

2. Copy your source exactly, including punctuation marks. If an error appears in the original, put [*sic*], meaning "this is the way I found it," in your notes.

3. Use an ellipsis mark of three spaced periods (. . .) to indicate omitted material within a direct quotation; avoid ellipses before quotations of only parts of sentences (see **58d** and the sample note card that follows).

4. Use square brackets for your own insertions in a quotation: "Last year [1984] Americans spent more than $3 billion on pet foods alone."

Paraphrase (rewording). Direct quotation is not the only way to record the material you will use. You can reword passages from your sources, being careful to capture the ideas of an author without copying his or her sentence structure or word choice. You do not have to change every word in your source; simply write in your own style, and note the exact location of the ideas you are rephrasing. When your source contains phrases that you think deserve direct quotation, you can combine paraphrase and quotation, but be sure to distinguish carefully between your words and those of your source.

Summary. Instead of copying or carefully paraphrasing background information or other material that you will not need to present in detail, write a brief summary. Record the important facts; skip unimportant details. Early in your note taking, you may want to take summary notes on sources you expect to investigate more carefully later. Rough summary notes can include abbreviations and incomplete sentences. Such notes give a quick sketch of material you may use and will be more fluently worded in your paper.

Précis. The précis, a very brief summary in your own words, is much more concise than a paraphrase and more polished in style than a summary. A précis note captures the tone of the original material and condenses it in your own language, quoting directly only distinctive words and phrases. In a précis, reduce paragraphs into sentences, articles into paragraphs, and full-length works into a page or two.

The following examples illustrate each of these four note-taking methods. Be sure to include source information (author and page number) on all note cards.

Note Card: Original Material

Nazi loyalty

"The early foreign policy triumphs of the Nazis and the intensity of their own convictions made it possible for Germans to overlook the excesses and brutalities of the regime. Long after the good days had passed and war had come and the shadow of defeat loomed before them, the majority of the people remained loyal to the regime and discountenanced disobedience or opposition. . . . Loyalty to Hitler persisted to the bitter end.

(Gordon Craig, "Facing up to the Nazis, <u>The New York Review</u>, February 2, 1989, p. 11.)

Note Card: Paraphrase

Craig, p 11   Nazi loyalty

Most Germans during the Nazi era remained intensely loyal to Hitler and his regime even after defeat seemed inevitable. Recalling earlier government successes, people tended to ignore Nazi savagery and to feel ashamed of any disloyalty.

Note Card: Summary

Craig, p 11   Nazi loyalty

Source deals with loyalty to Hitler and
his regime despite defeat. Reason: Early
Nazi successes led most Germans to
ignore brutal realities.

Note Card: Précis

Craig, p 11   Nazi loyalty

Most Germans remained loyal to Hitler
and his regime, overlooking their
inevitable defeat and government
brutalities because of earlier Nazi
successes and the "intensity of their own
convictions (Craig 11).

Careful note taking can help you avoid plagiarism (see p. 348) in your finished paper. It should also indicate your solid understanding of what you have read. For this reason, summaries and paraphrases are preferable to word-for-word copying. Some of the following examples are too close to the original wording to be effective paraphrases:

Original sentence: "*Gender* is a term that has psychological or cultural rather than biological connotations."

Poor paraphrase: *Gender* has psychological or cultural, not biological, implications.

Effective paraphrase: The word *gender* refers to behavior or culture, not biology.

Original sentence: "The ideal of strict objectivity is absurd."

Poor paraphrase: Complete objectivity is an absurd ideal.

Effective paraphrase: No one should strive to be completely objective.

Original quotation: "Human beings owe their biological supremacy to the possession of a form of inheritance quite unlike that of other animals: exogenetic or exosomatic heredity. In this form of heredity, information is transmitted from one generation to the next through non-genetic channels—by word of mouth, by example, and by other forms of indoctrination; in general, by the entire apparatus of culture."

(P. B. Medawar, "Unnatural Science," *The New York Review,* 3 Feb. 1977, p. 14)

Compare this with the following student note cards:

Note Card A (unacceptable)

Medawar, p. 14   cultural heredity

The biological supremacy of human
beings is due to their unique form
of inheritance called exogenetic or
exosomatic (p. 14). Such heredity is
transmitted from one generation to the
next through non-genetic, cultural
channels, such as example and word
of mouth.

This note is unacceptable because the first sentence is copied closely without acknowledgment; the second sentence closely follows the original wording. It will be difficult to determine later if these notes are quoted or paraphrased.

Medawar, p. 14   cultural heredity

Human beings have a biological
supremacy due to a type of inheritance
unlike that of other animals: exogenetic
or exosomatic heredity. This means that
one generation transmits heredity
information to another generation
through cultural, non-genetic channels.

This note is unacceptable because it will be unclear later whether the first sentence is quoted directly or not and whether the second is a paraphrase or summary from material on a different page.

Note Card C (acceptable)

Medawar, p. 14   cultural heredity

According to P. B. Medawar in <u>The New York Review</u>, man is superior to other animals because he possesses "exogenetic or exosomatic heredity (p. 14). This means that one generation transmits heredity to another generation through such non-genetic means as word of mouth, example, and other instruction; in short, says Medawar, through culture. (p. 14)

This note is acceptable because no plagiarism (see p. 348) will result; the source is clearly introduced and acknowledged while the expert's key terms are assimilated into the student's own writing.

As you read and take notes, consider possible subtopics which will complete the ideas in your rough outline (see **82**). These subtopics will help guide your reading and note taking, and your reading will provide ideas for more subtopics. You will then be organizing the paper as you prepare to write it. If you are investigating ways to restore the tarnished image of the Olympic Games, you might develop these subtopics:

flags and national anthems	presentation costs
drugs and steroids	security costs
permanent site	national scorekeeping

The order of the subtopics, as well as the subtopics themselves, will doubtless change as you find material and as your ideas develop.

Plagiarism. Plagiarism—presenting the words or ideas of others without giving proper credit—is both unethical and illegal. A writer cannot copy direct quotations without providing quotation marks and without acknowledging the source. When you put your name on a piece of writing, the reader assumes that you are responsible for the information, wording, and organization and that you will acknowledge the source of any fact or idea that is not your own.

Paraphrasing material or using an original idea that is not properly introduced and documented is a common type of plagiarism. This can result from sloppy note taking, in which you have not distinguished between your thoughts and those of your sources. To avoid plagiarism, follow these guidelines:

1. Introduce every quotation and paraphrase by citing in the text of your paper the name of the source of the material used.

2. Place quotation marks around all directly quoted material.

3. Rewrite paraphrased material so that it is faithful to the original ideas; it is not enough to rearrange sentences.

4. Document all source material used.

5. Include on the "Works Cited" page every source referred to in your paper.

EXERCISE

Read the following selections (documentation below), and then read the students' paraphrased versions. Revise the student paragraphs, rewriting and adding whatever documentation is needed to avoid plagiarism.

Original:

The secularization of sport, which began as soon as athletics were pressed into the cause of patriotism and character building, became complete only when sport became an object of mass consumption. The final stage in this process was the establishment of big-time athletics in the university and their spread from the Ivy League to the large public and private schools, thence downward into the high schools. The bureaucratization of the business career, which placed unprecedented emphasis on competition and the will to win, stimulated the growth of sports in another way. It made the acquisition of educational credentials essential to a business or professional career and thus created in large numbers a new kind of student, utterly indifferent to higher learning but forced to undergo it for purely economic reasons. Large-scale athletic programs helped colleges to attract such students, in competitive bidding for enrollments, and to entertain them once they enrolled.

—Christopher Lasch, *The Culture of Narcissism*
(New York: Norton, 1978), pp. 119–20.

Student:

Sports have become a major industry due in large part to

what has happened to athletics in universities. First,
as Christopher Lasch observes,
‸athletics were seen as a source of patriotism and character
(119–120).
building‸ Big-time sports, which helped colleges compete

for and attract students, spread from the Ivy League to

colleges elsewhere and then to the high schools. At the
, Lasch goes on,
same time‸the business world, with its emphasis on

competition, advanced the state of big-time sports by
"
making‸educational credentials essential to a business or
"(120).
professional career‸ As a result, many students began to

attend college for economic reasons rather than to pursue learning; and sports were essential in keeping them on the campuses.

Original:

For psychoanalysis, repression is not a simple forgetting of unpleasant things but an unconsciously compelled and traumatic forgetting that alters one's mental economy in certain drastic ways. The concept takes its scope from boldly universal assertions about the oedipal strivings of infants, the meaning of dreams and errors, the mechanisms whereby character and sexual preference are formed, and the causation and cure of psychoneuroses. Those claims have not been warranted by independent research, and much has been tellingly said against them. Thus, though something like repression may yet be found to exist, its loss of scientific favor in all the domains to which Freud applied it deprives the idea of explanatory force.

—Frederick Crews, "The Future of an Illusion,"
The New Republic, 21 January 1985, p. 28.

Student:

Frederick Crews says,
By repression,ₐpsychoanalysts do not simply mean the

forgetting of unpleasant things but ₐan unconsciously

compelled, traumatic forgetting ₐthat seriously affects the
(28).
individualₐ This idea is based on certain generalizations
, Crews asserts,
ₐabout sexuality, dreams, and the causes and cures of

psychoneuroses. Independent research has not validated

such generalizations, and many critics have attacked
them. Although ^Crews believes that "something like repression may yet be
found to exist,^ " he says, it has lost scientific credibility in those
areas to which Freud applied it^ (28).

---

84 | Organize, write, and revise the rough draft.

If you revise your rough outline as you collect information, you should be nearly ready to write your rough draft by the time you finish taking notes. But first review and refine the organization. Start with your thesis statement: does it clearly express what you now see as the central, unifying idea of the paper? (See **6**) If, for example, your initial thesis were "Library censorship is dangerous to our schools," your research might lead you to a more limited, precisely focused thesis:

> Censorship in high school libraries denies students their constitutional right to the free exchange of ideas.

A *sentence outline* can be especially useful at this point. Write a sentence stating each of the main ideas supporting your thesis. Then complete the outline with sentences that represent the subdivisions of your main points. You will be able to see how well the parts of your paper fit together, and you may be able to use many of the sentences as topic sentences for your main subsections. In its final form, the outline can serve as a guide for the reader to the contents of the paper.

To help make the organization of your material clear and logical, follow these conventions in outlining:

1. Make sure that *all* the divisions and subdivisions are complete sentences; do not mix phrases with sentences.

2. Type your thesis statement at the head of the outline, followed by capitalized Roman numerals for the main headings; then A, B, etc., for main subheadings; then 1, 2, etc.; then a, b, etc.

3. Always use at least two subdivisions. If you have "I. A.," you must logically have "I. B." As a general rule, subdivisions stand for blocks of material in the essay, not for single sentences.

4. Make the subdivisions logically consistent. If your first main division is "I. Students in four-year colleges" and your first two subdivisions are "A. Freshmen" and "B. Sophomores," then you must continue with "C. Juniors" and "D. Seniors," not "C. History majors" or "D. Student athletes."

A sentence outline is included with the research paper on pages 374 and 375.

Handling source material. Identify your sources so that readers can make their own judgment about the content and reliability. Make sure that material from your sources supports the points you wish to make and that your own voice is not drowned out by excessive quotations. If all the quoted and paraphrased passages were to be removed from the paper, it should still make sense. These guidelines will help you achieve that goal:

1. Write a topic sentence in your own words for each of your main paragraphs. Even if you later incorporate a quotation into a topic sentence or drop the topic

sentence altogether, writing it in your own words will help you make sure that the paragraph expresses your thought. (See **21**)

2. Use direct quotations only to emphasize significant points or to show your reader how your source expressed a key idea.

3. Avoid long paragraphs of quotations.

4. Make short quotations part of your own sentences: Frances FitzGerald says that history textbooks have changed so much that "many an adult would find them unrecognizable" (21).

5. Introduce quoted and paraphrased material so that your reader will know whose work you are citing: As B. F. Skinner said, "The goal of science is the destruction of mystery" (59).

6. After each paraphrase or quotation, place the page number in parentheses.

Revising the rough draft. You will probably need to revise your paper several times to make it read smoothly and say exactly what you want it to say. Check especially to see that your paragraphs are unified and sufficiently developed (see **22** and **24**) and that you have supplied transitions to guide your reader through the paper (see **23**).

Before typing your final draft, make sure that it is free of errors (spelling, mechanics, grammar, punctuation) and that its sentences are logical and its diction clear. Compare the final draft with your outline to make sure that they are consistent. (If not, decide which needs to be changed.) Type from your bibliography cards a "Works Cited" page for those materials you have cited in the paper. Eliminate sources you have not used, but include each source which appears in your annotation. Arrange the cards in alphabetical order by author (or title if there is no author), and type one continuous list according to the format outlined in **86**.

Documentation means including notes within your paper to tell readers where you located specific ideas and information and also including a list of your sources at the end of the paper. Documentation has two important functions: to give credit to the sources you have consulted and to enable your readers to look up the original material. Documenting also protects you against possible plagiarism (see p. 348): it distinguishes your thoughts and words from those of your sources.

The form followed in this book is the Modern Language Association's 1988 format, which uses parenthetical notes rather than footnotes or endnotes. Two other types of documenting, including that of the American Psychological Association, are briefly explained on pages 360–363. Many disciplines have their own style guides, for example:

American Psychological Association
American Chemical Society
American Mathematical Society
Council of Biology Editors

Consult your instructor about the preferred style guide in any course requiring a research paper.

According to MLA style, you document by using in-text citations of author and page, in parentheses, at the end of every sentence containing a quotation or paraphrase. For example:

American children need to learn traditional

information at an early age (Hirsch 31).

Under "Works Cited" at the end of the paper, you will provide in an alphabetical list the essential information about each source; your in-text citation must specify the page from which the quotation or paraphrase is taken.

What must you document? Since you have read extensively to prepare your research paper, you may think at first that nearly every sentence in the paper will have to be documented. But readers are interested in what *you* have to say, in how you have used your reading. Information that is common knowledge, short dictionary definitions, and well-known quotations do not require documentation. But every sentence taken from a source requires a citation so that the reader knows who says what—and with a minimum of disruption. Whenever possible, introduce each quotation and paraphrase with the name of the authority.

You must document the following:

1. All directly quoted material:

```
Paul Johnson asserts that "the outstanding non-

event of modern times was the failure of

religious belief to disappear" (698).
```

If you did not use the author's name to introduce the quotation, cite it along with the page:

```
(Johnson 698).
```

2. All paraphrased and summarized material:

```
The prestige of a college education, John W.
```

Gardner says, has led many people to assume
(falsely) that there is no other type of learning
after high school (103).

or:

According to John W. Gardner (103), the prestige
of a college education has led many people to
assume (falsely) that there is no other type of
learning after high school.

3. Facts and data that are not common knowledge:

Dylan Thomas was twenty years old when he left
Wales in 1934 for London (Ferris 23).

When two or more works by one author are listed in "Works
Cited," provide a shortened version of the title to prevent confusion. Here the complete title—*The Presence of the Word*—is
cited at the end of the paper:

Speech as sound, Ong says, is "irrevocably
committed to time" (Presence 40).

For repeated references to a primary source (such as a
play or poem), simple citations (such as to act, scene, and
line) will suffice once you have established the title of the
work:

Lear's dying words are, "Look there, look there!"

(5.3.316)

When several items are taken from the same source, such as four sentences in a paragraph giving statistics derived from a single book, use one citation at the end of the paragraph: this will indicate that all the data in the paragraph come from that book. In such cases, especially, introducing your sources is important. And strive for some variety in introducing quotations and paraphrases and incorporating them into your sentences fluently. Some possibilities are:

In his famous study of the Third Reich, William

L. Shirer describes the Nazi war machine (399).

Others, like Koehl (360) and Bloch (36-37),

present a different view.

From 1939 on, Johnson says, Hitler became a

militarist, ceasing "to play the politician, the

orator, the demagogue" (356).

As Bruce Pauley (102) has observed, . . .

Yet, according to one scholar (Fussell 245), the

issue in 1939 was . . .

Other historians disagree with this

interpretation (for example, O'Neill 52-59

and Binion 78-82).

Istvan Deak is surely right in agreeing with

Koehl that not even the SS in Nazi Germany was

totally committed (42).

Though you will most often combine quotation and paraphrase in short citations, occasionally you will use a longer
quotation to present an especially important point. If a quotation will take up more than four lines in your paper, indent
the quotation ten spaces from the left margin and omit quotation marks. Double-space the quotation but triple-space
between your text and the quotation. Introduce the quoted
material, using a colon to connect the introduction with the
quotation, as in this example:

Part of the reason for the Nazi party's

success was the German economy. In his 1983

survey of modern history, Paul Johnson provides

this summary evaluation:

Hitler's coming to power, therefore,

provided German industry with precisely

what it wanted to perform effectively:

government stability, the end of

politics and a sense of national

purpose. It could do the rest for

itself. Hitler was shrewd enough to

realize this. While he allowed the

```
party to invade every other sphere of

government and public policy, he kept

it out of industry and the army, both

of which he needed to perform at

maximum efficiency as quickly as

possible (295).
```

For subsequent citations to the same page in a source just cited, simply repeat the page (*Ibid.* and other Latin abbreviations are no longer used):

```
Another writer argues that "it may turn out that

apes do have a dim awareness of syntax" (Gardner

6). He also points out, however, that such a

discovery may not be major (6).
```

Content endnotes. Certain types of information cannot appropriately be included in the body of your paper. Such items include comments on your research process or on the sources you used, or acknowledgment of assistance you received. This information should be placed on a separate page labeled "Notes," following the last page of your text.

The accepted format for such notes is as follows:

```
1 On this point see also Kennedy (12) and

Garrett (119).

2 All citations to Shakespeare are to the

Bevington edition.
```

³ The data for this study were collected between 20 January 1989 and 7 August 1989 in Miami, Orlando, and Tampa, Florida.

⁴ This study has benefited from the research assistance of Brenda Gordon, graduate assistant, Department of English.

Include bibliographical information in "Works Cited," *not* in content endnotes. Place the consecutive note numbers in the text immediately following the relevant sentence, raised slightly above the line as in this example:

during the war.²

Other Forms of Documentation

A. APA style

In many business, social science, and other courses, you will be expected to follow the conventions of the American Psychological Association (APA). For full information, see *The Publication Manual of the American Psychological Association*, 3rd ed. (1983).

In general, APA style requires you to use an in-text parenthetical note for any passage requiring documentation and to list alphabetically all sources cited on a page titled "References" at the end of the essay.

1. The parenthetical note appears after the passage requiring documentation:

```
Most young adult users of marijuana, based on

1,325 persons interviewed, had also used other

illicit drugs and had "less conventional

lifestyles" (Kandel, 1984, p. 201).
```

or:

```
Kandel (1984) reports that most young adult users

of marijuana, based on 1,325 persons interviewed,

had also used other illicit drugs and had "less

conventional lifestyles" (p. 201).
```

The note is placed outside the quotation marks but before a period ending a sentence. An author's name need not be repeated in second and subsequent references to the same source; *p.* or *pp.* will suffice. If there are two authors, cite both names in all references:

```
(Melzoff and Moore, 1983)
```

Use ampersand (&), not *and*, if there are three or more authors. Cite all the names in the first note, and then abbreviate subsequent notes with *et al.* (and others):

First note: `(Kagan, Lein, & Romero, 1991)`

Subsequent notes: `(Kagan et al., 1991)`

If there is no author, use the title (abbreviated, if necessary) and the date:

```
("Newborn infants," 1989)
```

2. The "References" page at the end of the paper is a double-spaced, alphabetical list (by authors' last names) of the sources used. Begin each entry at the left margin, and indent subsequent lines three spaces. In titles, only the first word and proper nouns are capitalized, and quotation marks are not used for article titles:

For a book, follow this form:

```
Wilson, E. O.  (1984).  Biophilia.  Cambridge,

   MA: Harvard University Press.
```

(The last name of the author is followed by his or her initials and two spaces; the date in parentheses is followed by a period and two spaces; the title, underlined, is followed by a period and two spaces; the place of publication, followed by a colon, precedes the publisher, which is followed by a period.)

For articles in scholarly journals, follow this form:

```
Melzoff, A. N. & Moore, M. K.  (1983).  Newborn

   infants imitate adult facial gestures.

   Child Development, 54, 702-709.
```

For a magazine or newspaper:

```
Gardner, H.  (1981, December).  Do babies sing a

   universal song?  Psychology Today, pp. 70-76.
```

B. Alternate endnote/footnote style

Some instructors (in history, political science, philosophy, and other fields) may require you to document sources by using raised numbers in sequence to refer to endnotes or footnotes. Type each number half a space above the line directly after the final punctuation of the sentence:

```
Morrison refers to Sethe as a woman "of iron eyes

and a backbone to match."³
```

Endnotes appear on a page titled "Notes" at the end of the paper (preceding the "Works Cited" page). List each note consecutively (1, 2, 3, etc.), and double-space. Type the number without punctuation five spaces in from the left margin. Leave a space and type the author's name in normal order a half space below the number. Begin the second line (and subsequent lines) at the left margin. Note that commas replace periods and that parentheses surround publishing information. Place the page number(s) at the very end without punctuation or with the abbreviation *p.* or *pp.*

Endnote and footnote form:

```
³ Toni Morrison, Beloved (New York: Knopf,

1987) 9.
```

Works Cited form:

```
Morrison, Toni. Beloved. New York: Knopf, 1987.
```

Footnotes begin four lines below the last line of text on a page. Single-space footnotes but double-space between them.

86 Construct your list of Works Cited.

End the paper with an alphabetical list of the books, articles, and other sources you cite. This bibliography is titled "Works Cited." Although some instructors may require you to list all the works you consulted in preparing your research paper, the most common practice is to list only those sources you have used and cited. Copy on your bibliography cards the complete information for each such source, and keep the cards in alphabetical order by author's last name (or title if there is no author).

The following form for bibliography is that of the Modern Language Association.*

1. Since the list is alphabetical, place authors' last names first. (If no author or editor is given, alphabetize by title.)

2. Then list the full title. Use italics (underlining) for titles of books and periodicals; use quotation marks for articles, poems, essays, and parts of books.

3. Separate the items within the entry with periods.

4. For books, cite the publisher's city and a shortened form of the publisher's name: New York: McGraw-Hill, 1991. Use only the first city printed on the title page and the most recent copyright date.

5. For journals, cite the volume, year, and full pages: 12 (1984): 122–49. For magazines, the date and full

---

*For full information, see Joseph Gibaldi and Walter S. Achtert, *MLA Handbook For Writers of Research Papers,* 3rd ed. (New York: Modern Language Association, 1988).

pages: *Esquire* Feb. 1991: 60–62. (If pages are not continuous, use 60+.)

6. Double-space the lines of each entry, and indent the second line five spaces.

7. In listing two or more works by the same author, use three hyphens followed by a period instead of repeating the author's name:

Ong, Walter J. The Barbarian Within. New York:

    Macmillan, 1962.

---. The Presence of the Word. New Haven: Yale

    UP, 1967.

Works Cited Form: Books (MLA Style)

Single author:

Schiffhorst, Gerald J. John Milton. New York:

    Crossroad, 1990.

Two or three authors:

Marchetti, Victor, and John D. Marks. The CIA

    and the Cult of Intelligence. New York:

    Knopf, 1974.

Watson, David L., Gail deBortali-Tregerthan, and

    Joyce Frank. Social Psychology: Science and

    Application. Scott, 1984.

More than three authors:

Baugh, Albert C., et al. <u>A Literary History of</u>

    <u>England</u>. 2nd ed. New York: Appleton, 1967.

Translated and edited books:

Virgil. <u>The Aeneid</u>. Trans. Robert Fitzgerald.

    New York: Random, 1983.

Chaucer, Geoffrey. <u>The Works of Geoffrey</u>

    <u>Chaucer</u>. Ed. F. N. Robinson. 2nd ed.

    Boston: Houghton, 1957.

Gong, Victor, and Norman Rudnick, eds. <u>AIDS:</u>

    <u>Facts and Issues</u>. New Brunswick: Rutgers

    UP, 1986.

A work in an anthology:

Rubinstein, Arye. "Children with AIDS and the

    Public Risk." <u>AIDS: Facts and Issues</u>. Ed.

    Victor Gong and Norman Rudnick. New

    Brunswick: Rutgers UP, 1986. 99–103.

Note: The full pages of the article or chapter are cited; if you cite an article or essay in a collection of previously published works, list the earlier publication data along with *Rpt. in* (reprinted in):

C. S. Lewis. "Satan." <u>A Preface to "Paradise</u>

<u>Lost</u>." London: Oxford UP, 1942. 92-100.

Rpt. in <u>Milton: Modern Essays in Criticism</u>.

Ed. Arthur E. Barker. New York: Oxford UP,

1965. 196-204.

Encyclopedias:

"Melodeon." <u>Encyclopedia Americana</u>. 1985 ed.

Reprinted and revised editions:

Fitzgerald, F. Scott. <u>The Great Gatsby</u>. 1925.

New York: Scribner's, 1953.

Here the date of the original edition is included after the title
of a reprinted book. If an edition is other than the first, cite
Rev. ed. or *4th ed.* after the title.

Multivolume work:

If all volumes were used:

Parrington, Vernon L. <u>Main Currents in American</u>

<u>Thought</u>. 3 vols. New York: Harcourt,

1927-32.

If only one volume is used (with its own title):

Churchill, Winston S. The Age of Revolution.

    New York: Dodd, 1957. Vol. 3 of A History

    of the English-Speaking Peoples. 4 vols.

    1956-58.

Corporate author:

Committee on Telecommunications. Reports on

    Selected Topics in Telecommunications. New

    York: National Academy of Sciences, National

    Research Council, 1970.

Government publication:

United States. Dept. of Labor. Bureau of

    Statistics. Dictionary of Occupational

    Titles. 4th ed. Washington: GPO, 1977.

Works Cited Form: Periodicals

Article in journal (paged by volume):

Rofe, Yacov. "Stress and Affiliation: A Utility

    Theory." Psychological Review 91 (1984):

    235-50.

Article in journal (paged by issue):

West, Nancy M. "Order in Disorder: Surrealism in

 Oliver Twist." _South Atlantic Review_

 54.2 (1989): 41-58.

Article in monthly magazine:

Moffett, Mark W. "Dance of the Electronic Bee."

 National Geographic Jan. 1990: 134-40.

Article in weekly magazine:

Talbott, Strobe. "Rethinking the Red Menace."

 Time 1 Jan. 1990: 66+

Note: Abbreviate all months except May, June, and July. When the pages of an article are not continuous, list the first page followed by a plus sign. Otherwise always list the inclusive pages for all periodicals.

Article in newspaper:

Halprin, Mark. "A Single Bullet." _The Wall_

 Street Journal 12 Jan. 1990, Eastern ed.:

 A12.

(Most daily newspapers have section numbers that precede the page.)

Book review:

Anderson, Jarvis. "Life with Father: Duke

Ellington." Rev. of <u>Duke Ellington in</u>

<u>Person</u>, by Mercer Ellington. <u>New York Times</u>

<u>Book Review</u> 28 May 1978: 8.

Pamphlet:

Follow the form for books. If there is no date of publication, list *n.d.*; and if there is no publisher, list *n.p.*

Interview or letter:

Willis, Dr. Susan L. Personal Interview. 2 Feb.

1991.

Computer data:

Rosenberg, Victor, et al. <u>Pro-Cite</u>. Vers. 1.3.

Computer Software. Personal Bibliographic

Software, 1987. IBM PC-DOS 2.0, 256KB,

disk.

Database source:

Nevin, John J. "Doorstep to Free Trade."

<u>Harvard Business Review</u> 61 (1983): 88-95.

Dialog Information record no. 83-N43.

Film or TV program:

One Flew Over the Cuckoo's Nest. Dir. Milos

    Forman. With Jack Nicholson. Fantasy

    Films, 1975.

A Gathering of Men. With Robert Bly and Bill

    Moyers. PBS. WNET, New York. 8 Jan. 1990.

87 Research Paper Format (MLA style).

The following sample paper should answer most of your questions about the form of the research paper. It should be typed on white 8½″ × 11″ bond paper, double-spaced. Leave one-inch margins on all four sides of the page. Indent the first word of each paragraph five spaces from the left margin, and indent long quotations (more than four typed lines) ten spaces from the left margin. Such quotations, like the body and the list of works cited, are double-spaced.

Many instructors prefer a separate title page, as in the sample, with an accompanying outline as a guide for the reader, but these are not required by MLA style. Instead, on the first page you can type your name, the instructor's name, the course number, and the date on separate lines, double-spaced, starting one inch from the top of the page and flush with the left margin; this first page may also be numbered:

↑
1"
↓

87

1"→ Russell Thomas

Dr. Schiffhorst

ENG 1101

2 April 1990
↑
2 spaces
↓

Center the Title Here

Note that the title is not underlined, fully capitalized, enclosed in quotation marks, or ended with a period. Capitalize the first and last words of the title and all other words except articles (*the, an*) and prepositions and conjunctions with fewer than five letters (*in*). Double-space between the title and the first line of text.

Number your pages consecutively throughout the paper in the upper right-hand corner, one-half inch from the top. Type your last name, followed by the page number; this head is typed flush against the right margin. Double-space between this head and the text.

Year-Round Education: The Time Is Now

By

Russell Thomas

Composition 1

Dr. Schiffhorst

2 April 1990

Outline

Thesis: The time for year-round schools has arrived, for
         they can solve many of the mounting problems, such
         as overcrowding and inefficiency, that our
         educational system faces.

Type the thesis sentence at the head of the outline.

  I. Year-round schools are largely misunderstood.
      A. Parents' and students' misunderstandings are
          based on preconceived notions of how year-round
          schools operate.
      B. A wide variety of plans allows flexibility in
          implementing a year-round school system.
 II. Year-round schools offer advantages to those directly
      involved in education as well as to the community at
      large.
      A. Parents' and students' apprehensions about year-
          round schools are often dispelled after they have
          experienced such a system.
          1. Year-round schools offer greater flexibility
              in vacation planning.
          2. Students often retain knowledge more
              easily in a year-round plan.

For sentence outline form, see p. 43.
For sentence outline form, see p. 43.

        3.   Both marginal and gifted students benefit from a year-round school system.

    B.   Year-round schools provide economic benefits to school systems.

        1.   School facilities are used more efficiently.

        2.   Year-round schools relieve overcrowding.

    C.   Teachers also benefit from year-round plans.

        1.   Smaller class sizes make for less stressful situations.

        2.   Teachers have more time to plan curricula.

III. Some teachers point out drawbacks to year-round school plans.

 IV. Firsthand experience in a year-round school convinced the author of its merits.

  V. While year-round schools may not be the answer to every school system's problems, many communities are finding that the advantages of year-round schools far outweigh their disadvantages.

Use small roman numerals for preliminary pages (except for the title page and the first page of the outline).

Year-Round Education: The Time Is Now

One of the most misunderstood concepts in education
today is that of year-round schools. At the very mention of
this concept, many parents and students are ready with their
lists of the ways such a system will disrupt their lives. It
is ironic that although we Americans consider ourselves
pioneers, we are often unwilling to be objective when
confronted with a revolutionary idea. Most people's fears
concerning year-round schools are based on misconceptions
about the way they are designed to function. Some mistakenly
assume that classes will be held for twelve months, non-stop.
Students are often reluctant to give up their vacations; and
parents, convinced that the old system served them well,
resist the possibility that a new plan might be better.
While such preconceived notions are understandable, they can
be quickly dispelled once the opponents have experienced the
efficient and innovative nature of a year-round school plan.
The time for year-round schools has arrived, for they can
solve many of the mounting problems, such as overcrowding and
inefficiency, that our educational system faces.

A basic understanding of the way a year-round school
plan works is important to appreciate its merits. In setting

Repeat the title as the heading.

The opening paragraph provides background and leads to thesis sentence.

up such a system, a school board has many options, particularly regarding the number of tracks, or groups of students, into which each school will be divided. Under the simplest arrangement, called the single-track plan, all students in a school are on the same schedule, often a forty-five-day "on," fifteen-day "off" timetable, or some variation. This plan provides the traditional one hundred eighty days of classes, with four additional weeks allotted for winter holidays, spring vacation, and other holidays. Also common is the multitrack plan in which students are divided into two to four groups so that, except for a very brief schoolwide break at Christmas, the track vacations are arranged in such a way that one group of students is always on vacation at any given time of the year. The number of tracks and the number and length of holidays may vary from system to system, but the overall concept remains the same: students are divided into one or more tracks with staggered holidays.

Unfortunately, merely being informed about the advantages of year-round schools is often not enough to convince students and parents of the worth of the system. After undergoing the change to such a plan, however, most find their reservations dispelled. My research indicates

The student explains the concept, based on reading of various sources.

Information in this paragraph consists of widely known facts that do not require documentation.

that the chief objection to year-round education is its
potentially disruptive effect on family schedules. Parents
worry about planning family vacations around shorter
holidays, and students fear that they will have less vacation
time. In fact, the shorter but more numerous vacations
provided by a year-round school plan allow greater freedom of
choice in deciding where to go and what to do, since families
are no longer limited to one season of the year in which to
vacation. Many school boards further offset this anxiety by
scheduling tracks according to geographic area, ensuring
that siblings (and often friends as well) will be able to
vacation at the same time. Describing the conversion to year-
round schools in the Jefferson County, Colorado, school
district, William D. White notes that "parents resisted
going back to the nine-month school year after experiencing
the year-round calendar and the multiple vacations each
year" (105).

    Another benefit afforded students by year-round
education is better retention of what they have learned.
Since people learn all year long, it follows that a system
designed to take advantage of that fact will be more
efficient and productive. According to Lisa Gitlin in <u>The</u>

The quotation is made part of the student's sentence. The page number suffices since the source (White) is cited in the paper.

Education Digest, a sixth-grade teacher "spends less time
reviewing, since . . . his students generally retain what
they've learned for a three-week absence. In addition [he
says], the kids move along more quickly" (18).

Students who come from homes in which English is not the
primary language will also benefit from the shorter
vacations since they are not confined for long periods to
homes and neighborhoods in which only the foreign language is
spoken (Gitlin 18). Year-round schools provide distinct
advantages for marginal as well as gifted students, too,
since a student may choose to take an extra class during his
or her scheduled vacation, thereby gaining a head start on a
new subject or increasing proficiency in an area in which he
or she is weak.

Most existing studies indicate that students and
parents should experience a year-round program before
condemning it. For example, according to studies conducted
after the first year of year-round schools in the Chula
Vista, California, school system, 79 percent of the parents
polled favored the year-round school concept; and when
parents were surveyed about their perception of their
children's response to year-round schools, 84 percent

**Ellipsis
indicates
words
omitted
from quo-
tation;
bracketed
material
indicates
clarifica-
tions in-
serted into
quotation.**

**Place par-
enthetical
references
outside
quotation
marks but
inside final
punctua-
tion.**

**Para-
phrased
material
must still
be docu-
mented.**

believed that their children favored the system (Servetter 107).

Year-round schools also provide major economic benefits to the school system and, as a result, to the community. School facilities are used more efficiently than in a traditional nine-month plan, since they do not lie unused for extended periods. Just as in business it would be illogical and financially unwise to let resources remain idle for months, many school systems are realizing the economic advantages of using school buildings and grounds all year long. There are no economic advantages to long summer vacations; the days when children were needed to work on the family farm are almost entirely gone. Today, communities employing the year-round plan might open schools during brief schoolwide vacations for adult classes and other community-oriented functions.

More important for many communities, the increased efficiency of a year-round school plan means that more schools will not be needed to relieve overcrowding at existing facilities. Thus year-round schools are one important answer to the ever-present public clamor for more efficient school systems. Keeping existing schools open

Servetter, the source of the information in this paragraph, is cited in parentheses since he was not cited in the paragraph.

year round will result in higher maintenance and utility
costs, but these increases pale when compared to the great
expense of land and new buildings. White points out that the
Jefferson County School District turned to year-round
schools expressly for the purpose of relieving overcrowding
and found that a six-term plan with three attendance tracks
released one-third of its students every term, increasing
the rated capacity of year-round schools (over the nine-
month plan) by 50 percent (104). Since overcrowding can
adversely affect the attitude of students toward attendance,
their behavior and level of achievement in school, and
teacher effectiveness as well, the solution to this problem
offered by year-round education is too important to be
ignored. Stephen Walters, director of the Los Angeles
School Utilization Task Force, is quoted by Gitlin as
stating:

> Before year-round school, we had 3,800 students
> jammed into a school designed for 2,400. There
> were lines everywhere. With a thousand kids on
> vacation at any given time, we have far fewer
> discipline problems. We don't notice the pushing,

White's full name was cited earlier.

The source of the quotation is Gitlin.

Note that the colon (:) introduces a long quotation.

the shoving, the verbal accusations that we

did before, especially among the younger

students. (17)

Teachers also have much to gain from the year-round

school concept. Smaller class sizes resulting from relief

of overcrowding make for less stressful classroom situations

and allow more frequent breaks to plan new strategies and

courses. In addition, teachers find that more of their time

can be devoted to curriculum planning and less to organizing

the physical environment of the classroom than with a nine-

month plan, since the classroom has already been in use when

the teacher arrives after his or her short vacation. A

teacher contacted in Leonard Servetter's study[1] liked the

fact that "art supplies, textbooks, maps, and other basic

accessories were left in each classroom. All she needed was

to unpack her belongings, rearrange the furniture to her

liking, and she was ready" (55).

Some teachers have noted potential drawbacks in the

year-round school concept that need to be addressed by school

boards implementing the plan. In-service workshops and

college courses that teachers are required to take in order

A long quotation is indented ten spaces from the left margin, with no quotation marks, and is double-spaced. Place references two spaces after the quotation.

The raised number indicates a content endnote (additional information) listed on the Notes page.

to keep their teaching certificates current will be more difficult to attend because of the briefer vacations under year-round plans. A possible solution to this problem is for teacher unions and other organizations to petition schools of education at colleges and universities to offer "mini" courses designed to meet the needs of teachers working in year-round schools. Another potential disadvantage mentioned by Gitlin, White, and other sources is that because of low salaries in some areas of the country, many teachers have traditionally relied on summer employment to augment those salaries. This practice would be rendered less feasible by the year-round plan since it might be difficult for teachers to find employment during shorter vacation periods. An obvious solution is for teachers to be allowed to teach year-round, earning a full annual compensation and forgoing the reduced pay they often have to settle for in a temporary summer job. As to the complaints cited by Gitlin that teachers need the three-month summer vacation both to relax and to plan curricula, it seems that the shorter vacations throughout the year can serve a similar function (19).

As a former student in a year-round school, I can see

The summary of opposing views with the student's response makes the paper balanced.

how effective this system can be at reducing overcrowding and improving the learning atmosphere, issues that more than compensate for the drawbacks cited. In my junior year at Cypress High School in the Orange County, Florida, school system, my high school was one of two in the country to switch to a year-round plan on an experimental basis.[2] We were put on a four-track, forty-five-day on, fifteen-day off plan, which worked wonders in the school. Before the change, all of my classes had thirty to thirty-five students, and some days it was hardly worth the wait to stand in line for lunch. After the year-round plan began, my classes averaged twenty-two students, and teachers and students alike were in a better frame of mind. Some students and some parents (mine included) were apprehensive about the change, but most people overlooked their fears and supported the program because they realized that something needed to be done. We were not receiving a quality education, because of the rapid growth of Orange County, and the success of the year-round plan outweighed any inconvenience that my family and I experienced as a result of the change in my schedule.

Many educators, even those enthusiastic about year-round education, admit that such a plan may not be feasible

The student's experience provides good evidence.

for every school system. For example, Gitlin rightly observes that the "overwhelming majority of year-round schools are west of the Mississippi, where populations are expanding. Districts with stable or declining enrollments are not inclined to consider expanding the school year" (18). And in some school systems, year-round schools have been tried and abandoned in the face of parent complaints about family members being in different schools (and so on different vacation tracks) and the inability of their children to participate in such activities as Vacation Bible School, Little League, and summer jobs.

Not even proponents of year-round schools claim that the system is a cure for all of our nation's educational woes; but in many school districts, especially those facing overcrowding and inadequate funding for additional schools, year-round education is the most viable alternative to traditional plans. And though implementing and running such a system are enormous tasks, and overcoming negative public perception of the plan can be difficult, school boards across the nation are finding that year-round education is the right choice for the communities they serve.

The student indicates his agreement with the source.

The conclusion sums up the main points and restates the thesis.

Notes

[1] Other teachers quoted by Gitlin (18) make similar points.

[2] In Orange County, which has been among the fastest-growing areas of the country for more than a decade, the issue of year-round schools has recently become a heated political issue.

Content endnotes are double-spaced. The first line is indented five spaces from the left margin. Use content endnotes only when you have additional information that does not fit in the body of the paper. Put bibliographical information on the Works Cited page.

Works Cited

Gitlin, Lisa. "Does Year-Round Education Really Make
    Sense?" The Education Digest 54:3 (1988): 16–18.
Servetter, Leonard. Year-Round School Program: A Case
    Study. Chula Vista: People Education and
    Communication Enterprises, 1973.
White, William D. "Year Round High Schools: Benefits to
    Students, Parents, and Teachers." NASSP Bulletin
    72.504 (1988): 103–106.

Special Types

of Academic

Writing

The emphasis in most academic writing is on responding to what you have read, on demonstrating both your mastery of the subject and your ability to present it clearly and effectively. The writing techniques discussed in Part I of this book apply to many writing situations outside the composition class, including the three special applications treated in this chapter: writing essay examinations, reviews, and literary analyses.

88 Writing essay examinations.

Essay examinations test both your knowledge of material and your ability to organize and present it. They enable your instructor to determine how well you can put facts into perspective and draw conclusions from them. Some questions ask you to provide facts; most ask you to state an opinion based on your study of the facts. Although it is no substitute for studying the material, learning how to approach an essay question properly will improve the quality of your answers.

88a Read an essay question carefully to see what it requires you to do.

If you do not read a question carefully, you may end up writing about the general subject rather than answering the specific question. Look especially for key words that will help you determine how to approach and organize an answer:

analyze: Break the topic into its parts, and show how each part relates to the whole. In analyzing a play, for example, you might focus on how the author uses character, setting, and symbolism to convey a theme.

comment, criticize: State your opinion of the issue or statement in the question.

compare: Explain both the similarities and differences.

contrast: Explain the differences.

define: Give the meaning of a term or concept (and show how it is different from related terms and concepts).

describe: Explain what the subject is or looks like: what happened?

discuss: Examine the topic in detail.

evaluate: Judge the worth or quality of something by making positive and negative points about it.

explain: Make something clear or state the reason(s) for something.

illustrate: Provide examples to explain a general statement.

interpret: Explain the meaning of facts.

list, outline, review, summarize: Give the main points of a concept or story, often in a numbered series.

prove: Give reasons why a statement is true or false.

Before you begin to formulate an answer, make certain that you understand exactly what the question asks you to do. Do not squander valuable time summarizing a story or theory unless the question asks you to do so.

88b Develop an essay answer much as you would an essay.

Before you begin to write, decide on your basic answer, plan your overall organization, and begin deciding what specific details to use. You will usually not have time to develop a full outline, but you can take a few minutes to jot down notes. Consider also the length of time you will have. Plan an answer which you can complete in the time allotted.

Develop a good beginning that lets the reader (your instructor) know that you understand what is asked of you and that you do have an answer. Try in one or two sentences to state the essential answer, much as in a thesis statement in an essay. Often you can turn the question into your opening statement:

Question: Compare the motif of reality and illusion in *Hamlet, Macbeth,* and *Othello.*

Thesis: The motif of reality and illusion is interwoven with the theme in each of the three plays but in varying degrees of complexity.

After opening with this thesis, you could go on to identify the theme of each play and to show how the motif of illusion relates to the theme in each. You should illustrate your points with references to particular scenes, but you should not spend time summarizing the plots of the plays or simply describing the scenes in which illusion is particularly important.

If you were asked to evaluate the usefulness of solar energy in home heating, you might begin like this: "Solar energy is potentially useful in home heating, but neither the cost nor the available technology makes it a practical option, at least at this time." With this as an initial main idea, you can go on to develop each point (potential, cost, present technology) in more detail.

The middle section of your answer should expand each of the points mentioned in your brief introduction. Use as many specific details as time and space allow to clarify or defend your main point. Many weak answers are too general: they correctly provide the essentials but fail to support them. Remember that essay tests are not invitations to toss around vague generalities: the more specific the facts and figures you provide, the better will seem your grasp of the issues. But do not think that mere length will impress your instructor. Get to the point quickly, and give a concise but reasonably complete response.

Finally, write a brief conclusion. In a short answer, a single sentence will suffice; longer essays will require a short paragraph. Restate your main point clearly and emphatically, returning to the point with which you began (see **9**). Try to reserve a few minutes to check over your answers. Look for unclear statements, omitted words, or errors in punctuation or spelling. You will not attain the type of perfection which more time would make possible, but proofreading can make your presentation much more effective.

Consider the following responses to this essay question:

How did the cases of *Near v. Minnesota* and *New York Times v.*

U.S. (the Pentagon Papers case) influence freedom of the press?

1. In both *Near v. Minnesota* and *New York Times v. U.S.*, the U.S. Supreme Court limited the rights of state and federal governments to restrict the press. In *Near v. Minnesota*, the court held that suppression of *The Saturday Press* was unconstitutional censorship. The court acknowledged that although libelous statements may be punishable, the First Amendment guarantees the freedom to publish news without prior injunctive restraints. *The Saturday Press*, the court ruled, may have been guilty of publishing defamatory articles, but it had the constitutional right to do so.

   New York Times v. U.S. reaffirmed the Supreme Court's reluctance to allow politically controversial material to be suppressed. The court held that the government could not censor publication of the Pentagon Papers by the *New York Times*. The Justice Department argued that publication of some information in the Pentagon Papers could threaten national security. The *Times* replied that the First Amendment protects freedom of the press and that the government had not shown the need for "prior restraint" to halt publication of the papers. The *Times* also argued for the right of Americans to be truthfully informed about their government. Agreeing with the *Times*, the court stated that the government failed to meet the burden of proof showing how the papers endangered national security so as to justify prior restraint. However, the court conceded that the press may be censored in advance by the government in "exceptional cases" or in more urgent circumstances related to national security.

   The Supreme Court, in both cases, protected and upheld freedom of the press. The question of libel in *Near v. Minnesota* did not justify prior restraint to halt publication; and although the court found that national security did not justify censorship in the case of *New York Times v. U.S.*, prior restraint was held to be valid in exceptional situations.

2. Both cases dealt with a particular interpretation of the First Amendment to the Constitution. That amendment states that the government, federal or state, has no right to interfere with freedom of speech, freedom of the press, freedom to follow religious convictions, or the freedom to assemble and criticize the government. The specific and vital issue in *Near v. Minnesota* and *New York Times v. U.S.* concerns the freedom of press. One case had to do with a state government; the other, with the federal government.

The Saturday Press, a respectable Minneapolis weekly, published a series of articles accusing the city administrators of corrupt actions. Perhaps out of fear, guilt, or simple revenge, the city officials passed a statute that restricted any newspaper, magazine, or other periodical from publishing an article that was libelous with no good motive. The city officials determined that *The Saturday Press* did not comply with these terms: they had no good motive for publishing the articles. Consequently, the city officials attempted to close down the newspaper.

In 1971 secret government documents describing the early political decisions of the Vietnamese war were unlawfully given to the *New York Times*. Prepared by the Secretary of Defense in the Johnson administration, the Pentagon Papers revealed the clandestine actions of four successive administrations. Military and political decisions were made and executed without the knowledge or agreement of Congress or the people. The *New York Times* began publishing these articles until legal protests from the Justice Department temporarily halted publication.

The question of freedom of the press is particularly controversial today when government activity demands increasing amounts of security. Various excuses such as internal stability, external threat, or preservation of the national image discourage criticism. However, the Supreme Court continues to uphold the First Amendment and to follow its duty to protect the constitutional rights of Americans to publish the truth.

Note that answer 1 begins with a clear thesis statement, supports that statement with specific details, and closes with a brief summary. Above all, it answers the question that was asked. By contrast, answer 2 opens with a vague statement, wanders off into background material, and never addresses the original question. Although it includes as much detail as answer 1, it is not a satisfactory answer.

89 Writing reviews.

Reviews present an evaluation of a performance, product, person, or idea, based on specific criteria and on evidence that supports the evaluation.

You might be asked to write a critique of a book or film for a class or to recommend a new computer for your employer. In either case you will be expected to evaluate the subject objectively and fairly, using facts to support your evaluation, and to state your opinion of it.

There is no single standard form for all types of reviews, but the following advice is a guide to the process of writing them:

1. If you are free to select the work to be reviewed, begin by choosing a favorite writer, filmmaker, or

musical group, something you know enough about to discuss its quality. Think of similar works you can use for comparison and contrast. Examine reviews of books and movies in magazines and newspapers.

2. Consider your purpose and the needs of your *audience:* Will your readers use your review as a guide to seeing the movie, reading the book, or attending the concert? If so, your review may persuade them to experience (or avoid) the work for themselves, depending on your assessment. If the subject is a performance already concluded, your purpose will be to inform, not persuade. If your readers are consumers (of cameras, computers, or cars), your purpose would be to inform them about the product and to urge them to consider whether or not to buy it.

3. Decide what *criteria* you will use in evaluating the subject. If you are reviewing a novel, consider the author's description, characterization, plot, style, and ideas. Appropriate criteria for a rock concert would differ from those for a symphony concert. A restaurant reviewer would consider such elements as food quality, service, price, cleanliness, and location in relation to similar types of restaurants and would assume his readers' acceptance of these criteria. When readers are unfamiliar with a product, however, the reviewer might explain the criteria in detail. For each criterion, select specific standards you can defend. For example, in reviewing a play, one of your criteria would be good acting; one of your standards might be that "good acting seems natural, creates the illusion of reality, and interprets the character."

4. On the basis of your specific criteria, locate as much *evidence* (examples) as you can before reaching your judgment. Remember that generalizations, such as "good music" or "weak plot," will not be convincing. A play review, for example, might state that the three leading actors used distracting gestures, spoke in

unconvincing accents, and rushed their lines; therefore, the performance was seriously flawed. Anticipate possible objections to your views and answer them.

5. Choose an appropriate *writing strategy*. In reviewing a literary or dramatic work, you would rely chiefly on narration, telling the reader what happens in the plot but without revealing everything, such as a surprise ending. Remember that your readers may experience the work for themselves. A review of a concert would also present the events in chronological order. But since reviews must evaluate, not just summarize, you would analyze the work, much as a sportscaster's postgame analysis examines the various factors that influenced the outcome of the game. (See "Writing Literary Analyses," p. 400). Comparison is another common strategy. Be sure your criteria are fair and reasonable: you could not logically compare a gourmet restaurant with a fast-food restaurant or a luxury car with a compact economy model.

6. Finally, organize the review much as you would an essay. State your *thesis* (see **6**), indicating your attitude toward the work, in the opening paragraph. And identify the work fully:

The latest novel by Robertson Davies, one of Canada's leading writers, is an intelligent, complex work involving deception and supernatural romance. *The Lyre of Orpheus* (Viking; 472 pages; $19.95) is part of the author's third trilogy of novels and draws on his extensive theatrical background.

EXERCISE

1. Discuss the purpose and audience for a hotel or restaurant review, an album or compact disc review, and a television review.

2. What criteria would you use for each of the above? What standards would you use for each criterion?

3. What writing strategies would you use for the above reviews?

4. For a comparative review of two cars, list as many criteria as you can.

As the following sample book review shows, a review (evaluation) is not a report (summary).

Review of <u>Brideshead Revisited</u> by Evelyn Waugh.
Little, Brown, $7.95.

Why does love so often lead to unhappiness?
This is one of the questions explored in
<u>Brideshead Revisited</u>, the 1945 novel by Evelyn
Waugh. It is a study of friendship, romance,
failure, and the past, all viewed from the perspective of religious faith. The plot is less
compelling than the colorful characters, yet they
quickly draw the reader into their glamorous but
sad world. The style is as lush and richly orna-
mented as the baroque mansion called Brideshead.

Waugh's story is narrated by his main character, Charles Ryder, whose "sacred and profane
memories" begin during the dark days of World War
II. With his military company billeted at
Brideshead, once the scene of his youthful involvement with the Marchmain family, Charles
looks back to the 1920s and to his first meeting
with Lord Marchmain's younger son, Sebastian
Flyte, at Oxford. Sebastian is an immature,
spoiled young man "in love with his own childhood."

This charming aristocrat dominates Charles's reminiscence in the first half of the novel.

Charles, who has had no real home, is enchanted with Sebastian and his family, but puzzled by what he sees as their quaint Catholicism. He is gradually accepted as a friend by Lady Marchmain, the pious but manipulative matriarch, whose husband has long lived in Venice with a mistress. She tries to use Charles to spy on her son's drinking escapades.

Not long after their romantic friendship blossoms, Sebastian increasingly withdraws from Charles into solitary drinking; and when Sebastian is "sent down" from Oxford, Charles loses his only source of boyhood innocence. Hearing about Sebastian from his pompous brother, Bridey, and his young sister, Cordelia, among others, the reader comes to understand Charles's and the author's lament not only for the loss of youthful promise but more so for the inability to love. Fleeing from what he sees as his family's hatred, Sebastian, a hopeless alcoholic, ends up in Morocco, cared for by monks.

As the years pass, Charles tries to find happiness in his career as a painter and then in a loveless marriage. He becomes reacquainted with Sebastian's sister, Julia, and they become lovers. But their plans to marry are frustrated by Julia's sense of guilt: her first marriage to a divorced non-Catholic has been painful, and she refuses to continue living "in sin" with Charles, who is also about to be divorced.

The gloom of the second half of the book is reinforced by the return of old Lord Marchmain to Brideshead. He has come home to die. His death-bed repentance and return to the Church affect Julia's decision to break off with Charles. As his long reminiscence draws to a close, we learn that Charles--having failed to find fulfillment in marriage, his profession, or the army--has found some peace in the Catholic faith of the Marchmains.

Throughout the novel, the great house, built of old stones from an earlier house, symbolizes the continuity of faith; it is a source of whole-ness and permanence in a world of change, ugli-ness, and war. From the house and from Sebas-tian's family, Charles has seen the need for something beyond the physical. He has sought transcendence with Julia, following the loss of Sebastian, but finds that human love is an imper-fect source of happiness. Waugh's melancholy theme seems to be that the values of the world offer no real solace compared to those of the spirit.

The purpose of the novel--to show Christian faith at work in a world of materialism and al-ienation--is as ambitious as its plot, which at points is burdened by excessively detailed de-scriptions. But the vivid, often comic charac-ters and the scenes of lost innocence and tragic failure make <u>Brideshead Revisited</u> a memorable work.

Responding to what you read and putting your responses into words is a basic part of most college courses, which often require you to summarize, analyze, or discuss various texts. Analyzing literature is an excellent way of developing these writing skills and of learning about your own experiences as a reader.

Most college essays that entail writing about other writing are analytical: you explain the reasons for an economic downturn, the effects of a disease, or the meaning of a poem. That is, you explain relationships and what they mean. Rather than merely summarizing a work or event, you will most often comment on and interpret it, pointing out why a work or event means what it does. Explaining the reasons for your opinions about a piece of literature requires critical reading and thinking, skills that will be of value in many real-world tasks. All serious thinking is analytical since it is only by mentally taking a subject apart and then reconstructing it that a person can understand how it functions, why it occurred, or what it is.

90a Analysis requires interpretation.

In explaining the reasons for your opinions of a novel, short story, poem, or play (as well as essay, film, song, or advertisement), you learn about yourself, your values, and the values of your society as well as those of the author. You read such texts not merely for information but for pleasure and for insight. Writing a good analysis adds to your original pleasure and deepens your first insights by bringing you closer to the work and to your own thoughts and feelings about it. You analyze a text to explain what it means to you and why it moved you as it did.

Your assignment might be to write a *response statement* that indicates your personal reactions to a work. Or you might be asked to write a *review* (see **89**). Sometimes you will write a *summary* of the action or plot. But most often you will be expected to write an *analytical essay* that explains how the elements of the work (plot, character, setting, point of view, among others) add up to some overall meaning or theme. To develop a convincing analysis, you will provide evidence from the text to substantiate your *interpretation*, your explanation of a meaning not readily apparent. You may discover that a work reveals meanings other than what the author intended; there is no single "right" interpretation. An interpretation, however, is not merely a subjective reaction but a reasoned evaluation, supported by examples and quotations from the text. As long as you can support your interpretation and prove your solid grasp of the work, your readers will be satisfied that your opinions are worth considering.

90b   Read the work carefully.

Unlike newspapers, which are read quickly for facts, literary texts are meant to be read slowly and carefully, not just for information but for understanding. The first reading serves mainly to discover what the work is about. In your second reading of a work, have a pencil handy to mark passages that strike you as important, interesting, or revealing. Check the dictionary for the definitions of any unfamiliar words. With each reading, you will be conscious of your reactions to different aspects of a work and to its cultural background; its meanings will gradually become clear to you.

90c   Choose a limited topic.

As you reread a work, consider possible topics that interest you. Although you will be considering the significance of the whole work, you must find a limited approach. To write an essay about everything in a novel or even a short story would result in general, superficial comments. A limited topic—on a symbolic color, unusual title, or revealing setting, for example—will not be trivial or dull; in fact, if developed properly, it can shed light on the whole work, helping you and your reader understand it from a specific viewpoint. (See **5**.)

Literary analysis has one advantage over many other types of writing. The text is filled with human experiences; it provides many subjects for you to analyze and provides the source of the evidence needed to develop the essay. You can always return to the text for ideas, and many more topics than you can use will occur to you as you read. Selecting the most interesting and appropriate topics, those that mean the most to you and your readers, may be the most challenging task.

90d Formulate a thesis statement.

Once you have your topic, take an attitude toward it. This attitude or stance should be expressed in a sentence to give your writing a unifying purpose. If the subject of a poem is death, try to determine what the poet's attitude toward death is—and how it reflects or differs from yours. Be sure to formulate your own thesis so that you will develop *your* views and not rely on those of critics. If you are assigned a topic, consider the importance of this topic in relation to the work as a whole. If, for example, your topic is "The Importance of the Town in William Faulkner's 'A Rose for Emily,'" your thesis statement might be: "The town in Faulkner's 'A Rose for Emily' is one of the principal characters." Once you have your thesis, read the story again, this time with the eye of a defense attorney eager to make a good case. Look for evidence—examples, descriptive details, quotations—that proves the importance of the town. (See **6**.)

90e Assume that your reader has read the work.

Unlike the readers of a book report or review, readers of a literary analysis are familiar with the work and do not require summaries or long quotations. (In explicating a poem, you may need to supply the text of the poem for the readers' convenience.) Summarize only those events of the plot necessary to make your observations clear. In the following paragraphs, you can see the difference between reporting on a work by retelling what happens and analyzing it by explaining the reasons for what happens:

A. Paul Morel in D. H. Lawrence's *Sons and Lovers* is a sensitive, tormented character. As a very young man, he begins a long relationship with the spiritual Miriam that is never fulfilling. Later, he has a more mature, physical relationship with Clara, but this, too, is unsuccessful. Throughout his life, a dominating presence is that of his strong, possessive mother. It is not until her death that Paul is able to free himself.

B. Paul Morel in D. H. Lawrence's *Sons and Lovers* is a sensitive, tormented character whose failure is linked to his mother's strong presence. He has a relationship with Miriam, whose reserved, spiritual character is an extension of his mother's. Paul therefore never sees her as a woman but as a soul who wants to possess him. In his more mature relationship with Clara, Paul finds no genuine satisfaction because he sees in her only the womanly aspect of his mother, to whom he is forever tied. By failing to relate to either Miriam or Clara, Paul is unable to find himself or the freedom he needs to break away from his mother's domination, which ends only with her death.

Whereas the first paragraph relies on plot summary, the second paragraph develops the *reasons* for the opening statement by exploring the relationship between the women in Paul's life and his lack of freedom and fulfillment. Literary analysis, then, presents ideas, reflections, and judgments about the work rather than merely facts; it explains *why*, not just *what*.

90f Write an interesting introduction.

90

The opening paragraph should capture the reader's interest and clearly state your main point (see p. 44). Identify the full title and author of the work being treated.

90g Develop the body of the essay with evidence.

Rather than follow the structure of the work you are analyzing, arrange your body paragraphs according to major ideas. Each paragraph should support one aspect of your thesis statement (see p. 34) and should contain examples or quotations from the work. If, for example, your introduction mentions that two characters in a play have some similarities despite their many differences, you could devote one paragraph to their differences and two paragraphs to their similarities. Or you could have a thesis statement such as the following: "Through his references to darkness, robbing, and animals, Iago establishes the pervasive atmosphere of evil in *Othello*." You could structure such an essay in terms of the three types of references. An essay will be convincing to the extent that it contains evidence from the text in support of your main point. The sample paper (p. 406) shows how you can combine your comments with supporting quotations.

Note that the verb tense in an essay about literature is the present. Include only your final views of the work, and eliminate any sentences that do not advance your thesis. Your purpose is not to congratulate the author, not to discuss his or her life, not to preach to the readers about your philosophy, not to find fault, as a reviewer might, but to express your grasp of the ideas and artistry of the work.

90h   Use quotations correctly.

In developing the body of the essay with selected quotations, be sure to copy each quotation exactly as in the original. Place the page number(s) from the original in parentheses at the end of the sentence: Connie "knew she was pretty and that was everything" (212). Brief essays of literary analysis usually do not require bibliographical citations from primary sources, but any secondary (critical) sources should be acknowledged (see p. 355). For repeated references to your primary source, simple citations will suffice once you have identified the work in your essay; in this example from a play, the act, scene, and line are cited:

> Othello speaks of himself as one "that lov'd not wisely but too well" (5.2.344).

You will rarely use long quotations (more than four lines); when you do, they are indented (set off ten spaces from the left margin without quotation marks). Incorporate all other quotations into your own sentences. Short passages of poetry (one or two lines) should be included in your text: Butler speaks of "a leering company/Of unholy ghosts" (lines 10–11). But longer quotations of poetry (three or more lines) are set off (indented ten spaces from the left margin), with the line numbers in parentheses at the conclusion of the quotation.

90i   Develop an effective conclusion.

Conclude your analytical essay by summarizing your main points and assessing the significance and impact of the work. Do not introduce new ideas, cite critics' views, or provide quotations; instead, emphasize what your analysis has discovered.

Here is a poem by Robert Frost, titled "Fire and Ice," followed by a sample student analysis of the poem.

FIRE AND ICE

Some say the world will end in fire,
Some say in ice.
From what I've tasted of desire
I hold with those who favor fire.
But if it had to perish twice,
I think I know enough of hate
To say that for destruction ice
Is also great
And would suffice.

Analysis of "Fire and Ice" by Robert Frost
    by Rick Speer

    "Fire and Ice" by Robert Frost is a short
but powerful poem about the end of the world,
expressed in an ironically offhanded style.
Frost uses several surprising devices to express
his bleak theme.
    The tone is playful and deceptively simple,
the result of the poet's carefully planned
rhythm, rhyme, and diction. "Fire and Ice" is
written mostly in an iambic meter, with the last
syllable of each line stressed. Each line (if
the eighth and ninth lines constitute one line)
has a total of eight syllables, except for the
second line, which has only four: "Some say in
ice." This contrast makes the reader pause after
"ice" to reflect on the major idea of the poem,
before continuing. If the second line had flowed

along in perfect harmony with the first, the reader would be tempted to proceed directly to the next. But the lone four syllables say, in effect: "Stop! Think about this theme--the end of the world. Do you believe it will happen? Let me tell you what I think. . . ."

The perfect iambic pattern of the lines that follow gives the poem an almost nonchalant air, complemented by Frost's informal diction, which clashes with the vast, cosmic scale of the subject matter. Examples of the clash can be found in the lines "I hold with those who favor fire" and "ice is also great and would suffice." The speaker's casual attitude parallels the cold detachment of those who might bring about the ultimate global cataclysm.

The elegant rhyme scheme of the poem also belies its horrific theme. "Fire" rhymes with "desire," and "ice" with "twice" and "suffice." Together with the meter, the rhymes create a mood of easy, almost whimsical contemplation about the most unwhimsical subject of all, the end of the world. It is precisely the easy, gentle flow of the poem that brings about in the reader a reaction of delayed terror: if one can consider the earth's destruction with such back-porch nonchalance, then how concerned are people about rescuing humanity from its impending doom?

An obvious interpretation of "Fire and Ice" is biblical, for the idea of Armageddon is presented in the Bible (Revelation 16:14-16) as a religious certainty: the world <u>will</u> end. Frost's poem rests on this hypothesis, for the issue his speaker debates is not <u>if</u> the world will end but <u>how</u>. Will fire--the fires of Hell, the forces of evil, the power of Satan--destroy the earth? The poet seems to believe that the answer is "yes." The possibility of a nuclear Armageddon has become popular among many theologians since Frost's poem was written. And it is appropriate that the precursor of nuclear destruction (fire) is the Cold War (ice). Ice also reminds the reader of Dante's conception of the lowest level of Hell, where Lucifer sits encased in ice. Light (heat, fire) is likened to God, and darkness (coldness, ice) to the absence of God. Thus, while the most flagrant and immediately destructive sins may be committed in the mad heat of passion, the journey to spiritual depravity is often seen as distancing oneself from God.

Another possible approach to the poem is that Frost intended it to be interpreted scientifically. Twice he refers to what experts theorize in contrast to his own hypothesis. Thus the reader is led to speculate about whether the earth will be engulfed by flames in a few trillion centuries, as many modern astronomers maintain, or whether the older theory that the sun will gradually die out, freezing all human life, is valid.

But it seems most likely that Frost wrote "Fire and Ice" in a moralistic vein. His focus is on human motivation. He equates "fire" not with love but with "desire." But if desire will bring about the global apocalypse, the reader wonders, "Desire for what?" Does desire mean romantic passion or, more likely, a greedy lust for power? Frost equates "ice" with "hate." Yet hatred is a fiery emotion, morally incinerating all it touches. Does Frost mean that "hate" is only that frigid, malicious brand of contempt that chills the blood? The poet leaves these questions open to interpretation. His most astounding line, "But if it had to perish twice," suggests that hate and desire are not so much opposed as related.

"Fire and Ice" assumes the inevitability of the apocalypse and speculates as to its nature. The poem's flowing rhythm and elegant rhyme are ironically opposed to its grim subject matter. Religiously, the poem brings Armageddon to mind. Scientifically, it unintentionally coincides with modern astronomical theory. And morally it lets the reader decide what constitutes "fire" and "desire," "ice" and "hate." However one reads "Fire and Ice," the poem produces a somber reflection on one of the most profound questions imaginable.

90

1. Study the selections and the advice in an anthology of poetry, prose, and drama. Select a work that interests you. After a careful reading, jot down your initial reactions and the reasons for your reactions. Why does the work interest you? How does it relate to your own experience?

2. Choose a poem, and write down your impressions of the speaker's tone (the attitude toward the subject). Try to sum up in your own words what each stanza says.

3. Choose a minor character in a work you are studying, and explain the relation of this character to the significance of the work. Or explain the importance of the setting in establishing the mood of a short story.

4. Select a Shakespearean sonnet as the subject for an explication, that is, a detailed line-by-line or stanza-by-stanza reading. Comment on the structure, imagery, tone, and theme. Or analyze W. H. Auden's poem "The Unknown Citizen," explaining who you think the speaker is.

13

Job-Related

Writing

The techniques of clear, effective writing are essentially the same in all situations, whether in the composition classroom, in another classroom, or on the job. But some types of writing have special requirements in addition to those already discussed in this book. This chapter is designed to help you with some of the special types of writing you will be likely to face in college or in business.

Use conventionally accepted style and form for business letters.

No other type of writing today is as stylized as the business letter. Although conventional practices concerning letter form and tone vary somewhat, you must follow some standards if you want your reader to accept and respect your letters. The suggestions below present the most commonly accepted conventions.

91a Arrange the parts of your letter according to standard form.

The eight parts listed below are required in all business letters. Arrange them as shown in the sample. Single-space within each part, but double-space between parts and between paragraphs. Use at least one-inch margins at the sides and one and one-half inches at the top and bottom. Balance a short letter to fill as much of the page as possible.

Letterhead or return address. If no printed letterhead is available, type your return address so that it ends at the right-hand margin. Start one and one-half inches from the top.

Dateline. Center the correct date two lines below the letterhead. If you type your return address, type the date immediately below the last line of the address.

Inside address. Four to eight spaces below the dateline, put the name, title, and mailing address of the person to whom you are writing. The inside address may require three, four, or five lines, each starting at the left margin.

Salutation. Write the salutation flush with the left margin two spaces below the inside address. If the letter is addressed to an individual, use *Dear Ms. X, Dear Mrs. X*, or *Dear Miss X* for female addressees and *Dear Mr. X* for males; when appropriate, use a title such as *Dr.* or *Professor*. If the letter is addressed to a job title without a specific person's name (such as Director of Personnel), use *Dear Sir* or *Dear Madam*. Some writers prefer *Dear Sir or Madam*. If the letter is addressed to a group, such as a company or department, use *Gentlemen* or *Ladies*. Put a colon (:) at the end of the salutation.

Body. Begin the body two lines below the salutation. Either indent the first line of each paragraph five spaces or start it at the left margin. Double-space between paragraphs.

Complimentary close. Put the complimentary close two lines below the end of the body, starting five spaces to the right of the center. Use only standard closings such as *Sincerely yours* or *Yours truly*. Capitalize the first word and put a comma after the last.

Signature. Type your name four spaces directly below the complimentary close. Women may type *Mrs., Miss,* or *Ms.* in parentheses before their names to indicate their preference.

Written signature. Sign your name in the space between the complimentary close and the typed signature.

In addition to these eight required elements, certain others are sometimes needed:

Identification line. When typing someone else's letter, list that person's initials before your own in the following manner:

```
DEF: lf.
```

Start it at the left margin two lines below the typed signature.

Enclosure notation. If you enclose anything with the letter, place an enclosure notation two spaces below the identification line or typed signature. Use one of the following forms:

```
Enc.  or  Encs. 2.
```

Carbon-copy notation. If anyone other than you and the addressee is to receive a copy of the letter, include a carbon-copy notation. Put it on the left margin two spaces below the previous notation. Use the following form:

```
cc: Mr. Anthony Canteras
```

Second-page heading. If a letter requires more than one page, use plain paper instead of letterhead for the second and subsequent pages. Leave a one-inch margin at the top, type a second-page heading as shown below, skip three spaces, and then continue the letter. A second page must have at least two lines of body.

```
Mr. Ralph Bushee          2          February 2, 1991
```

Envelopes. Placement of the address is important so that the address can be read by the post office's optical scanners. The last line should be no more than three inches and no less than one-half inch from the bottom of the envelope. Leave at least one inch from the end of the longest line to the right-hand edge.

91b Use the all-purpose letter pattern.

Nearly any letter you will have to compose can be developed using a three-phase pattern. Begin by getting to the point

5100 Fair Oaks Blvd.
Winter Park, FL 32790
September 25, 1990

Ms. Elise J. Schiller
Sawyer Incorported
18 Orange Trail
Orlando, FL 32802

Dear Ms. Schiller:

I am submitting the enclosed résumé in response to your
advertisement in the Orlando Sentinel (Sept. 20, 1990). I
have been interested in your firm since you visited us at
Creative Systems a few months ago and have heard many good
things about your company from friends in the local business
community.

The production control system that you saw during your visit
here is now nearly complete and is simultaneously managing
ten batch production projects. The system, which I established
and supervise, interacts with inventory control, payroll, and
accounting. It provides guidance for purchasing materials,
projects work force requirements, and estimates the effect of new
projects on completion dates of existing work. At its most
basic level, it assigns tasks to individual production workers.
This system, which has allowed us to increase our level of production considerably, reflects my background and experience in
computer systems.

If you find my work to be of interest to you as you develop
your operations at Sawyer and if my qualifications fit your
needs, I hope you will feel free to call me at your convenience.
However, since I have not definitely decided to leave my present
job, I would ask that you not contact Creative Systems. I look
forward to hearing from you.

Sincerely,

Edmund J. Bryan

Edmund J. Bryan

Enc.

within the first two sentences, stating the basic purpose of your letter much as you would the thesis of an English composition. Then develop your point by adding specific details and examples as needed. Be concise, and use short paragraphs so that your reader can refer quickly to each specific point you make. Finally, write a brief one- or two-sentence paragraph to close the letter smoothly. Note how the sample letter on the next page follows this pattern.

Adapt your tone to your reader and the situation, and be cordial but businesslike. Avoid the jargon often associated with business letters: *in reference to, pursuant to, yours of the 12th received*, and so on. You can communicate more clearly and effectively without such phrases (see **77**).

92 Prepare a clear, concise résumé to emphasize your strengths.

Few things you ever write will be as important to you as the résumé you submit to prospective employers. The facts do not speak for themselves; a well-prepared résumé will enhance your qualifications.

92a Include the appropriate information in your résumé.

When preparing a résumé, select facts about your background that will present you as positively as possible. Do not lie or concoct fictitious credentials, but select those that present the best impression.

Personal data. By law, you do not have to furnish personal data to prospective employers, but many people include it on their résumés. You might choose to include such information as date of birth, height and weight, sex, marital status, number of children, religious preference, health, military status.

Educational background. Begin with the college you are currently attending and work backward to the high school from which you graduated. Give dates of attendance or degrees, names of degrees or majors and minors, memberships in organizations and honor societies, and grade point average if it is impressive.

Work experience. Begin with your present or most recent job and work back to your high school graduation date; you may include significant part-time work from your high school days. Give your past employers' names and addresses, dates of employment, and job descriptions.

Professional skills. If you have experience or training in the field you are applying in, develop a special section summarizing your skills. The exact skills will vary with your field, but the following suggestions should help: equipment, procedures, or special techniques used; supervisory positions held; unusual promotions or awards; certifications or registrations.

Related skills or activities. If you have acquired through elective courses, hobbies, or other means any skills that might be useful in the desired position, you may include them. You may also mention community activities. Include anything that might give you a slight edge over other candidates. Do not bother listing interests or hobbies merely to give the reader a notion of what you are like.

Position desired. Many applicants name the actual position being sought; others list a broader "objective." Use either if you wish, but your accompanying letter of application should state the position you are seeking; stating that position in your résumé may prevent your being considered for other openings.

Résumé
Edmund J. Bryan
5100 Fair Oaks Blvd., Winter Park, FL 32790
Telephone: 305-555-6416 (home)
305-555-1018 (office)

Position Desired
Computer Programming Manager

Educational Background

1978-1981 University of Central Florida, Orlando, FL B.S. in
Engineering Mathematics and Computer Systems, 1981. GPA:
3.96 of 4.0. Member, Alpha Pi Mu (National Engineering
Honor Society). Courses included graduate-level study in
microprocessor design and operations research.
1976-1978 Case Institute of Technology, Cleveland, OH and
Cleveland State University, Cleveland, OH Major: Chemistry.
GPA: 3.67 of 4.0. No degree.
1972-1976 John Carroll High School, Cleveland, OH Diploma
with honors.

Work Experience

1982-present Creative Systems, Inc., Orlando, FL
Computer Programming Manager. Responsible for technical
supervision of programming staff. Participated in design
of computerized production tracking and control system and
wrote all programs used by this system. Supervisor Ralph
Phillips.
1980-1982 Tech-Systems, Inc., Maitland, FL
Programming Consultant with small area businesses. Supervisor Harold G. Williams.
1978-1980 Orlando Naval Training Center, Training Analysis and
Evaluation Group, Orlando, FL Part-time programmer.
Supervisor Thomas Porter, Jr.
1976-1978 Cleveland State University Library, Cleveland, OH
Student library assistant. Supervisor Mary A. Greer.

Related Skills and Activities

Consultant, Institute for Technical Documentation, University
of Central Florida, 1983-present; member: Society for
Technical Communication; East Central Florida Regional
Planning Council; Orlando Jaycees; St. John's Episcopal
Church
References available upon request
August 1990

References. Including references is usually unnecessary, but feel free to do so, especially to fill out an otherwise very short résumé. If you do include references, give the names, titles, and business addresses of three or four people who know you well and who can be trusted to speak favorably about you. Try to get variety, selecting people who know you in various ways.

92b Carefully prepare your résumé in an effective form.

The following checklist will help you to prepare an effective résumé:

1. Put your name, address, and telephone number at the top.
2. Use correct grammar. You may use phrases and clauses instead of complete sentences, but be sure you are consistent.
3. Use common abbreviations to save space.
4. Single-space within sections; double-space between sections.
5. State everything as positively as possible.
6. Make the final copy clean and neat, even if you must have a professional typist prepare it.

93 Writing memos.

A memorandum is used to communicate within an organization. Memos (memorandums) are frequently short and always direct, highlighting essential information in clear, easy-to-read form.

Structure

A memo has a standard two-part structure: a heading followed by a message. The heading, clearly separated by white space from the message, is divided into four sections:

1. TO: Identify the person to whom the memo is addressed, including that person's organizational title.
2. FROM: Identify yourself, including an organizational title.
3. SUBJECT: Include a brief description (a short phrase) of the subject matter contained in the message.
4. DATE: Include the date when the memo is written.

The message that follows is separated by enough white space to clearly distinguish between the heading and the body, which is single-spaced. At the end of the message there is no complimentary close or signature.

Content

Most memos inform individuals about a course of action, recommend policies, or announce decisions. Because it is circulated inside an organization, a memo takes for granted a general knowledge concerning the products, practices, or personnel of the organization. Background information and formal documentation are also frequently omitted.

A memo is a concise type of business writing meant to be read, understood, and acted upon amid the noise and routine of the office. It therefore quickly reaches the issue at hand and frequently includes outlines to save the reader time.

Style

Since you are writing to people with whom you work, an informal style is appropriate. Avoid long sentences and big

---

MEMO

TO: Dr. Cynthia Barr, Chair
                Department of English

FROM: Dave Herrick, Instructor

SUBJECT: Prizewinning Student Essay

DATE: 19 Oct. 1990

A Comp II student of mine, Lee Donegan, won second place in this year's NCTE essay writing contest. Her topic, the growing influence of drugs on elementary school kids, uses the experiences of her younger brother. It's dynamite work, nicely unified with excellent coherence.

I have a copy of her paper if you want to use it for department and/or university publicity. Let me know how I can help get the word out. Thanks.

cc: K. Higgins

---

words. Abbreviations, contractions, in-house jargon, and technical terms (provided everyone knows them) are all routine.

Glossary of Terms

absolute construction A phrase that qualifies a sentence but is not grammatically related to it: *This being true,* she left.

abstract A brief summary in paragraph form of the key ideas in a work.

active voice See *voice.*

adjective A word that describes or limits a noun or pronoun: The *rude* remark.

adverb A word modifying a verb (ran *quickly*), an adjective (*very* grateful), or another adverb (*quite* smoothly).

analogy The use of a comparison to note a resemblance between two otherwise very different things. Analogies often explain complex things by showing how they resemble simpler things.

analysis A type of writing in which you explain a subject by examining the parts that constitute it.

antecedent A noun to which a pronoun refers: The men are coming; here they are. (*They* refers to, or stands for, *men,* the antecedent of *they.*)

appositive A noun, noun phrase, or pronoun placed next to a noun to explain it: Sam, *the teller,* was wrong.

argumentation Writing that uses logic and persuasion to prove a point and convince the reader.

auxiliary verb A form of *be, can, could, do, get, have, may, might, must, ought, shall, should, will,* or *would* used in a verb phrase (*had* seen, *will be* going).

case The grammatical category of a noun or pronoun that indicates its relationship to other elements in a sentence. The nominative case is used for subjects of verbs (*he* is); the objective case is used for objects of verbs and prepositions (I hit *him*); and the possessive case indicates ownership (*his* arm).

clause A group of words containing a subject and a verb that is used as part of a sentence. An independent clause can stand alone as a sentence; a subordinate or dependent clause cannot stand alone: *Although he ran his fastest race.* When a sentence contains both a dependent and an independent clause (Although he ran his fastest race, he lost to Juan), the independent clause may also be called the main clause.

coherence The logical flow from point to point in an essay or paragraph.

collective noun A word that names a group of persons or things, for example, *class* or *committee*; it may take a singular or plural verb.

comparison and contrast Explaining by showing similarities (comparison) and differences (contrast) between two or more things.

complement A word or phrase that completes the verb. A subject or nominative complement is a word or phrase that follows a linking verb and belongs to the subject: Her paper is a *masterpiece.* An objective complement completes the action of the verb and follows its object: The jury found the defendant *innocent.*

conclusion The end of an essay, summing up the main points and restating the thesis; it does not introduce new ideas.

conjunction A word used to connect parts of a sentence or to relate sentences. Coordinating conjunctions (*and, but, or, nor, for, yet, so*) link equal elements; subordinate conjunctions (such as *because, although, if*) link a dependent clause with an independent clause.

conjunctive adverb A word such as *thus, moreover,* or *however* that connects one independent clause to another.

coordinating conjunction See *conjunction.*

deduction The type of reasoning that moves from a general proposition to a specific conclusion.

dependent clause   A clause that functions as an adjective, adverb, or noun and that cannot stand alone as a sentence.

description   Developing a topic by using sensory experience to show the reader what a person, place, or object is like.

draft   The text of an essay in progress, from its first to its final version.

editing   Making corrections and final additions or deletions to the final draft of a paper.

elliptical construction   A phrase or clause in which clearly understood words are omitted: he is taller than you (are tall).

evidence   Facts, examples, statistics, etc., needed to support an argument and to make it convincing.

exposition   Writing that explains a topic.

fallacy   An error in logical reasoning.

figurative language   The use of metaphor, simile, personification, and other imaginative devices to express a meaning beyond the literal.

freewriting   A form of prewriting in which you jot down whatever thoughts you have about a subject as they occur to you.

future tense   See *tense.*

gerund   The *-ing* form of a verb used as a noun: *Making money* (gerund phrase) is his only concern.

idiom   An expression that cannot be logically explained but is commonly understood.

independent clause   A clause that can stand alone as a sentence; see *clause.*

indirect object   See *object.*

induction   The type of reasoning that proceeds from specific evidence to a general conclusion or hypothesis.

infinitive The form of a verb usually preceded by *to*; it sometimes functions as a noun: Sally decided not *to smoke* (infinitive as direct object). Sometimes the infinitive can appear without *to*: He does nothing but *complain*.

interjection A word used as an exclamation: No!

intransitive verb See *verb.*

introduction The opening of an essay that expresses the writer's purpose, thesis, and tone and that captures the reader's attention.

irregular verb See *verb.*

linking verb Any form of the verb *to be* as well as such words as *seem, feel, become,* and *look* that link the complement with the subject: Jack *is* a hunter.

modifier A word that describes or limits another word or word group.

mood The form of a verb that indicates whether the action or condition it expresses is a factual question or statement (indicative mood), a command or request (imperative mood), or a wish or condition contrary to fact (subjunctive mood).

narration A type of writing that tells a story.

nominative See *case.*

non-restrictive A modifying phrase or clause that gives non-essential information about a noun; it is set off by commas. A restrictive modifier gives essential information about the noun it modifies and is not set off by commas.

noun A word that names something: *lady, squirrel, patience, writing* (common nouns); proper nouns, for specific names and places, are capitalized.

number A grammatical term used to establish the singular or plural status of nouns and verbs: *Colleges* is plural in number.

object A noun or pronoun that receives the action of a verb. The object may be direct (Susan hit *the ball*) or indirect (She gave *him* a kiss). Participles, gerunds, infinitives, and prepositions take objects to complete their meaning (turning the *corner*).

objective See *case.*

outline A diagram of an essay's organization in which the main points are listed as major items in a column, with subordinate points indented under the main points to which they belong.

paragraph A group of related sentences that develop one subject.

participle A verbal that may be in either one of two tenses. The present participle, which always ends in *-ing,* is used with forms of *be* in verb phrases (is *sinking*) or as a modifier (*sinking* ship). The past participle, which ends in -ed for regular verbs, is used as part of a verb phrase (*has sunk*) or as a modifier (*used* car). See also *verbal.*

parts of speech The classification of words according to their function in a sentence: nouns, pronouns, adjectives, adverbs, verbs, prepositions, conjunctions, and interjections.

passive voice See *voice.*

past tense See *tense.*

person A grammatical term used to distinguish the person speaking (first person) from the person spoken to (second person) and from anyone or anything else (third person). Nouns, except those in direct address (*John,* please leave), are always considered third person.

persuasion A type of writing that aims to convince the reader to do or believe something.

phrase A group of words that can function as a noun, verb, or modifier and that does not contain a subject-verb combination.

plagiarism Using the words or ideas of another without giving credit to their source.

possessive See *case.*

predicate The verb by itself (simple predicate) or the verb with all its modifiers, complements, and objects (complete predicate).

preposition A word that relates a noun or pronoun to another word in the sentence: *after, before, by, for, from, in, of, on, to, up,* and *with* are some commonly used prepositions.

present tense See *tense.*

prewriting Any device you use to get started before beginning the first draft of an essay.

principal parts The three basic forms of a verb: infinitive (*to eat*), past tense (*ate*), and past participle (*eaten*).

pronoun A part of speech that stands for or refers to a noun.

proper noun See *noun.*

purpose Your reason for writing; your answer to the question: "Why am I writing?"

regular verb See *verb.*

relative pronoun A pronoun that introduces a subordinate clause: *who, whom, whose, that, which, what, whoever, whomever, whichever, whatever.*

report An essay in which a writer summarizes the content of another person's work.

restrictive See *non-restrictive.*

review An evaluation in which a writer assesses the

strengths and weaknesses of another's work by using supportive evidence.

revising The part of the writing process that enables you to alter and clarify what you have written by rethinking, rereading, and rewriting.

sentence A word group that expresses a complete thought, consisting of a subject and a predicate. A simple sentence contains one main clause; a compound sentence has two or more main clauses. A complex sentence contains one main or independent clause and at least one dependent clause. A compound-complex sentence contains two or more main clauses and at least one dependent clause. Sentences also differ in purpose: declarative (statement), imperative (command), interrogative (question), and exclamatory (strong feeling).

subject The word or word group about which the predicate says (or asks) something in a sentence.

subjunctive See *mood.*

subordinate conjunction See *conjunction.*

syllogism The standard form of deductive reasoning in logic, consisting of two premises and a conclusion.

tense The form of a verb that expresses time: present, past, future. Perfect tenses express completed action: present perfect (I have run), past perfect (I had run), future perfect (I will have run). The progressive tense expresses continuing action (I am running).

thesis A sentence that states your main point, usually placed in the introduction of an essay.

topic A specific aspect of a broad subject.

topic sentence A sentence that states the main idea of a paragraph, guiding and unifying it much as a thesis statement guides the development of the essay.

transition   A word, phrase, or sentence that guides the reader from one point to another by linking sentences or paragraphs.

transitive verb   See *verb*.

verb   A word or word group expressing action, process, or being. Regular verbs form the past and past participle by adding *-d* or *-ed* to the infinitive: walk, walked, have walked. Irregular verbs (drink, drank, have drunk) do not follow this rule. A transitive verb requires an object to complete its meaning: He *wrote* [verb] a *letter* [object]; an intransitive verb does not require an object: he *sings* well. See also *linking verb, mood, tense,* and *voice*.

verbal   A word formed from a verb and used as an adjective, adverb, or noun: *laughing*. Gerunds, participles, and infinitives are verbals.

GL

voice   A verb is in the active voice when the subject names the doer of the action: Joan read the book; it is in the passive voice when the subject names the receiver of the action: The book was read by Joan.

Glossary of Usage

This glossary discusses words that are commonly confused and usages that appear frequently, especially in speech, but are disapproved of by many dictionaries and books on style. Look over the entries, noting any usages with which you are unfamiliar, and refer to this glossary or to a good college dictionary whenever you are unsure of the way you are using a particular word. For a discussion of the varieties of writing referred to in this glossary, see **67**.

a, an Use *a* before a consonant sound, *an* before a vowel sound: *a* university, *a* horror; *an* uncle, *an* hour.

absolutely Often meaningless intensifier (*absolutely* the finest cook); redundant with such words as *complete* and *perfect*.

accept, except See *except, accept*.

adapted, adopted *Adapted* means "changed"; *adopted* means "accepted." After the mayor **adopted** the housing rule, it was **adapted** to suit local needs.

administrate Use *administer*.

adverse, averse *Adverse* means "opposite" or "unfavorable": *adverse* criticism, *adverse* winds. *Averse* means "reluctant" or "disliking": He is *averse* to manual labor.

affect, effect *Affect* (to influence) is usually a verb; *effect* (result) is usually a noun. As a verb, *effect* means "bring about":

His injury did not **affect** his performance.

The protest had little **effect.**

The new chair **effected** several changes.

afflict, inflict *Afflict* typically takes *with* and an animate object: He was *afflicted with* measles. *Inflict* takes an inanimate object: The judge *inflicted* the maximum penalty.

again, back Unnecessary after words meaning *again* or *back*, such as *refer, revert,* and *resume.*

> In reaching its decision, the court **referred** [not *referred back*] to a 1948 Supreme Court ruling.

ahold Use *hold:* Dan tried to get *hold* [not *ahold*] of himself.

ain't Most writers avoid this colloquial contraction.

all ready, already *All ready* means "fully prepared" or that everyone or everything is ready: The letters were *all ready* to be signed. *Already* is an adverb meaning "at or before this time": The book has *already* sold a million copies.

all right Use this spelling. *Alright* is not a standard spelling.

all the farther Use *as far as:* This is *as far as* we can go.

allude A verb meaning "mention indirectly": He often *alludes* to Shakespeare. Do not confuse it with *refer,* "to mention directly." Also do not confuse the noun *allusion* with *illusion,* a false perception or impression.

a lot Two words; do not spell as one.

alternate(ly), alternative(ly) As an adjective, *alternate* means "by turns, first one and then the other": *alternately* hot and cold weather. *Alternative* means "another choice," such as an *alternative* course of action.

altogether, all together *Altogether* is an adverb meaning "completely": *all together* is an adjective phrase meaning "in a group":

> The hikers were **all together** at the campsite.
> They were **altogether** unprepared for the storm.

alumnus, alumna, alumni A male graduate is an *alumnus,* a female graduate is an *alumna; alumni* is the plural for both sexes (although *alumnae* is sometimes still used for female graduates).

among, between   Use *among* with more than two, *between* with two.

amoral, immoral   *Amoral* means without moral principles; *immoral* means contrary to such principles.

amount, number   Use *number* for things that can be counted, *amount* for quantities of things that cannot be counted:

> A large **number** of books have been stolen.
>
> The old furnace wasted a large **amount** of fuel.

analyzation   Use *analysis.*

and etc.   See *etc.*

anyone, any one   *Anyone* means "any person"; *any one* refers to a single person or thing from a group:

> **Anyone** can learn to spell better.
>
> Choose **any one** point of view and stick with it.

anyway, any way   Use *anyway* to mean "in any case" or "nevertheless," *any way* to mean "any course" or "any direction." To mean "in any manner," use either one.

> We played well but lost **anyway.**
>
> The traffic will be heavy **any way** you go at that hour.
>
> Do it **any way** [or **anyway**] you choose.

Anyways is non-standard.

appraise, apprise   *Appraise* means to set a value, as on real estate (The house was appraised at $65,000); *apprise* means to notify, tell, or inform: The attorney was *apprised* [not *appraised*] of the facts of the case.

apprehend, comprehend   *Apprehend* means to catch the

meaning of something, whereas *comprehend* means to understand it fully.

as   Often ambiguous when used to mean *since, when,* or *because:* She forgot her lines *because* [not *as*] she was nervous. *As* is often unnecessary: He was voted [as] the most likely to succeed. Do not use *as* to mean "whether" or "that": I can't say *that* [not *as*] I understand. See also *like, as.*

as regards   See *concerning.*

awhile, a while   *Awhile* is an adverb; *a while* is a noun: wait *awhile;* wait for *a while.*

bad, badly   Use *bad* as an adjective, *badly* as an adverb:

> I wanted a drink so **badly** that I was ready to do almost anything.
>
> It was **bad.** I feel **bad.** He looks **bad.**

basically   Like *essentially* and *ultimately, basically* is overused and often adds little emphasis: [*Basically,*] the problem is serious.

being   Often a weak connective in sentences: He writes well, being the son of a novelist. Instead of *being that* or *being as,* use *because* or *since:* He writes well *because* [not *being that*] he is the son of a novelist.

beside, besides   *Beside* means "at the side of"; *besides* means "in addition to"; either may be used to mean "except":

> The map lay **beside** the lamp.
>
> **Besides** her regular job, she plays bass in a blues band.
>
> No one **beside** [or **besides**] you had a key.

better   Avoid as a synonym for *more: More* [not *Better*] than half of the workers were present.

between   See *among, between.*

both Redundant with words such as *agree* or *together:* We [both] agreed to stop bickering.

but Avoid redundant combinations such as *but however* or *but nevertheless.* Use *that* rather than *but that* or *but what* in sentences such as "I do not doubt *that* [not *but that*] he will succeed."

can, may In strict usage, *can* expresses ability; *may* expresses permission:

> **May** I go fishing?
> Yes, if you **can** find your rod.

cannot Spell as one word unless you wish to place especially heavy emphasis on the *not.*

can't hardly, can't scarcely Avoid these double negatives; use *can hardly* or *can scarcely.*

case, line Both are often deadwood:

> In [the case of] English, single adjectives usually precede nouns.
> I would like to buy [something in the line of] a mystery.

center around *Center on* is more exact, but either phrase is usually roundabout and imprecise:

> The story **concerns** [not *centers around*] a jewel thief.

cf. The abbreviation of the Latin *confer* ("compare"). Except in notes, *compare* is preferable.

climactic, climatic *Climactic* refers to climax (as in a story), *climatic* to climate (weather).

close to Not a substitute for *nearly* or *almost:* Nearly [not *close to*] fifty guests are coming.

complement, compliment *Complement* means "to complete"; *compliment* means "to praise."

considerable, considerably Avoid using the adjective *considerable* as an adverb:

The injury to the first-string center hurt the team **considerably** [not *considerable*].

consist in, consist of *Consist in* means "to reside in" or "inhere": Virtue *consists in* doing good. *Consist of* means "to be composed of": The book *consists of* seven chapters.

continual, continuous *Continual* means "frequently repeated" and is not the same as *continuous,* "uninterrupted":

Robbery is a **continual** problem in our neighborhood.
Chicago suffered forty-three days of **continuous** subfreezing weather.

convince Use *convince* when someone changes his or her opinion; use *persuade* when someone is moved to take action:

The dean *persuaded* (not *convinced*) us to cancel the meeting.

could of An error for *could have.* See *of.*

council, counsel, consul A council is a governing body; counsel is advice or the act of giving advice; a consul is a government official in a foreign country:

The town **council** met last night.
Mr. Adamson **counseled** me to choose a career other than medicine.
The **consul** was expelled from the country.

couple *Couple* takes a plural verb when it refers to people, as does *pair:* The couple *are* [not *is*] in Bermuda.

credible, credulous, creditable All have to do with belief, but they are not interchangeable. *Credible* means "believable"; *credulous* means "naive"; *creditable* means "deserving praise."

data   Plural for the rarely used singular *datum*. *Data* is best used as a plural.

different   *Different from* is standard usage: Frye's approach to the poem is *different from* [not *than*] Ellman's approach. Watch for needless use of *different:* I read three [different] novels last winter. Use *various* to indicate diversity unless you wish to stress unlikeness. *Differ from* indicates dissimilarity (Boys *differ from* girls); *differ with* indicates disagreement (She *differed* with his view of the film).

disinterested, uninterested   *Disinterested* means "impartial"; *uninterested* means "not interested."

done   Non-standard as a substitute for *did:* They *did* [not *done*] the work already.

due to the fact that   Use *because.*

each and every   Use one word or the other.

economic, economical   *Economic* usually concerns economics (*economic policy*), whereas *economical* always means "thrifty."

effect   See *affect, effect.*

e.g.   The abbreviation for the Latin *exempli gratia* ("for example"). Use *for example.*

elicit, illicit   *Elicit* is a verb meaning "draw forth": The article *elicited* an angry response. *Illicit* is an adjective meaning "unlawful": The police cracked down on *illicit* gambling.

emigrate, immigrate   *Emigrate* means to move out of a country; *immigrate* means to move in. An American who emigrates to England is immigrating from the English standpoint.

eminent, imminent   *Eminent* means "prominent" or "famous"; *imminent* means "upcoming, about to happen":

An **eminent** economist predicted **imminent** disaster.

enthuse A colloquial substitute for "be enthusiastic" or "show enthusiasm."

equally as Just *as* is sufficient. The film was [*equally*] *as* good as the book.

etc. An abbreviation of the Latin *et cetera* ("and other things"). It is often a lazy or evasive substitute for specifics: Work was delayed by rain, etc. Do not use *and etc.,* in which *and* is redundant.

everyone, every one See *anyone, any one.*

except, accept *Except,* meaning "other than" is not a substitute for *but.* Also, do not confuse *except* with *accept,* "to receive" or "to agree."

> The British might have scored a decisive victory, **but** [not *except*] they did not pursue the retreating American army.
>
> Everyone **except** Aunt Agatha **accepted** the invitation.

expect Informal when used to mean "suppose" or "think" as in "I expect it will rain." *Suppose, assume, think,* and *believe* are preferable.

explicit, implicit *Explicit,* meaning "expressed directly," is the opposite of *implicit* (suggested, expressed indirectly).

factor A factor helps to produce a given result, so *contributing factor* is redundant. *Factor* is often misused to mean "item" or "point": There are several *points* [not *factors*] in favor of the new proposal.

farther, further *Farther* usually refers to physical distance, *further* to additional time or degree.

> We managed to drive **farther** than we expected during the first three days.
>
> The economists decided to wait for **further** developments before making a decision.

feature As a verb, *feature* should not be used to mean "contain" (The magazine *contained* [not *featured*] many recipes) but to mean "give prominence to" (The magazine *featured* an article by Truman Capote).

few, little; fewer, less *Few* and *fewer* refer to things that can be counted; *little* and *less* to things that cannot be counted: *few* apartments, *little* space; *fewer* calories, *less* food.

finalize Jargon for *complete*.

former, first; latter, last Use *former* and *latter* when you refer to one of two items; with three or more items, use *first* and *last*.

goes Not acceptable as an equivalent for *says:* Then he *says* [not *goes*], "I didn't mean it."

good, well *Good* is an adjective: The air smells *good*. *Well* is usually an adverb: The choir sings *well*. *Well* is also used as an adjective referring to health: I have stayed *well* since I started the new diet.

half Use *half a* (can) or *a half* (can), not *a half a* (can).

hardly See *can't hardly*.

hisself Non-standard for *himself*.

hopefully Colloquial substitute for "I hope" or "it is hoped."

idea, ideal *Idea* (thought or notion) can be confused with *ideal* (a conception of something in its most perfect state): He did not have a clear *idea* of the ancient Greek *ideal* of heroic virtue.

i.e. The abbreviation for the Latin *id est* ("that is"). Use *that is*.

if and when Like *when and if*, a wordy and trite phrase. Use one word or the other.

imminent See *eminent, imminent*.

implicit See *explicit.*

imply, infer *Imply* means "to suggest"; *infer* means "to conclude." Writers imply; readers infer.

> The press secretary **implied** that the President would fire the attorney general.

> From the press secretary's remarks, I **inferred** that the President would fire the attorney general.

inflict, afflict See *afflict, inflict.*

in regards to The standard forms are *in regard to* or *as regards.* But *concerning* is usually preferable to either phrase.

inside of Use just *inside* or *within.*

irregardless Non-standard for *regardless.*

its, it's *Its* is the possessive (belonging to *it*): The company issued its report. Compare *his, hers. It's* is the contraction for *it is* or *it has.* There is no such word as *its'.*

kind of/sort of are colloquial: The lecture was [kind of] interesting.

kind of a Drop the *a:* That kind of [a] story always amuses young readers.

latter See *former, first; latter, last.* Do not confuse *latter* with *later.*

lay, lie See *lie, lay.*

learn, teach Students learn; instructors teach:

> My grandfather **taught** me how to cast a fly.

> I **learned** to cast a fly before I was six years old.

leave, let *Leave* means "to depart or go away from"; *let* means "to permit." Do not use *leave* for *let.*

less See *few, little; fewer, less.*

GL

let's us Since *let's* is the contraction for *let us,* do not add a second *us.*

liable See *likely.*

lie, lay *Lie* means "to rest" or "to recline"; *lay* means "to put or place (something) down." The past of *lie* is *lay;* the past of *lay* is *laid:* She *laid* the book on the table and *lay* down to rest.

like, as In making comparisons, use *like* as a preposition; use *as, as if,* or *as though* as a conjunction introducing a dependent clause:

> **Like** Hamlet, he is indecisive.
>
> The lab researcher will examine the slides **as** she always has—slowly and carefully.
>
> After the race, all of the runners looked **as though** they might faint.

Some writers mistakenly go out of their way to avoid using *like:* The hotel looks *similar to* [preferably *like*] the one in Johnstown.

likely, liable *Likely* expresses probability; *liable* expresses obligation but is sometimes used loosely to mean *likely:* She is *likely* (not *liable*) to receive an award.

line See *case, line.*

loose, loosen, lose A *loose* screw (adjective); *loosen* a tie (verb); *lose* a bet (verb).

may, can See *can, may.*

media The plural of *medium.* Compare *criterion, criteria; phenomenon, phenomena.* The media are (not *is*) often accused of bias.

might of An error for *might have;* see *of.*

GL

most Informal as a substitute for *almost*, as in "he comes here *most* every evening."

myself *Myself* can be used as a direct object referring to the subject of the sentence (I hurt *myself*) or as an intensive (I will do the job *myself*). Do not use it as a substitute for *I:* Two of us finished the puzzle: John and *I* [not *myself*].

nohow, nowheres Non-standard forms. Use *in no way, not at all, nowhere.*

nowhere near Colloquial for *not nearly:* Sam's pizzas are *not nearly* [not *nowhere near*] as good as Tony's.

not too, not that Colloquial substitutes for *not very*, as in "I'm *not that* concerned with politics."

number, amount See *amount, number.*

of Do not use *of* for *have* in verb phrases: *could have, would have, might have, must have:* I should *have* [not *of*] attended the meeting.

off of Use just *off:* He would not get *off* [*of*] the subject.

oftentimes Use just *often.*

on account of Use this phrase as a preposition (*on account of* the rain), not as a conjunction (*on account of* it rained). *Because* or *because of* is preferable: *because of* the rain; *because* it rained.

opinionated An *opinionated* essay (as opposed to an essay of opinion) is one that unreasonably or obstinately maintains the writer's own opinions.

orientate *Orient* is simpler and preferable.

ought Do not use with auxiliaries such as *had* and *did:* Eve wondered if she *ought* [not *hadn't ought*] to leave.

outside of Use just *outside.*

party Except in law, *party* is a poor substitute for *person:* Would the *person* [not *party*] who requested a change in seating please come to the counter?

per Jargon for "according to"; Use the insecticide *according to* (not *per*) the instructions.

percent, percentage Use *percent* with numbers (*ten percent*), *percentage* without numbers: A high *percentage* [not *percent*] of those responding rated inflation as the chief problem. Do not use *percentage* loosely for *part:* A large *part* [not *percentage*] of the work was done before we arrived.

persuade See *convince.*

plenty Informal as an adverb meaning "very": She must be *very* [not *plenty*] rich.

plus *Plus* is technically a preposition meaning "with the addition of," not a conjunction:

> After the game, Bill was tired **and** [not *plus*] his leg hurt.
> The principal **plus** the interest comes to $368.55.

practical, practicable Something *practical* works well in practice; something *practicable* can be put into practice but has not yet been shown to work:

> Conversion to solar energy is **practicable** in many parts of the country, but few systems have so far proved **practical.**

precede, proceed See *proceed, precede.*

predominant, predominate *Predominant* is the adjective (the *predominant* opinion); *predominate* is the verb: For twenty years, conservative opinion *predominated* in the court.

presently Use *now.*

previous to, prior to Use *before.*

principal, principle *Principal* can be an adjective or a noun: the *principal* cause; the *principal* of our school; the *principal* plus the interest charged by the bank. *Principle* is always a noun meaning "basic rule or truth": Although customs vary, the *principles* of good behavior are the same in both countries.

proceed, precede *Proceed* means "to go forward," "to continue"; *precede* means "to go before." *Proceed* is not a good choice if the meaning is simply "go."

quite, rather See *rather, quite.*

quotation, quote *Quote* is the verb, *quotation* the noun: an apt *quotation* [not *quote*].

raise, rise *Raise* takes a direct object (*raise something*); *rise* does not:

> They **raise** the flag every day.
>
> Farmers **rise** early.

rather, quite Both can weaken the force of a strong modifier: a [quite] huge fireplace. *Rather* often adds no meaning and produces ambiguity: does *rather clear* mean "very clear" or "a little clear"?

real, really *Real* is the adjective, *really* the adverb: a *real* distinction; *really* late. But *really* is often just an empty word: They [really] worked hard.

reason is, because Redundant. The reason is *that* [not *because*] he is shy.

refer back See *again, back.*

relevant If you call something *relevant* or *irrelevant*, be sure to say *to what* it is relevant or irrelevant.

respectfully, respectively *Respectfully* means "with respect"; *respectively* means "singly in the order given":

They treated the ambassador **respectfully.**

Her three children weighed **respectively** eight, nine, and ten pounds at birth.

rise, raise See *raise, rise.*

sensual, sensuous *Sensual* refers to bodily (usually sexual) pleasures; *sensuous* refers more generally to sensory appeal.

set, sit *Set* takes a direct object (*set* something down); *sit* does not (*sit* down). See p. 217.

shall, will The distinction between these words has largely broken down. See p. 208.

should of An error for *should have.* See *of.*

so Not a substitute for *very* (It was *so* cold); as an adverb, *so* requires some further explanation: It was so cold that the pipes froze.

some In writing, avoid the colloquial use of *some* for *somewhat:* I feel *somewhat* [not *some*] better today.

somewheres Non-standard for *somewhere.*

stationary, stationery *Stationary* means "fixed in course or position"; *stationery* refers to writing materials.

supposed to, used to Be careful not to drop the *-d* from the end of *supposed* or *used* before *to.*

sure, surely *Sure* as an adverb is colloquial; in writing, use *surely:* We *surely* [not *sure*] enjoyed the concert.

teach, learn See *learn, teach.*

than, then *Than* is a conjunction used in comparisons; *then* is an adverb indicating time:

> The balloon rose faster **than** they expected.
> **Then** it drifted out over the lake.

their, there, they're Watch for misspellings: *Their* books are here (possessive adjective); *there* are my glasses (adverb); *they're* coming tonight (contraction of *they are*).

theirselves Non-standard for *themselves.*

thusly Error for *thus.*

till, until Both are acceptable; *til* and *'til* are not.

to, too, two Spelling errors with these words are common but unnecessary. *To* is a preposition (*to* the fair) or the sign of an infinitive (*to* run). *Too* means either "also" or "excessively." *Two* is a number.

> John, **too,** found the path **to** the top **too** steep.
>
> It takes **two to** argue.

try and *Try to* is preferred by many stylists, though *try and* is common.

-type This suffix should usually be omitted in phrases: *a temperamental-type person.*

unique *Unique* means "single" or "without equal" and therefore does not need qualification: not *very unique* or *quite unique* but just *unique.*

used to See *supposed to, used to.*

utilize Often bureaucratic jargon for *use,* especially with reference to people.

wait on Use *wait on* to mean "serve" but not as a substitute for *wait for.*

> The army stopped to **wait for** [not *on*] reinforcements.
>
> She feigned illness and persuaded everyone to **wait on** her.

ways Use *way* for distance: a long *way* [not *ways*] to go.

where   Avoid using *where* as a substitute for *that;* I read in the paper *that . . .* [not *where . . .*].

whose, who's   Be careful not to confuse the possessive *whose* (*Whose* notes are these?) with *who's,* the contraction for *who is.*

-wise   Avoid this suffix, a common type of jargon: *gardenwise, profitwise.*

your, you're   *Your* is the possessive (*your* copy), and *you're* is the contraction for *you are.*

Acknowledgments

MARGARET ATWOOD, excerpt from *Cat's Eye.* © 1988 by O. W. Toad Limited. Reprinted by permission of Doubleday, a division of Bantam, Doubleday, Dell Publishing Group, Inc. and O. W. Toad Limited.

RACHEL L. CARSON, excerpt from *The Sea Around Us*, Rev. Ed., by Rachel L. Carson. Copyright 1950, 1951, 1961 by Rachel L. Carson; renewed 1979 by Roger Christie. Reprinted by permission of Oxford University Press, Inc.

KENNETH CLARK, excerpt adapted from "The Italian Alter Ego of Thomas Jefferson," *Virginia Quarterly Review*, Autumn, 1972. Reprinted by permission.

MALCOLM COWLEY, excerpt from *The View from 80* by Malcolm Cowley. Copyright © 1976, 1978, 1980 by Malcolm Cowley. Reprinted by permission of Viking Penguin, a division of Penguin Books USA Inc.

GORDON CRAIG, excerpt from "Facing Up to the Nazis," *The New York Review of Books*, February 2, 1989. Reprinted with permission from *The New York Review of Books.* Copyright © 1989 Nyrev, Inc.

FREDERICK CREWS, excerpt from "The Future of an Illusion," *The New Republic,* January 21, 1985. Reprinted by permission of *The New Republic,* © 1985, The New Republic, Inc.

NORA EPHRON, excerpt from "A Few Words About Breasts," *Esquire,* May 1972. Reprinted by permission of International Creative Management, Inc. Copyright © 1972 by Nora Ephron. First published in *Esquire.*

ROBERT FROST, "Fire and Ice" from *The Poetry of Robert Frost* edited by Edward Connery Lathem. Copyright 1923, © 1969 by Holt, Rinehart and Winston. Copyright 1951 by Robert Frost. Reprinted by permission of Henry Holt and Company, Inc.

CHRISTOPHER LASCH, excerpt reprinted from *The Culture of Narcissism, American Life in an Age of Diminishing Expectations,* by Christopher Lasch, by permission of W. W. Norton & Company, Inc. Copyright © 1979 by W. W. Norton & Company, Inc.

C. S. LEWIS, excerpt from *The Essential C. S. Lewis,* Collier Books, 1988.

P. B. MEDAWAR, excerpt from "Unnatural Science," *The New York Review of Books,* February 3, 1977. Reprinted with permission from *The New York Review of Books.* Copyright 1977 Nyrev, Inc.

FLANNERY O'CONNOR, excerpt from "A Good Man is Hard to Find" from *A Good Man is Hard to Find and Other Stories,* copyright 1953 by Flannery O'Connor and renewed 1981 by Regina O'Connor, reprinted by permission of Harcourt Brace Jovanovich, Inc.

WALKER PERCY, excerpt adapted from "Southern Comfort," *Harper's,* January 1979. Copyright © 1978 by Walker Percy. Reprinted by permission of McIntosh and Otis, Inc.

PHILIP ROTH, excerpt from "The Newark Public Library" from *Reading Myself and Others* by Philip Roth. Copyright © 1969, 1975 by Philip Roth. Reprinted by permission of Farrar, Straus and Giroux, Inc.

LEWIS THOMAS, excerpt from *The Lives of A Cell* by Lewis Thomas. Copyright © 1973 by the Massachusetts Medical Society. Originally published by the New England Journal of Medicine. Reprinted by permission of Viking Penguin, a division of Penguin Books USA Inc.

SIR FREDERICK TREVES, excerpt from *The Elephant Man and Other Reminiscences.*

WEBSTER'S NEW WORLD DICTIONARY, entry for "rare" from the book, *Webster's New World Dictionary* © 1986. Used by permission of the publisher, Prentice Hall Press, a Division of Simon & Schuster, Inc., New York.

GILBERT WHITE, excerpt adapted from *The Natural History of Selbourne,* Oxford University Press, 1974. Reprinted with permission.

DONALD J. WILCOX, excerpt adapted from *In Search of God and Self, Renaissance and Reformation of Thought.* Copyright © 1975 by Houghton Mifflin. Adapted with permission.

Index

Subject (*Cont.*):
    compound, 174–175, 187–189
    nouns as, 165
    relationship of, to predicate,
      150–151
    separation of, from verb, 240–
      241
Subject complements, 162, 176
Subjective case (*see* Nominative
    case)
Subjunctive mood, 218–219, 425
Subordinate clauses, 123–125,
    169–170, 287, 423
    comma after, 227–228
    with semicolon, 247
    as sentence fragment, 178–180
Subordinating conjunctions, 123–
    124, 167–168, 170, 178, 183,
    423
Subordination of sentences:
    to avoid choppy and stringy sen-
      tences, 122–127
    excessive, 127
Subtitles:
    capitalization of, 272
    colon with, 252
Subtopics, 347
Suffixes, 280–281
    hyphens with, 269
Summary, 339–340, 343, 383, 401
Superlative forms, 205–206
Supposed to, used to, 444
Sure, surely, 444
Syllables, division of, by hyphen,
    269
Syllogism, 78, 428
Symbols, plurals of, 266
Synonyms, 142

Teach, learn, 439
Team, agreement with, 193
Technical language, 315–316
Television programs, bibliography
    form for, 371
Tense, 162, 208–212, 404, 428
    avoiding shifts in, 221–222
    future, 208–209, 428
    perfect, 209–210, 428
    progressive, 210–211, 428
    simple, 208–209
    of verbals, 211–212
Tests (*see* Essay examinations)

Than, then, 444
That, 153, 233
    vagueness of, 198–199
The, 273
Their, there, they're, 445
Theirselves, 445
There, sentence beginning with, 187
Thesis statement, 34–37, 40–43,
    90, 351, 374, 396, 401, 404,
    428
    preliminary, 337–338
Third person, 200, 426
This, vagueness of, 198–199
Thusly, 445
Till, until, 445
Time:
    with colons, 250, 252
    as figure, 276–277
    and verb tense, 208–212
Title page, 371, 373, 375
Titles (personal):
    in business letters, 413
    capitalization of, 272
Titles (written work):
    capitalization of, 272–273
    colon with, 250, 252
    commas with, 238
    italics with, 262
    quotation marks with, 262
    of research papers, 372
    underlining with, 262
To, too, two, 445
To be, 187, 205
Topic, 428
    and audience perception, 27–28
    evidence to support, 70–73
    limiting, 6, 31–33, 401–402
    selection of, 5–6, 326–328
Topic outline, 42–43
Topic sentences, 56–58, 91–93, 95–
    96, 352–353, 428
Transition, 141–142, 429
Transitional devices, 90, 91, 99,
    104–109, 231, 235–236, 246
Transitional sentences and para-
    graphs, 108–109
Transitional terms, 105–108
Transitive verbs, 217, 429
Translations, bibliography form for,
    366
Trite language, 310–311
Try and, 445
-type, 445